Nenad Zivanovski

r no and why not

To my colleague Charlie, with sincere wishes for success in his professional career!

P.S. Why not a diplomat in North Macedonia?! :)

WIMBLEDON
29/06/2024

Nenad Zivanovski

Nenad Zivanovski

Hate speech: yes or no and why not

Multidisciplinary theoretical overview of US and European treatment of hate speech in political discourse

LAP LAMBERT Academic Publishing

Impressum / Imprint

Bibliografische Information der Deutschen Nationalbibliothek: Die Deutsche Nationalbibliothek verzeichnet diese Publikation in der Deutschen Nationalbibliografie; detaillierte bibliografische Daten sind im Internet über http://dnb.d-nb.de abrufbar.
Alle in diesem Buch genannten Marken und Produktnamen unterliegen warenzeichen-, marken- oder patentrechtlichem Schutz bzw. sind Warenzeichen oder eingetragene Warenzeichen der jeweiligen Inhaber. Die Wiedergabe von Marken, Produktnamen, Gebrauchsnamen, Handelsnamen, Warenbezeichnungen u.s.w. in diesem Werk berechtigt auch ohne besondere Kennzeichnung nicht zu der Annahme, dass solche Namen im Sinne der Warenzeichen- und Markenschutzgesetzgebung als frei zu betrachten wären und daher von jedermann benutzt werden dürften.

Bibliographic information published by the Deutsche Nationalbibliothek: The Deutsche Nationalbibliothek lists this publication in the Deutsche Nationalbibliografie; detailed bibliographic data are available in the Internet at http://dnb.d-nb.de.
Any brand names and product names mentioned in this book are subject to trademark, brand or patent protection and are trademarks or registered trademarks of their respective holders. The use of brand names, product names, common names, trade names, product descriptions etc. even without a particular marking in this work is in no way to be construed to mean that such names may be regarded as unrestricted in respect of trademark and brand protection legislation and could thus be used by anyone.

Coverbild / Cover image: www.ingimage.com

Verlag / Publisher:
LAP LAMBERT Academic Publishing
ist ein Imprint der / is a trademark of
OmniScriptum GmbH & Co. KG
Heinrich-Böcking-Str. 6-8, 66121 Saarbrücken, Deutschland / Germany
Email: info@lap-publishing.com

Herstellung: siehe letzte Seite /
Printed at: see last page
ISBN: 978-3-659-78148-3

Zugl. / Approved by: Rousse, University of Rousse, Bulgaria, 2013

Copyright © 2015 OmniScriptum GmbH & Co. KG
Alle Rechte vorbehalten. / All rights reserved. Saarbrücken 2015

NENAD ZIVANOVSKI

HATE SPEECH
YES OR NO AND WHY NOT

*To my parents
Aleksandar-Titre and Blagica Zivanovski*

CONTENT

CONTENT III
INTRODUCTION .... - 1 -
CHAPTER ONE .... - 6 -
HATE SPEECH .... - 6 -
1. TERM AND DEFINITION OF HATE SPEECH .... - 6 -
  Criteria on identification of hate speech .... - 10 -
  Phase model of hate speech .... - 14 -
2. HISTORICAL OVERVIEW OF THE EMERGENCE OF
HATE SPEECH .... -19-
  EUROPE .... - 19 -
  Germany in the thirties - creating an environment for crimes .. - 19 -
  The role of Nazi media in promoting hate speech .... - 22 -
  Art in the function of racial policy and hate speech .... - 30 -
  Italy - manipulation and hatred for the triumph of fascism - 35 -
  Racial policy in fascist Italy .... - 40 -
  Hate speech in post-war Europe - from condemnation to controversy .... - 43 -
  AMERICA .... - 49 -
  Twenties of the 20th century - a decade of intolerance .... - 49 -
  The Thirties and the impact of National Socialism .... - 53 -
  Creating a national policy on hate speech in the forties ... - 57 -
  The post war period - victory for freedom of speech .... - 62 -
  Hate speech in the 80s and 90s of the last century - crisis in university campuses .... - 66 -
  Hate speech in the new millennium .... - 70 -
3. INTERNATIONAL DOCUMENTS AND NATIONAL LAWS RELATED TO HATE SPEECH .... - 72 -

International documents..- 74 -
European documents..- 78 -
The internet and hate speech..- 83 -
Sexist and homophobic speech...- 87 -
National laws and hate speech..- 90 -
4. HATE SPEECH AND/OR FREEDOM OF EXPRESSION- 93 -
Introduction..- 93 -
Europe: dignity of the other before the freedom of expression- 98 -
5. CRITICAL OBSERVATIONS OF THE EUROPEAN AND US APPROACH TO HATE SPEECH ....- 120 -
Selectivity in the application of the prohibition ....- 121 -
Hate speech as a weapon of the weaker ....- 126 -
6. POSSIBLE TENDENCIES OF RAPPROCHEMENT BETWEEN THE TWO APPROACHES...- 135 -
7. CONCLUSION 140

CHAPTER TWO...145
POLITICAL DISCOURSE AND HATE SPEECH.............145
1. DISCOURSE ANALYSIS..145
Introduction..145
Definition of discourse 146
Discourse analysis as a research methodology....................150
2. CRITICAL DISCOURSE ANALYSIS 152
Introduction..152
Theoretical approach to CDA 153
Creation and application of CDA 157
Access and control of the discourse 158
Control of subject, text and context.....................................162
Mind control 166

Social issues as a CDA subject for research 170
Gender inequality 170
Media discourse 170
Political discourse 171
Ethnocentrism, anti-Semitism, nationalism and racism 172
Discursive structures and strategies 174
Modalities for US and against THEM 175

3. POLITICAL DISCOURSE 179
Introduction 179
Political discourse and political cognition 180
Knowledge 182
Opinions and attitudes 184
Ideologies 185
Structures of political discourse 186
Context 187
Themes 189
Schemes 190
Techniques and tactics in the use of political discourse 190
Political discourse and violent conflict 197
Use of emotions in the political discourse for causing conflict 198
Recontextualization of own crimes 202

4. LANGUAGE MANIPULATION IN POLITICAL DISCOURSE
.... 205
Propaganda techniques 207
Methods of misinforming 214

5. NONVERBAL ASPECTS OF HATE SPEECH 217
Categorization of gestures 219
Hate speech through nonverbal communication 220

6. SYMBOLISM IN POLITICAL DISCOURSE 224

7. STYLISTIC FIGURES IN THE POLITICAL DISCOURSE AND PROMOTION OF HATE SPEECH 229

Introduction 229

Methaphor 230

- The metaphor in political discourse and hate speech..232

Irony 234

Antithesis 238

Rhetorical question 239

Allusion 242

Litote - Euphemia 244

8. CONCLUSION 248

Bubliography 250

INTRODUCTION

Offensive speech and words that cause pain are phenomenon that appeared in the communication process since people started to verbally communicate with each other. Every news or message in that act of information exchange has not always had positive criticism, or affirmative and complimentary. In the long history of speech, there has always been speech that is negative, hurt someone's feelings or disqualified other views and attitudes and such an attitude was at first noticed only on interpersonal level of communication between people and together with the development of the community it became institutional with the official bodies addressing the individual, but also in the communication between institutions. Thus, throughout history there have cases when the institutions whether they are foreign, occupational, conquest or colony addressed the domicile population with abusive language or cases when domestic institutions were, figuratively speaking, "our", but occupied by authoritarian, totalitarian and undemocratic regimes and in their repressive policies toward the population did not avoid using language as a means of domination and coercion. In a situation of war between two countries the hostilities were clearly demonstrated in the language of communication led by both warring sides.

However, in the 20-ieth century this kind of speech became most wisely used as part of the politic strategy of the authorities. That's the period when abusive language is not only orderly and systematically used in public discourse but is also identified by the science as a problem and interest appears for its organized and systematic study. The provocation for the scientific thought to become motivated in this social phenomenon is the result of two world problems that happened in the last century, and those are the emergence of fascism and National Socialism in Europe and the culmination of racial policy towards black people and segregation of immigrants and natives on American soil. Although, separated by thousands of miles, on two different continents, these processes did not develop independently but had a common substrate in its basis, which is hatred of everything that did not originate of the white race and had no Anglo-Saxon and Aryan roots. The peak of such a racist policy was the attitude of Nazi Germany towards the Jews, the so callled final showdown that culminated in the Holocaust atrocities, and the US the organized persecution, violence and murders of black people, Jews, immigrants and other minority communities. The secret organization that conducted these crimes in the United States was the Ku Klux Klan, although the triumph of National Socialism in Germany had its reflections in the US through associations of "brown shirts" formed on American soil.

Certainly this eruption of crimes did not happen overnight and that some preparation preceded. The preparation actually constituted of spreading hatred and indoctrination of the population in order for this idea to gain greater acceptance and approval. The massiveness was achieved with public use of the language in which words are not chosen to denounce the fixed enemies. The social phenomenon of using such language, which exploded on the eve of World War II, was not only fascinating for the uneducated masses, but found its supporters among the then social elite (most impressionable example of anti-Semite of the time is the famous car designer Henry Ford, who published his book "The International Jew - The World's Biggest Problem" in 1922).

At first, these processes were new to science itself, which found no sufficient attraction to get interested in them, so, although widely spread and applied, the language that spread intolerance and hatred towards other nations did not even have scientifically codified denomination under to be recognized under. Commonly used term at the time was *racist language* or *language that infringes*, but all that was far from universally acceptable term and only shows how science was caught off guard by the new situation in society. In the late eighties of the last century the end of the Cold war led to an appropriate social environment for science to comprehensively and holisticly get interested in this problem and to access it with multiple scientific disciplines. In that period was the first time when today generally accepted name 'hate speech' appeared, which is in fact the US neologism that has no adequate linguistic transcription in other world languages. Although the period is relatively short, this problem began to be widely reviewed by several sciences, as law that deals with his sanction, linguistics, semantics above all, interested in its recognition in language, communicology focused on its impact and effects on the process of communication, journalism and the media for their role as most direct actors in the process of transfer of hatred to the audience through language, social psychology deals with cognitive processes that occur under the influence of hate speech and how it is manifested in the individual as part of a group, while, for example, politicology which studies hate speech as deviant factor of pragmatic politics, etc.

As reflected in order for this problem could be fully qualified and researched and scientifically founded it takes a lot of actors from science to be included. For its part, the absence of just one scientific approach would make the study of the problem incomplete, improperly disregarding an important link in the scientific chain. On the other hand, today's modern democratic society increasingly encounteres this problem – hate speech is directed in all directions, on national, ethnic, religious, racial, gender, sexual, political, age and other grounds. Radical and extreme discourse are becoming increasingly recognizable speech, not only for the authoritarian and totalitarian societies, but also in the west liberal democracy. Thus, the weakness of the moderate politicians to offer answers and solutions to problems that threaten the existence of the western man leave room for extreme options that most effectively attract the electorate through pointing a finger towards those responsible for the crisis in the society. As a rule, immigrants are always the target of hate speech.

If such speech finds favorable basis to spread and be accepted in a traditionally tolerant environment like, for example the Scandinavian, then for the Balkans, with its rich history of ethnic hatred and wars it could be said that it is a space where hate speech can be felt like on its own ground. An indication for the use of hate speechare present in all possible inter-state and inter-ethnic relations: Serbs↔Albanians, Bulgarians↔Turks, Croats↔Serbs, Bosniaks↔Serbs, Greeks↔Turks, Maceodnians↔Greeks, Macedonians↔Bulagrians. Except on inter-state level, it is present in each of these traditionally ethnocentric societies - towards the fellow citizens from other ethnic community, towards the Roma towards the sexual minorities, towards women on gender grounds, towards the political opponents and not just in election cycles but as constant of the political discourse in the permanent political "struggle".

The relevance of the problem with hate speech for our societies and the personal impression that this phenomenon is not enough theoretically processed, especially not with the inclusion of the contributions of each science in particular, were the main motives to tackle with this research challenge and problem to process it as much as possible through its interdisciplinary character. Therefore, the tasks that were asked were related to a wide range of theoretical analysis of the problem of hate speech. Hence, the first chapter refers to the concept and definition of hate speech, then historical overview of the emergence of hate speech from the early twentieth century until recently, a review of international documents and some national laws that treat the problem of hate speech, one chapter addresses the conflict of freedom of speech and hate speech, as well as critical observations of the two concepts of treatment of hate speech - European and American and the possibility of their approaching. The task in the second chapter was to linguisticly-socio-communicationally approach the topic. Researched and defined are the terms discourse analysis, critical discourse analysis and political discourse, manipulative functions of language such as promotional techniques and methods of disinformation, then some non-verbal aspects of hate speech, symbolism in political discourse and hate speech and use of some stylish figures for public manifestation of hate speech.

I would like to inform the readers that this paper is part of a larger research on the subject "Is there hate speech in the Macedonian media towards Bulgaria", which actually was my doctoral work at the University of Ruse, Bulgaria. Therefore, I should necessarily say that this whole thing would be inconceivable if I did not encounter continued support and provided academic comfort and tranquility in the work all the time on its preparation by my scientific tutor Mrs. Juliana Popova, Ph.D. from the University of Ruse, which resulted to be crucial to successfully bring to an end the engagement on such a controversial social topic. I give the results of this labor on insight to the reading audience to judge whether the end product justified the invested energy, time and knowledge.

The Author

CHAPTER ONE

HATE SPEECH

1. TERM AND DEFINITION OF HATE SPEECH

Almost on a daily baisi in a public speech in Macedonia one can hear words like *Cigan* (offensive word for Roma), *Shiptar* (offensive word for Albanian), *Kaurin* (offensive word for Orthodox people), *turski kopilinja* ("Turkish bastards", offensive word for Macedonian), *peder* ("faggot", offensive word for gay population). Very often, the street arguments are filled with such insults, while sports competitions between different national teams inevitably contain derogations on ethnic grounds, and often the media does not remain immune to such vocabulary. If you want to insult a Roma person in Bulgarian you will call him *mangal*, Romance *mamaliga* and you will address the Turk with *fes* or *sechen* ("cut penis"). Turk will answer the Bulgarian addressing him with *gaur* ("unbeliever"). In the western public discourse inherent words to disregard any foreign group are *zhabar* for an Italian or *shvaba* for a German. In the USA *nigger* is pejoratively used for black person, *spic* for a Hispano, *chink* for a Chinese or the yellow race, *gringo* is a Mexican term for foreigners, mostly Americans, *dago* is disparaging name primarily for Italians, but also for the Portuguese and Spaniards, *kike* for Jews and African Americans use *honkey* for whites, while *limey* is a cynical expression for the English in the USA. All these designations which are colloquially called *offensive words*, because, in essence, they are intended to cause offense or disregard of the person they are addressed to.

Insults between people on racial or ethnic grounds are present since long time ago. Such occurrences are as old as old as the identification and recognition of the differences between people. The ancient Greeks considered those who do not speak Greek are barbarians. The English and the French also did not use kind words for each other in the past. The Great British Empire, as well as the French, Spanish and Portuguese conquistadors, based their colonizers expeditions on spreading hatred towards the indigenous people, which often preceded the mass killings and massacres. Such practices are also typical for white Americans towards the

Indians and the Blacks in the 17th and 18th century. European great empires, as the Ottoman and Austro-Hungarian as also relied on spreading hatred towards the enslaved local population. No war of one nation against another, whether France and Germany or China and Japan were not only wars between nations, but also of ethnic groups against ethnic groups. Insult and hatred have seemed to be an integral part of ethnic conflicts.

However, only in the 20th century, the horrors of the Holocaust and what preceded the "final showdown" with the Jews in Germany, initiated the organized dissemination of insult and humiliation of an entire ethnic group to begin being treated separately in most sciences, primarily in law , linguistics, sociology, psychology, communicology and other sciences. By deepening the scientific treatment, special terms that more accurately determine the phenomenon were differentiated. Historically, hate speech preceded designations with several different terms. In the late 20ies and early 30ies of the 20th century hate speech was known as *racial hatred*. At the beginning of the 40s he was called *group defamation*, reflecting the specific legal question whether the law of defamation should be expanded to include groups, and not just individuals.[1] The term hate speech, which very accurately determines the meaning of the more general expression abusive speech, appeared in widespread use only in the late eighties and, above all, during the nineties of the last century, along with the disintegration of the block division and the establishment the new world order. The origin of the term is from the Anglo-American expression *hate speech*, which means speech that contains hatered. From a linguistic aspect it is intriguing that in European languages, the literal translation of the English or the original expression is mainly used to describe the phenomena of expressing hatred. The reason is that it is about a neologism which in a very short period became widespread for public use, as evidenced by the fact that the authoritative encyclopedia of English language *Webster's Encyclopedic Unabridged Dictionary of the English Language*, in the edition from 1996., includes the term *hate speech*. Instead that abstract term, *Webster's* lists the terms related to the subject, that is, the source of hatred: *hate monger* is "a man who spread hatred, hostility or

---

[1]Walker, Samuel, "Hate Speech: The History of an American Controversy 8 (University of Nebraska Press 1994).

prejudices among others and "*hate sheet* are "newspapers or other publications that consistently express biased hatred towards a race, nationality, religion or other groups". In German, the literal translation of the English term *hate speech* as *Hassrede* is so unusual that it can not be found either in the latest editions of relevant encyclopedias (eg., *Wahrig - Kompaktwörterbuch der deutschen Sprache* from 2002.). The same is true of the French language and its encyclopedias (eg., "*Le Robert Micro - Dictionnaire de la langue française* from 1998.). Anglo-American origin of the term hate speech indicates, before all, the fact that the public debate about hate speech has historically been primarily an American feature.[2]

However, the general adoption of the new neologism "hate speech" was much easier than managing to build a universal definition to mark its implication. In the broadest possible sense, the term hate speech can be defined as any statement that calls for violence, hatred and discrimination against individuals or groups, most often based on their racial, religious or sexual affiliation.[3] According to the scientific literature on hate speech, whose volume in the nineties of the 20th century rose sharply, the definitions of the term hate speech can be summarized as follows: hate speech includes statements that intimidate, offend or disturb individuals or groups or such statements that incite violence, hatred or discrimination against individuals or groups. The reasons for hatred or discrimination, mainly "race, religion, gender or sexual orientation".[4] Therefore, the issue of hate speech falls primarily on the issue of "inciting racial hatred" (*Rassenhetze, racial hatred*). Certain messages of hate speech are often part of a complex ideology as, eg., the theory of "racial superiority".[5] What is essential to hate speech as a term (*hate speech*) is a public labeling, disqualification and demonization of a certain social group, which can

---

[2]Beham, Mira. 2004: "Govor mržnje u politici i medijima". Objavljeno u Vacic, Z. (ur.) 2004 Etika javne rijeci u medijima i politici, Centar za liberalno demokratske studije, Beograd, 2004.
[3]Ibid
[4]Brugger, Winfried, Verbot oder Schutz von Hassrede? Rechtsvergleichende Beobachtungen zum deutschen und amerikanischen Recht, u: Archiv des öffentlichen Rechts, vol. 128 (2003), s. 372-411.
[5]Zimmer, Anja, Hate speech im Völkerrecht - Rassendiskriminierende Äußerungen im Spannungsfeld zwischen Rassendiskriminierungsverbot und Meinungsfreiheit, Heidelberg: Max-Planck-Institut für ausländisches öffentliches Recht und Völkerrecht, 2001.

often be (especially in military terms) an announcement of a possible physical liquidation.[6]

The search for a universal definition of hate speech is futile because, in reality, the social categories to whom hate speech is addressed have increased over time Walker outlines the fluidity of the definition of the term hate speech. According to him, it traditionally includes any form of expression considered offensive to any *racial, religious, ethnic or national group*. In the 80s of the 20th century, some speech codes in university campuses in the USA expanded the definition with *sex, age, sexual orientation, marital status, physical disability and other categories*. This development was also recognized by "*Human Rights Watch*" that defines hate speech as any form of expression considered offensive to racial, ethnic and religious groups and other minorities and women. For Rodney Smola hate speech is a generic term that includes voice attacks based on race, ethnicity, religion and sexual orientation.[7]

However clear and obvious the aforementioned definitions seem, in practice, it is often difficult to determine exactly what fulfills the actual state of hate speech because it is about complex communication, cultural and socio-psychological processes. Therefore, the more particular definition of hate speech depends on the wider social, historical and political context. So in the USA, the definition of hate speech firmly binds the right to freedom of expression, which is enshrined in the *First Amendment of the US Constitution*.[8] In Europe, the distinction between the notion of freedom of speech and hate speech is very clearly set so that the most relevant definition is the one the Committiee of Ministers of the Council of Europe passed in 1997 in its Recommendation R (97) 20. There, hate speech is defined as "all forms of expression which spread, incite, promote or justify racial hatred, xenophobia, anti-Semitism and other forms of hatred based on intolerance, including: intolerance expressed by

---

[6]Beham, Mira. 2004: "Govor mržnje u politici i medijima". Objavljeno u Vacic, Z. (ur.) 2004 Etika javne rijeci u medijima i politici, Centar za liberalno demokratske studije, Beograd, 2004.
[7]Walker, Samuel, Hate Speech: The History of an American controversy 8 (University of Nebraska Press 1994).
[8]We will look in more details in the historic development of the term hate speech in the following chapters.

aggressive nationalism and ethnocentrism, discrimination and hostility against minorities, migrants and people of immigrant origin".[9] Accordingly, the European Court of Human Rights in Strasbourg defines the term as "any form of expression which spreads, incites, promotes or justifies hatred based on intolerance, including religious intolerance."[10] It is important to note that this is a "autonomous" concept because the Court does not consider itself bound to the classification of the domestic courts. That's why it sometimes refutes the classifications adopted by the national courts, or otherwise, classifies certain phenomena as "hate speech" even when domestic courts did not adopt such classification. Since hate speech is an element which the Court takes into account, the question arises when that expression can be classified as hate speech in the absence of a precise definition, how to identify hate speech?

Criteria on identification of hate speech

The identification of statements that could be classified as hate speech is exercised harder, because this kind of speech is not always manifested by expressing hatred or emotions. Hate speech can be concealed in statements which, at first glance, may seem rational or normal and therefore acceptable. However, from the principles in the legal provisions of the Court of Human Rights or other bodies it is possible to draw certain parameters to distinguish expressions which, although with offensive nature, are fully protected by the right to freedom of expression of those who do not enjoy such protection.[11]

The concept of hate speech, according to the Court, encompasses a diversity of situations:

- firtstly, incitement to racial hatred or, in other words, hatred directed towards persons or groups of people on the basis of belonging to a certain race;

---

[9] CoE hate speech Factsheet, www.coe.int/t/DC/Files/Source/FS_hate_en.doc,December 2009
[10] Ibid
[11] A whole chapter will be dedicated to hate speech against freedom of expression.

- secondly, incitement to hatred on religious grounds, which can be equated with incitement to hatred based on discrimination between believers and atheists;
- lastly, incitement of other forms of hatred based on intolerance "expressed by aggressive nationalism and ethnocentrism."

Numerous definitions of this term indicate the importance of the wider social context for defining hate speech which, as a key aspect, emphasizes the identities they constructed as "marginal" in those contexts. Thus, Macuda highlights racial discrimination as a defining aspect of hate speech. According to her, it is for each message containing:

1. Message of racial inferiority;
2. Messages addressing a group that has a history of oppression;
3. Messages that are haunting, impatient and degrading.[12]

Individual authors are critical to the term "hate speech" itself which lays stress on the emotion of hate, which blurs the understanding of the true nature of discriminatory discourse (racial, sexual, ethnic and others) [13]. The essence of this speech is not the emotions, but the understanding and confirmation of the balance of power: hate speech is a strategy of establishing and maintaining domination of the privileged groups over stigmatized "others".[14] Terms are proposed which would be clearer and more applicable in the law itself as "conflicting words" (conflict words). A judge of the Supreme Court of the United States, Delgado offers "words that hurt", stressing that despite possible physical hate speech also has serious psychological consequences on the target group.[15] Its content and meaning are not determined only with direct and explicit expression of "hatred" - they largely rely on contextually-connotative meaning, defined by a wider system of symbolic expression of the power relationships. Precisely for that reason, it is difficult for hate speech to be universally

---

[12]Sbury, Mary Beth. and Haas, John, 2008: "An Exploratory Investigation of Whether Individuals Differentiate between Hate Speech and Offensive Language" An essay presented at the Annual Convention of NCA 94th Annual Convention, TBA, San Diego, CA, 20. novembar, 2008. godine.

[13]Kaminskaya, Elvira, 2008: "Hate Speech: Theory and Issues", CASE-UC Berkeley Field Project - Spring 2008 Work Products: 3-4:
http://iseees.berkeley.edu/sites/default/files/u4/iseees/caseproject_/KaminskayaFR.pdf

[14]Ibid

[15]Paull, Miller and Paull 2004, "Freedom of speech", Cambridge University Press: 24

defined and legally regulated, while those who know the respective social context and those who have felt discriminationcan easily recognize it.[16]

A universal definition is impossible because an act of "symbolic violence" does not have to have the same meaning in different social and historical contexts. As noted by Panchikj, every society tends to penalize precisely those forms and manifestations of hate speech perceived as harmful in the context of its "social trauma."[17] Taking all this into consideration, the discursive approach to the problem of hate speech embraced by Judith Butler is of particular importance for our analysis. As a form of "ideological recruitment" hate speech simultaneously violates subject, but also constructs it in within the specified discourse.[18]. Its key elements are - the identity of groups that become the target of hate speech; assigning negative characteristics of those identities; putting identity in symbolic order within the specified context, as well as encouraging or spreading violence and intolerance as a mechanism that determines, or gives the status of a particular identity. This last element is particularly important to distinguish hate speech from other symbolic forms of discrimination (such as, for example, the under-representation of minority identity in the public space, which is a form of discrimination, but not the hate speech). Hatred expressed through this kind of symbolic violence is not necessarily a guide to physical violence, nor is lynch the ultimate goal of hate speech - it is a strategy to construct, maintain and reaffirm privileged and marginalized identities, in accordance with the existing relations of power in a certain society.[19] Hate crime Itself can be defined as

---

[16] Asbury, Mary Beth. and Haas, John, 2008: "An Exploratory Investigation of Whether Individuals Differentiate between Hate Speech and Offensive Language", Paper presented at the annual meeting of the NCA 94th Annual Convention, TBA, San Diego, CA, Nov 20, 2008: 4.

[17] Klaric, Željko (ur.) 2009: "Govor mržnje u medijima", Cenzura, Novi Sad: 49.

[18] Kaminskaya, Elvira, 2008: "Hate Speech: Theory and Issues", CASE-UC Berkeley Field Project - Spring 2008 Work Products: 3-4; page 2. Text availbale at: http://iseees.berkeley.edu/sites/default/files/u4/ iseees/caseproject_/KaminskayaFR.pdf

[19] Individual cases suggest that the biggest problem of hate speech is that it causes, promotes or justifies hate crimes - one of the most unfortunately examples are war crimes in Bosnia and Rwanda, in which the media are often cited as "inspiration" and whose role in the production of the crimes is still being investigated (see more: Budimir, V. 2009, „Odgovornost medija za ratne zlocine", published on http://www.media.ba/bs/etikaregulativa-novinarstvo-ratni-zlocini-etika/odgovornost-medija-za-ratne-zlocine-1).

an act that includes intimidation, threats, destruction of property, assault, murder, motivated by an attitude or hatred towards an individual who belongs to a specific group. If it can proven that the act of hate crime was preceeded by hate speech or it appeared during the crime, hit can be treated as a motive and can become the subject of criminal investigation.[20]

Cortese writes in detail how societies have used hate speech to attach a stereotype to a group as stupid, dangerous or corrupted - and later they developed that stereotype to justify cruelty as slavery, expulsion of Indians or genocide. Currently, under the law in the United States of America, hate speech is regulated only if it represents an imminent threat. But Cortese shows that hate speech is most dangerous when it is built slowly and it is concentrated. Occasional brawl that occurs as a result of "fighting with words" is rather less dangerous than the campaign of defamation as the one that led to the massacre in Rwanda or extermination of Native Americans with the banner "only the dead Indian is a good Indian."[21]

In its foundation, hate speech based on stereotyping an individual or a group. Stereotypes and social distance play a major role in the development of ethnocentrism because they are based on common beliefs that members of a group have of the members of another group in the same or in other societies. Hate speech, prejudices, discrimination and hostility towards members of another group and privileged treatment of the own group, are the expected results of ethnocentrism.[22] This way, the feeling of confidence of the individual can rise through an exaggerated view of the value and importance of their own group or through disregarding the value and importance of other groups. Pride of a particular group can become exaggerated and cause hate speech and prejudices as well as the sense of self-worth in children who grow as members of an ethnic minority group, which has a position of lower status in the social division, which is also dangerous. When anger appears in one social group towards another social group, the members of the target group usually react by becoming bolder

---

[20]See more on: OSCE/ODIHR, Hate Crime Laws: A Practial Guide, OSCE / ODIHR, 2009; or: http://legal-dictionary.thefreedictionary.com/bias+crime
[21]Cortese, Anthony Joseph Paul, Opposing hate speech, Westport, Conn. : Praeger Publishers, 2006.
[22]Stephan, Walter G. "Intergroup Relations", In Gardner Lindzey and Elliot Aronson, eds., Handbook of Social Psychology. 3rd ed. New York: Random House, 1985

and more determined to maintain their social identity. Thus, the dominance of one group over another may initiate a vicious circle called self-fulfilling prophecy.[23]

Phase model of hate speech

One should know that not every hate speech is the same and indicates on a discriminatory statement. There is a big different between an insulting statement and an encouragement to commit murder, just as there is a substantial difference between intentional and unintentional discrimination. In order to classify discriminatory statements a "development model of the seriousness of hate speech in four phases" is proposed which is developed by cultural exchange, group identification and critical racial theories.[24] The model is developed and follows a logical flow from the smallest accident to the most serious case, often culminating in violent hate crime. At each phase of the model intervention strategies are also presented.

Phase 1: Unintentional discrimination: these incidents are happening beneath the surface of ordinary, everyday social behavior and when you talk about micro violations you think about these incidents. They are sudden, small meetings with racism, sexism or homophobia from the members of the majority race or group. or example, a white woman approaches a black woman she had never met before and, without permission, takes the liberty to touch her hair. Another example is a rich white woman from the American South, who does not understand why black people hate to be called "colored". Education and proper upbringing are the biggest intervention for unintended discrimination so it could stop and not allowed to become a factor in social communication processes. When someone hears hate speech he should react in order to teach the offender that what he said is stereotypical, discriminatory and hateful.

Phase 2: Intentional discrimination: firstly, here education is also the biggest intervention for its elimination from the public discourse; secondly,

---

[23] Merton, Robert K., "Social Theory and Social Structure", Rev. ed. Glencoe, IL.: The Free Press, 1957
[24] Cortese, Anthony Joseph Paul, Opposing hate speech, Westport, Conn. : Praeger Publishers, 2006.

speech code which prohibits hate speech may be introduced in institutions; third, there must be court proceedings against intentional violation supposed to cause emotional pain. Proving such a case is particularly difficult and therefore the question is under what conditions is hate speech considered harmful? In order to receive compensation from this activity, the plaintiff must meet four basic criteria:

1. Intention
2. Extreme and cruel behaviour
3. Cause
4. Serious emotional pain

It is clear that in phase 2 giving cause satisfies the search for intention. However, much of the hate speech existing does not cause serious emotional pain. Also, hate speech, exists which does not include an extreme and cruel behavior. Perhaps for these reasons, civil penalties would be more typical for hate speech which is referred to in phase 3.

Phase 3: Raising discriminatory hate: this form of hate speech is more serious than that in phase 2. Although education shows its negative side that will not change the stance of a convinced fanatic. Therefore this hate speech falls in the area covered by the code speech prescribed in the institutions. However, very often, hate speech is spoken in public, for example on the streets and therefore it is out of reach from any institutional speech code. Therefore, the severity of the hate speech in this phase makes it is easier for court litigation than the one in phase 2.

Phase 4: Raising discriminatory violence: this type of hate speech inevitably arouses criminal behavior - action that could never be protected by the judiciary never. Phases 2, 3 and 4 correspond to the definition of hate speech.

x x x

Although we did not manage to establish a universal definition of what constitutes hate speech, the many variations summarized would mean that hate speech disparage people based on their race or ethnic origin, religion, sex, age, disability, sexual orientation etc.[25] Hate speech consists of words that are used to terrorize, humiliate, degrade, ambush, hit, insult and injure. We have seen that even in recent times, it appropriated additional groups to which it relates and which should be protected from. Since the mid 80s of the 20th century, the hatred became to be used in a much broader form to characterize the negative beliefs of the individual, especially the feelings of members of another category of people based on their ethnicity, race, gender, sexual orientation, religion, age, physical or mental disability.[26] As is contained in the "concept of hate speech", this extended use includes prejudice, racism, hate towards women, homophobia, intolerance of elderly people, bias, xenophobia.

Such definitions of hate speech clearly mark the target groups to which they refer, however, in reality there is an easy backsliding and quick qualification of hate speech in discourse that may seem covered by the definition, however, does not constitute hate speech. Vasovic explains this as follows: although one campaign is followed by political speeches full of invective, offensive metaphors, denigrating and belittling the opponent, ignorance, hysterical irony and rash qualifications, however, major imaginativeness and and social creativity are needed for the whole political circus to be attributed as hate speech. Too strong a word must, despite the saturation of strong emotion, animosity, and even personal hatred, meet some more important criteria in order to be interpreted and branded as "socially relevant hatred" to which the aforementioned phrase refers. Those who abuse it in the daily political purposes deliberately bypass the fact confirmed by all serious social theorists, that hate speech does not belong in the area of interindividual but intergroup relations. This means that the term is in theory applied to explain relations (primarily conflicts) that exist between large social groups (race, nation, class, political group, sexual minorities), i.e. those on social level, not everyday disputes between two or more individuals. It is a *par excellence* collective phenomenon, even when manifested through individual actions. This means that, unlike the

---

[25] Sedler, R., "The Unconstitutionality of campus Bans on 'Racist Speech': The View from Without and Within", University of Pittsburg Law Review 53: 632-683, 1992

[26] Jacobs, James B., and Kimberly A. Potter, "Hate Crimes: A Critical Perspective", In. M. Torny, ed. Crime and Justice: A Review of Research Chicago: University of Chicago Press, 1998

individual hatred in personal relationships, hate speech is not determined by the personal characteristics of the actors, but by their belonging to different social groups or categories that permit promote and encourage such conduct. Not any quarrel between two grocers or even every verbal exchange between two presidential candidates can be characterized as hate speech, no matter how many personal insults and moral disqualifications they exchanged. Even when some of them in that duel expressed personal prejudice and intolerance or used stereotypes to label the opponent (as fascist, nationalist or mobster), his act can be assessed as unfair and morally unacceptable, but can hardly be assessed as hate speech. This phenomenon is not simply individual and private, but general and public morality. In order to be able to talk about it at all, the hatred and intolerance must be relatively common and socially relevant phenomena. That means, above all, it has to rely on a system of dominanat moral values prescribing and regulating the relations of the members of one against the members of another group, and not on personal morality and personal relationships. Moreover to be presented to individuals who are differentiated according to social criteria (those are nationality, religion, social status, political affiliation, sexual orientation) and not personal characteristics. Finally, they have to actually or potentially have some implications for all (not just some) individuals as members of the hate group. Only after individuals, as members of other, different group, are attributed negative characteristics (all are equal and all are bad) and in accordance with it, acts of discrimination are plotting against them, even more so when it is justified with a certain ideology that is common to many people and it is widespread in society, we can confidently say that we are in the courtyard of socially dangerous hatred. In the first case, it comes to spreading negative social stereotypes and prejudices, and other social discrimination.[27] Unjustified replacement of theses, i.e. reaching conclusions about the existence of social pathology, such as ethnical, racial or any other kind of hatred and intolerance, based on incidents that happen in the limited context of personal attitudes and interpersonal relationship (be it a discussion of

---

[27]Vasović, Mirjana, „Govor mržnje", mesečne političke analize „Prizma", Izdavač „Centar za liberalno–demokratske studije", Beograd, oktobar, 2002

political rivals in the fight for power), is nothing more than a rough political abuse.[28]

At the end of this chapter, in which we tried to define the term and meaning of hate speech, we would ask a seemingly rhetorical question that many encounter: are hate speech and language of hatred synonyms? In a working-colloquial terminology, hate speech or language of hatred are synonyms. However, in a professional and science-founded, psycho-social, socio-cultural, anthropological and cultural and communicational elaboration, the language of hatred is primarily bound to manifesting the spirit of intolerance through mediation of the media, while hate speech is linked to public appearances in other channels of communication, both formal and informal. It also includes the complete public sphere: politics, culture, art, science/pseudo-science, education, sports. There is a private area which also generates a spirit of intolerance that encourages hate speech - sports grounds, cafes, streets, etc.[29] However, we will leave this "de Saussure's" discussion to the linguistic theory, and our choice in the continuation of this study would be hate speech and its English transcription.

---

[28] In other words, in order for a political discourse to be marked as a promotion of hate speech the hate should be pointed not on an individual basis, but the collective background of the target entity. If we say for person X say thathet is unintelligent, thus we would personally offend him, yet not rushing hate speech. However, if we say that person X is unintelligent because he is black, Roma, gay, adult, female, deaf, then the condition for expressing hate speech on racial, ethnic, sexual, age, gender or disability grounds is met.

It should be taken into consideration that any offensive speech is not hate speech, but any hate speech in its semantic basis, offensive speech. The same is true of profane or vulgar speech, which usually is not considered hate speech, but rather a stylistic feature of one's personal discourse and as such it gives the impression of morality and (un education of the one who uses it. On the other hand, application of vulgarity in different artistic expression can represent and promote hate speech such as pornographic movie, and it is the leading force of hate speech against women in the ideologies of women haters.

[29] Babić, Dušan, "Jezik mržnje u javnoj sferi: fenomenološko-tipološke naznake karakteristične za ove prostore", regionalni glasnik za promociju kulture Manjinskih prava i međuetničke tolerancije, tema broja: jezik mržnje, 15. august 2004.

2. HISTORICAL OVERVIEW OF THE EMERGENCE OF HATE SPEECH

We already mentioned that the organized expression of hate speech began in the first decades of the 20th century, initially naming the problem of hate with different names. FInally in the eighties of the last century began the systematic and in-depth study of hate speech in most sciences that led to the generally accepted term. The two processes that happened in the 20th century influenced science to become more seriously interested in this phenomenon. One happened in Europe - the emergence of fascism in Italy and National Socialism in Germany, with racial policies for supremacy of the Aryan race and discrimination against Jews that culminated in the Holocaust. In the same period, in the United States again strongly influenced by racist theories of the supremacy of the white race, a similar process of discrimination and persecution of blacks, immigrants Catholics and Jews took place.

This chapter will broadly address the historical overview of hate speech by looking at the most typical cases in Europe and the USA during the 20th century and until today.

EUROPE

Germany in the thirties - creating an environment for crimes

Under the influence of racist theory, which was developed in the 19th century by some European anthropologists who studied "primitive people" at the beginning of the 20th century appeared the most radical form of racist theory – National Socialism. Soon after gaining power in Germany in 1993 the Nazis started realizing their two most important program objectives: convincing the German population in the superiority of the Aryan race[30] and eradicating any influence of the Jews in German politics,

---

[30] The term Aryan race is a concept in European culture, current between the late 19th century and early 20th century. It developed from the idea that the original speakers of Indo-European languages and their descendants to this day constitute a separate race. In his most famous version as part of Nazism, it says that the earliest Aryans were identical to Nordic nations. The belief in the superiority of the Aryan race is sometimes called

economy and culture. One of the leading ideologists of National Socialism was Alfred Rosenberg and he was considered the main author of the racist theory, the persecution of Jews, the annulment of the Treaty of Versailles and the opposition of modern "degenerate art". He is also famous for his rejection of Christianity.[31] In 1929, he founded the Militant League for German Culture (*Kampfbund für deutsche Kultur*), and later the Institute for the Study of the Jewish question, which assailed the Jewish influence on German culture and studied Jewish history of anti-Semitic position. In 1930 he published the book "The Myth of the Twentieth Century" (*Der Mythus des 20. Jahrhunderts*), in which he expressed his racial, sociological and pseudo historical ideas. This book together with Hitler's "My struggle" (*Mein Kampf*), represented the most important source of ideas of the Nazi movement. His ideas were based on the writings of previous authors who have affirmatively written about the racial theory and the superiority of the Aryan race, as Arthur de Gobineau, Houston Stewart Chamberlain and Madison Grant.

His views as well as the views of the party changed over time, but the ideas of the superiority of the white race, extreme German nationalism and anti-Semitism always dominated. At the bottom of his racial list were Blacks and Semites, and at the top, the white, Aryan race. The Nordic nations were considered most superior of Aryan nations, and among them Scandinavians are listed (including Finns), Germans, Dutch, Flemish and British. Of them all, at the highest position were Germans who formed the top of the list and were the only true descendants of the ancient Nordic people who have been credited with the overall progress of civilization. Rosenberg proclaimed a new religion of blood, based on ideas of racial spirit, especially the spirit of the Nordic race which, according to his understanding, fought against the degeneration caused by Jews.[32] He also condemned the teaching of the Protestant and Catholic churches, which he

---

aryavism. Aryan race is divided into two parts: northern or European Aryans and southern or Asiatic Aryans. Southern Aryans can be divided into three main branches: Armenians, Persians and Indians. Kurds and Avghans are of less ethical importance. Armenians and Celts are now few in number, but eaelier they spanned a larger area, from Armenia to Italy under the names Phrygia, Thracians, Pelasgians, Etrurci, and other places.

[31] Evans, Richard J (2004). The Coming of the Third Reich. London: Penguin Books.

[32] Cecil, Robert, The Myth of the Master Race: Alfred Rosenberg and Nazi Ideology,

called negative Christianity, and advocated the so-called positive Christianity based on the assumption that Jesus Christ had the origin of Nordic enclave Galilee and that he actively opposed to Judaism; Rosenberg primarily wanted to achieve the religious ideas to serve the racial ideas and to link the individual with his supposed racial nature. At the Nuremberg Trials he was being tried and sentenced to death and he was executed as a war criminal.

In the thirties in Germany, anti Jewish campaign was operationalized by adopting a series of regulations, which culminated with the proclamation of the Nuremberg laws (Law on the citizens of the Empire and the Law on Protection of German Blood and German Honor) from 1935, In their making participated yet another influential politician - Wilhelm Frick.[33] The Nuremberg laws were based on the racial theory that Jews as Semites (like Roma, non- Aryans), were perceived as the lowest race that should be isolated and, finally, eliminated. With these laws the Jews were forbidden to perform state and public services (which especially affected intellectuals: scientists, professors, doctors, lawyers, journalists etc.), marriages and relationships with Aryans were forbidden, they were forbidden to take Aryans in service, as well as to participate in cultur, sports and so on. Jews lost their German citizenship and their children could not attend public schools; the presence of Jews in public places (parks, libraries, museums, etc.) was prohibited.[34] These laws were later applied in all affiliated countries and occupied areas. Under German pressure, in 1938 Italy also introduced anti-Jewish legislation.

All these theories, laws and regulations were just preparation for what was to follow. At the start of World War II in 1939 started the so-called "final showdown" with the Jews. he decision was made at the secret conference near Berlin (Vance) on 20.01.1942, known as the Conference in Vance. At the meeting it was agreed to have all government agencies to participate in the extermination of Jews under the leadership of SS police. It was determined that that all people incapable of work should be immediately killed, while others were taken to forced labor under minimum

---

[33]He was sentenced to death for war crimes and crimes against humanity. His last words were: "Long live eternal Germany!".
[34]Hunt, L. (2009). The Making of the West: Peoples and Cultures, Vol. C: Since 1740. Bedford/St. Martin's.

living conditions until they died of exhaustion. As a form of mass liquidation killing with gas and shooting was ordered. A few months after the conference, in the camps of Auschwitz and Treblinka the first gas chambers were introduced.[35]

The role of Nazi media in promoting hate speech

The so planned systematic destruction of the Jews and other non-Aryan races was supposed to be generally accepted and implemented by the German people. Therefore, propaganda in the media, culture and art were used to spread hatred of Jews and were crucial in Hitler's triumphant path since the seizure of power by the end of his life. There is no doubt that Hitler and the National Socialists quickly understood the power of the media in ruling with the masses, and experts even today recognize Hitler's great insight and understanding of the importance of the media, which he in impressively skillful way used to his advantage. In his retrospective on the situation of the media in the Third Reich, Vladimir Barovic outlines not only the contemporary media, but also the social context and impact of the media with its propaganda function performed on the population.[36]

At the beginning of the conquest of power, a newspaper which was called "People's Observer" (*Volkischer Beobachter*) played a significant role. This newspaper had distinctively anti-Semitic sentiment, and one of the specific titles in the early twenties of the last century in this newspaper was "Let's clean up the Jews once and for all" (*Mancht Ganze Arbeit mit dem Juden* - 10.03.1920). The General Editor was the already mentioned, Alfred Rosenberg, party ideologue who had a column in which he popularized racial doctrine and National Socialist ideology. As part of the propaganda campaign against the Jewish people art has also been abused, and in the cultural section readers could see anti-Semitic songs and many pamphlets against "tainted Jewish art." "People's Observer" was considered one of the pillars of German propaganda, which is especially expressed after the start of World War II. Another newspaper was "Illustrated

---

[35] Browning, Christopher R., The Origins of the Final Solution (University of Nebraska Press 2004),

[36] Barović, Vladimir, „Mediji u Trećem rajhu", CM Časopis za upravljanje komuniciranjem, broj 5, godina II, Decembar 2007., Beograd

observer" (*Illustrierter Beobachter*), and the first number was published in November 1926, under the editorship of Nazi publishing house *Eher Verlag*. Once Hitler consolidated his power, the newspaper received a strong polemical tone and took an antisemitic course, in which roughest forms of attack on the Jewish people were often used. To illustrate an article named "Talmud" (*Talmud*), under the text editors set a drawing which showed a Jew watching a naked woman, and another picture showed crucified Jesus under whose feet Jews burned fire.[37] However, the infamous title of one of the most aggressive anti-Semitic newspapers in the Third Reich could bear the newspaper *Der Sturmer*. This journal is an example of the lowest form of journalism, which combining with pornography, attacked all possible aspects of Jewdeism (bizarre accusation that referred to Jews as the Jewish sexual crimes, ritual murders and conspiracy activities. News of Jewish crimes were received from the Gestapo, as well as various pornographic images and documents pertaining to the Jews), the Freemasonry and the Communism. There columns and sexual scandals and cartoons about Jews and illustrations of "Jewish people" attacking Christian women or stalking young German children. Especially grotesque were the anti-Semitic cartoons that presented Jews as characters with nonhuman, distorted faces and bodies (choice of Nazi caricatures in *Der Stürmer*, see the picture below). The most famous cartoonist was Philip Ruprecht, known as Phillips, whose cartoons are still popular in anti-Semitic circles.

---

[37] Snyder, L.Louis (1998). Encyclopedia of the Third Reich. Hertfordshire: Wordsworth Editions Limited

Der gute Onkel
Eltern
Der Stürmer
Der Jude
Kriegsanstifter
Kriegsverlängerer
Der Stürmer
Wirtschaft und Judentum
Die Juden sind unser Unglück!

Der Stürmer was an influential factor in the Nazi propaganda machine, especially among the lower social strata, with a major focus on anti-Semitism; the bottom of the front page saying "Jews are our misfortune!" (*Die Juden sind unser Unglück!*), under the headline it was written "German weekly to fight for the truth" (*Deutsches Wochenblatt zum Kampfe um die Wahrheit*) (Figure 1). It stopped being published in February 1945, and the latest news were mainly concerning the belief that news of the recent defeat of the German people are just Jewish propaganda. Together with the mentioned cartoonist Phillips, chief man in the newspaper was Julius Streicher, who gained fame and fortune with his work in the newspaper. His publishing house also published three anti-Semitic children's books, such as "Poisonous mushroom" (*Der Giftpilz*, 1938), which represented one of the most widespread propaganda which warned about the seductive danger of Jews, using metaphor attractive but deadly mushroom (Figure 2). Because of his work, that is the extreme hate speech and incitement to crimes against Jews in the Nuremberg Trials he was sentenced to death and hanged.

Figure 1　　　　Figure 2

Most Nazi organizations had their own specialized magazines and the official organ of the SS police was the weekly "Black Order" (*Das Schwarze Korps*). Heinrich Himmler used to write in it and he often expressed his racist views on the world by explaining the theory of pure Aryans. The essay newspaper attacked jazz music because it incited the wild instinct in people, "such as homosexuality". In several numbers of the weekly Himmler published an articles with a clear message that "illegitimate (illegitimate) children are the most beautiful thing in the world" and the newspaper began a real campaign in order to increase the birth rate of the German people. n one of the published readers' letters posted by the editorial board of " Black Order" one female reader wrote:

> *I read the excellent article in your last number really carefully. I'm impressed, I must admit! I also have an illegitimate child of a Nazi who I do not know. But don't worry. I am proud that I can give a child to our beloved Fuhrer, who I now reluctantly separate from myself in order to be brought up in a new spirit. I am almost dying for the little toddler with blonde hair and blue eyes. I understand that with my seventeen years I'm still too young to raise my son in the spirit of our National Socialist views. Therefore, in the name of the love of our Führer, our movement and our German people, I will give him in a National Socialist home for infants, as I was advised. You are probably wondering why I am writing to you, dear Black Oreder? Because we so sincerely committed to our brave breeds.*[38]

There were many similar reader's letters in the Nazi newspaper, as well as different articles and texts on racial characteristics, on the significance of National Socialism, on the German worldview. All the above elements list this newspaper in the worst form of propaganda and media which had no need for truth, but for ordinary ideologuesation.

The main inventor of the Nazi propaganda was Josef Goebbels, who was very adept at propaganda techniques, and wrote ten commandments for good propaganda, which represent the first codified and precise form of media manipulation. In March 1933, Goebbels was appointed Minister of Propaganda in the Third Reich, and he introduced the so-called "equalization" (*Gleichschaltung*) in public administration and all spheres of social life. In this system all the media were put under state supervision and the newspapers, radio and film had to align their creations with the Nazi wishes. The National Socialist ideology would not even from far been so quickly accepted by the German people if it wasn't for the Goebbels's information breakthrough performed through all mentioned media, including television, which was in its infancy.

---

[38] Helms-Liesenhoff, K.H.(1976). Gretchen u uniformi. Zagreb: Globus

From the very beginning of his mandate Goebbels organized attacks on German Jews, starting with the so-called one-day boycott of Jewish businessmen, doctors and lawyers on April 1, 1933. His attacks on the Jewish population culminated in the Crystal Night in 1938, which marked the beginning of organized persecution of Jews across Germany, in which many synagogues were burned, and hundreds of Jews were attacked and killed. Goebbels openly admitted that in its propaganda he used the lowest instincts of the German people - racism, xenophobia, class envy and insecurity. In his editorial, written in November 1941,in the newspaper *Das Reich*, Goebbels cited Hitler's "prophecy" from 1939 that the Jews will be losers in the upcoming World War.[39] "Now the prophecy of Hitler is becoming reality: Jews gradually suffer in the process of destruction which they allocated to us... They are now collapsing under their own rule 'Eye for an eye, tooth for a tooth!'[40], wrote Goebbels.

Besides the already mentioned ten propaganda commandments, Goebbels also introduced the rule that every editor in Germany had to be "politically and racially pure", as the Law on the Press of 1933 declared the journalistic profession a public profession and all the editors had to be German nationals, with Aryan origin, and were not allowed to marry non Aryan partner. Head of the state press and Goebbel' sassistant in the Ministry of Propaganda became Otto Dietrich who, along with his supervisor, caused real terror among German journalists. After taking the key positions in German society, the Nazis began to extinguish the liberal media, and that's how *Vossische Zeitung* , which had a tradition of 250 years vanished, as well as the Jewish publishing house "Ulistein". All Jewish owners had to sell their shares to Aman Nazi publishing house *Eher Verlag*.

German newspapers could intensify the anti-Semitic campaign, and as a process of confiscation of Jewish property and ownership in the German

---

[39]In 1939, in a speech to the Reichstag, Hitler told before the crowd: "If international Jewish finance, inside and outside Europe, managed to push nations into another world war, then the result will not be Bolshevisation of the world, and thus victory of the Jews, but the destruction of the Jewish race in Europe!".
[40]Browing, Christopher R., The Origins of the Final Solution, University of Nebraska Press, 2004, p 391.

media developed, Max Amman described the procedure before the Nuremberg Tribunal:

> Since the party came to power 1933 (...) many of these corporations, as Ulistein, that had been in the possession or under the supervision of Jewish capital or have been in political or religious conflict with the Nazi Party, considered desirabile to sell their newspapers or their part in them to Eher Verlag. For such sales no free market existed and Eher Verlag, usually, was the only bidder.

It is this tendency that soon became the most important target of Nazi cultural policy and the Ministry of Propaganda and the National Enlightenment founded in 1933. The removal of Jews from the cultural life has become a priority of the Nazis, following claims that the Jews, were not only in the leading areas of significant public media, publishing houses and theaters, but were also undermining German culture with modernist creations as atonal music and abstract painting.[41]

Besides newspapers, radio was a new means of informing in the expansion, which Goebbels considered an extraordinary technological achievement, which enabled him to every German at the same time to listen to the leader no matter that he is kilometers away from the site of the party meeting. Head of the radio propaganda in the Ministry of Propaganda was Hans Fritsche, whose show "Hans Fritsche Speaking!" (*Hier spricht Hans Fritzsche!*) earned enormous popularity and 16 million listeners. He wrote the best radio commentary in the Third Reich and was in charge of the national network to interpret the actions and attitudes of the party and the Government on the most important issues. Fritsche was inspired by the ideology of "Mein Kampf" and spoke to the listeners about the world Jewish conspiracy, plutocratic democracy that was destroying the power of the people, the Bolshevik danger, the advantage of the Firer's principles and its benefits for the country and the people. Before the war he spoke about Hitler's ingenuity, which, as he explained to the listeners, no one in German history had reached. Fritsch bombasticly announced the first wins of the German army in the West on the radio, while he later falsely billowed morality that increasingly lost weight because of the defeats and

---

[41]Evans, R. J. (2003). The Coming of the Third Reich. London: Penguin Books Ltd.

the faith for final victory was slowly but surely disappearing. Although there were many Nazi-minded journalists who spread insults at the expense of Jews and opponents of the Hitler regime, Fritsche, together with the editor of "Jurishnik" Julius Streicher, it is one of the few propagandists who, because of their actions, were found guilty by the court in Nuremberg.[42]

If we summarize the media image during the Nazi rule, as concluded by Barovic, we can be sure that we are not making a mistake when we say that it was completely eclipse of the media in the modern sense of the word and that any freedom of speech and free journalistic question were impossible and, in such an undemocratic system, almost unnecessary. The Idealess broadcast of party meetings, rallies and speeches were reimbursed with slogans and template texts, in which except hatred and new outbursts of rage, the reader already knew in advance what he will read. All non-Nazi dailies experienced their end, and anti-Semitic, party and racist press abruptly spread in favor of Hitler's regime, while specialized SS newspapers had a large circulation. The bottom of journalism and German media lasted until the collapse of the Nazi regime in 1945 and it should be added that any appearance of freedom of speech was stifled at the very beginning ...[43] The end of the war was marked by the Nuremberg Trials, which, besides the generals and governors of the concentration camps, who were directly blamed for killing millions of Jews and others who did not belong to the Nazi regime, were being tried and and the ideologists and propagandists of National Socialism were alsp imposed punishments, which sent a symbolic message to humanity that hatred "planted" by the media is equally as poisonous gas chambers.

---

[42]He was sentenced to nine years in prison, but was released in 1950. He died of cancer shortly after his release from prison. He was released because the tribunal was clear that he never advocated extermination of the Jews, and in two cases even tried to stop the publication of the anti-Semitic newspaper Der Stürmer.
[43]Barović, Vladimir, „Mediji u Trećem rajhu", CM Časopis za upravljanje komuniciranjem, broj 5, godina II, Decembar 2007., Beograd

Art in the function of racial policy and hate speech

The new German government believed that film is a very important propaganda tool and on the matter Goebbels said: "We are convinced that film is generally one of the most modern and most far reaching methods to influence the masses." Firstly, the German film was purified from the unwanted elements so that films were banned to "degenerate artists' (*Entarteter Künstler*), and were " German films. " highlighted. The state generously financed state projects which directly promoted the Nazi organization, which was presented as a messenger of a new era. In these projects, particularly notable was Leni Riefenstahl, who has filmed his life work "Triumph of the will (*Triumph des Willens*)in 1934 on the Congress of the Hitler party in Nuremberg. From a technical and artistic view this was a remarkable film that represented Hitler as a messiah of a new era who landed from the clouds among the people who euphorically followed him through the town while he firmly but cordially, hailed. The party was presented as a comprehensive organization that united the whole German people, and in their pathetic speeches "gaulajters" showed loyalty to the leader who was represented as a Roman god. As a sign of gratitude, Hitler made available unrestricted funds to Riefenstahl for the next project. These were the Olympic Games held in Berlin in 1936, which were recorded with the same artistic temperament and promoted the sports competitions, but with a clear allusion to the racial superiority of the Aryan man.[44]

However, the Nazi regime was not satisfied only with indirect propaganda, but wanted an open movie humiliation and insults for the Jews, so in 1940, Eric Vasnek has recorded "Rothschilds" (*Die Rothschilds Akten von Vaterloo*), and in the same year "The Eternal Jew" (*Der ewige Jude*) by Fritz Hipler, that is "The Jew Zis" (*Jud Suss*) from the author White Harlan were broadcasted.[45] If we analyze these films we will see that these works are a classic example of abuse of the arts in party purposes, and despite the propaganda they are works full of anti-Semitism, insults to

---

[44]Ibid
[45]Kuk, A.Dejvid (2005). Istorija filma I-II. Beograd: Clio.

the "lower races and nations" and besides praising the leader and the party do not have some artistic qualities worth mentioning.[46]

Immediately after coming to power, the Nazis attacked the modernist trends in art, trying to overthrow the alleged Jewish "cultural Bolshevism", which, according to their claims, "spread contagion in painting, music and literature in the Weimar Republic".[47] The heads of the Nazi cultural policy actually simply repeated similar already indicated, claims of the German historian R. Von Trichke who also claimed that Jews undermine German culture and popularized the phrase "the Jews are our misfortune" which in the following years became a slogan of the Nazis and anti-Semites.[48] Almost identical to the position of Trichke was the position of the popular German writer of the late 19th century, J.Lanben, and a half century ago, the composer R. Wagner. In the book "Judaism in Music" (Das Judenthum in der Musik), from the early fifties of the 19th century, the famous composer wrote that the Jewish spirit is "detrimental to the musical depth."[49] The key works of the National Socialist worldview "Mein Kampf" by A. Hitler, and "The Myth of the 20th century," by A. Rosenberg, contained racist views on art. In Paragraph 25 of the program of the Nazi party in 1920, legal prosecution was even required for all tendencies in art and literature which could disintegrate the life of the German nation. Thirteen years later, the Law on Reconstruction of the Professional Civil Service (*Gesetz zur Wiederherstellung des Berufsbeamtentums*) allowed Nazi officials to expel from work all civil servants who weren't with Arian origin. In accordance with this, since April 7, when the law was enacted by the end of the year, 20 managers of museums and curators were fired.[50]

The aesthetics of modern painting Was also attacked. It was believed that it doesn't posses recognizable elements from the German tradition, so all schools of modern art in Germany were quickly closed. Modernistic

---

[46]Barović, Vladimir, „Mediji u Trećem rajhu", CM Časopis za upravljanje komuniciranjem, broj 5, godina II, Decembar 2007., Beograd
[47]Evans, R. J. (2003). The Coming of the Third Reich. London: Penguin Books Ltd.
[48]Kuljić, T. (2002). Prevladavanje prošlosti, Uzroci i pravci promene slike istorije krajem XX veka, Beograd: „Zagorac".
[49]Evans, R. J. (2003). The Coming of the Third Reich. London: Penguin Books Ltd.
[50]Atlagić, Siniša, Nacistička umetnost i propaganda CM Časopis za upravljanje komunicira,njem, broj 11, godina IV, 2009, Beograd

painting for Hitler was the product of "Jewish subversion and dismal set of crazy and degenerate people." The cruelest attack on contemporary art, during the reign of the Nazis, was the "Exhibition of degenerate art" (*Entartete Kunst*), which was opened in Munich on 19 July 1937. On this occasion, 650 works were exposed - paintings, sculptures, books and other printed content that just weeks earlier, consisted the parts of 32 museum collections across Germany. The purpose of collecting and presenting these works in one place was to show how art that is unacceptable looks like, because in its foundation it is non-German. During the four months, in which the exhibition was opened in Munich, it was visited by more than two million people, and over the next three years, which is how long it "traveled" through Germany and Austria, it was visited by several million people. Until then no exhibition of contemporary art in Germany was organized with such success and attendance. According to the news reports, five times as many people visited the "Exhibition of degenerate art" then the "Exhibition of the great German art" (*Grosse Deutche Kunstaussiellung*). The parallel organization of these two "exibitions" had propaganda character. The aim was to make a comparison between the two arts, to emphasize the character of the anormal character of modern painting with motifs of deformed and sick people, on the one hand, against "valuable" German painting in which constant motifs became the typical representatives of the higher race: strong personalities of men - the builders of the great German future and women - mothers of German Superman. The audience was left to choose between "sick" and "healthy". In the background of this comparison were the contours of one of the basic methodological principles of propaganda - simplifying the image of the world. The overall approach to the exhibition was "designed" as early as 1933, when the messenger "Report on German Arts" (*Deutscher Kunstbericht*), under the jurisdiction of Goebbels, a Manifesto in five items was published, which stated "what German artists expect the new Government". The first item introduced that "all works that have Bolshevik-cosmopolitan character" should be removed from German museums and collections. However, before that was done they should be presented to the public, which should be informed about the details about how they got there, and then to be burned. Most of the content of the

Manifesto was prepared by the artists who in the previous period remained outside the mainstream of the avant-garde.[51].

The same propaganda principle made of the exhibition, was previously emphasized by P. Schulze-Naumberg, an architect and racial theorist who in the work "Art and Race" of 1928, pointed out the similarities of modernist images of Modigliani, Dix and others with the pictures of sick people, concluding that modernists generally represent inferior aspects of modern German culture. In dichotomy, whose poles carried strong emotional charge (good - bad, acceptable - unacceptable), the negative elements were closely related to "modern" and "Jewish" and positive the with the "traditional" and "German". This way the "guilty" was found in the image of the Jews, and everything that was unacceptable was identified with the "enemy" in order to eliminate him from the political scene.

Literary works also under severe attack of theNazi ideology were filled with racist and anti-Semitic content. The poet D. Ben said that since 1918 literature in Germany developed under the term "jazz", "cinema", "exotic", "speed" and "technology" and that the spiritual problems of Germany were completely neglected. He wrote that he was against Americanism in art and thought that the philosophy of pure utilitarianism does not correspond to the Western man and his history.[52] This critics close to him and attacked the then Western art, calling it besides "Americanism" also "cultural Bolshevism". This sharp criticism went hand in hand with a strong anti-Semitism that is patronizing with efforts to put an end to the alleged Jewish domination in art.

Such social climate influenced Germany to lose its most important writers: Brecht Remarque, the brothers Mann, Zweig, Werfel, Hesse, Kesten and many others. It is estimated that since Nazis came to power some 2,500 writers left Germany. According to Evans by the end of 1933 no significant and talented writer stayed in Germany.[53] "Mein Kampf" by

---

[51]Barron, S. (2001): „Modern Art and Politics in prewar Germany" in Barron (ed.), Degenerate Art: The Fate of the Avant-Garde in Nazi Germany. Los Angeles: County Museum, Pp 9 – 23.
[52]Palmer, T., Neubauer, H. (2000). The Weimar republic Through the Lens of the Press. Könemann
[53]Evans, R. J. (2003). The Coming of the Third Reich. London: Penguin Books Ltd.

Hitler was promoted as the ultimate literary work, and until 1940 over six million copies of this book were sold. New standards for German literature were established and four thematic categories were determined in which the authors should write: 1. *Fronterlebnis* - experiences of the war, with an emphasis on the friendship between military comrades, 2. *Weltanschauung* - Nazi worldview; 3. *Heimatroman* - works in which local German themes prevailed, with emphasis on the national mysticism and 4.*Rassenkunde* - contents in which racial doctrines are highlighted, which indicated the difference between the gifted Germans and people with defective non-Aryan origin.[54]

While Nazi propagandists led the campaign against fine art under the slogan "Against degenerated art" the actions in the field of literature and theory of society were conducted under the moto of struggle "against anti-German spirit." Like many others simingly spontaneous folk activities the action of burning a book with "anti-German spirit" of May 10, 1933, was also organized by the Ministry of Propaganda. The action was intended with its meaning, mass and shock effect to cause propaganda effects on the participants and witnesses of the event, but also on those who were transferred the testimony of the event. The place where the event of burning the books took place - the Opera Square in Berlin – students were present who were close to the National Socialist party, several junior professors, and himself Goebbels also joined. The presence of the Minister was supposed to show the solidarity of the new state with "popular sentiment". On this occasion, Goebbels, among other things, said: "The soul of the German people can be expressed again. This flame not only illuminates the end of an old era, but sheds light on the new age".[55] Above all, it was a "personal example" as a form of propaganda an action based on a general psychological principle of looking up, that is identification.

After the National Socialist party came to power, work in the field of music, also fell under the control of the Ministry of Propaganda and the National Enlightenment. The Law of the Reich on Reconstruction of the Professional Civil Service made possible the dismissal of all Jewish

---

[54]Atlagić, Siniša, Nacistička umetnost i propaganda CM Časopis za upravljanje komuniciranjem, broj 11, godina IV, 2009, Beograd
[55]Snyder, L.Louis (1998). Encyclopedia of the Third Reich. Hertfordshire: Wordsworth Editions Limited.

musicians from the symphony orchestras and opera. They were fired and the famous professors and Schoenberg and Shremer, lecturers of the Prussian Academy of Arts in Berlin. Most music critics and musicologists, who had to leave their jobs, were denied access to the press. Because of their Jewish origin works composed by Meyerbeer nad Mendelsson and were not performed. German orchestras were forbidden to perform works of Hindemith, a world recognized and, at that time, leading German composer. Mainly works of Hitler's favorite composer Richard Wagner were performed.[56]

According to Altagikj this position of art in Nazi Germany had only one function – to fulfill the imperative of creating a picture of Hitler in the role of messiah. Propaganda initiated a mass psychosis and a belief through art that a new, desired type of German man, a man of the future is created. German art "adjusted" the Nazi myth of the Aryan race and contributed in shaping the Nazi society and, in this sense, allowed exceptional conditions for the action of the propaganda.[57] The main victims of this propaganda were Jews and political opponents who, before their mass killings and deportations, were first exposed to strong racist speech (then-expression hate speech), which found a successful application and manifest in all kinds of arts and creations.

Italy - manipulation and hatred for the triumph of fascism

Along with the success of National Socialism in Germany, a similar process of totalitarian rule with the country occurred in Italy. Despite the similarities both regimes had which mirrored in the great brutality with which with which they used to deal with opponents of the rule and infatuation with the world, however, fascism in Italy had some specifics that made it different from the Hitler regime. Just as for Hitler with the Germans with, the main priority Mussolini was also to win the Italian people with its totalitarian policy. To accomplish this he strongly used propaganda. The press, radio, education, films, were all carefully

---

[56] Atlagić, Siniša, Nacistička umetnost i propaganda CM Časopis za upravljanje komuniciranjem, broj 11, godina IV, 2009, Beograd
[57] Ibid

supervised as to create the impression that fascism is the new successful doctrine of the twentieth century which was to replace liberalism and democracy. The dominant feature of this regime propaganda was building and maintaining the cult of the personality of Mussolini. All editors of newspapers were personally selected by him and no one who did not have a certificate from the fascist party could not be engaged in journalism. These certificates were secretly issued, by which Mussolini skillfully created an illusion that the press is free. Besides control of the press and public speech, he relatively successful dealt with political opponents, by which he closed another outlet for critical speech, besides the non-free press. Thus the road to party rule was completely open and the the masses led by the idea of Italians as a chosen people, destined to continue the glory of Roman legionnaires were completely under his hypnosis.

The entire political doctrine of Mussolini, which encountered massive approval of the population, was called *spazio vitale* ("vital space"), and represented a fascist concept, analogous to the German National Socialist *Lebensraum* ("living space"). The concept of spazio vitale was first published in 1919, and in it the entire Mediterranean was declared as an exclusive sphere of influence of Italy. This was justified with the explanation that Italy suffered from overcrowding and it is necessary to colonize other areas of the Mediterranean, populated as it was claimed, with less developed nations. Borrowing this idea first developed by Enrico Corradini before 1914, the natural conflict between on the "plutocratic" nations such as Britain and "proletarian" nations such as Italians, Mussolini claimed that the principal problem of Italy was that "plutocratic" nations blocked Italy to achieve the necessary vital space that would lead to the growth of the Italian economy.[58]

With this, Mussolini has paralleled the national potential for economic growth with territorial size, by which, in his view, the problem of poverty in Italy could only be solved if the necessary vital space was conqured. Although biological racism was less visible than in Fascism than in National Socialism in Germany, from the very beginning of propaganda for the required vital space, it had strong racist idea in it, in which Mussolini claimed that a "natural law" is the stronger nations to manage and dominate

---

[58]Kallis, Aristotle. 2000. Fascist Ideology. London: Routledge

the "inferior peoples", as were, according to him, the "barbaric" Slavic peoples of Yugoslavia. In the same way, Mussolini claimed that Italy is entitled to pursue imperialist policies in Africa because black people were "inferior" compared to whites.[59] His conquering ambitions were realized with the occupation of Ethiopia, which was explain ed with the fascist rhetoric as "advancing civilization". Other European states were invited to back Italy against the "savage and cannibals from Ethiopia".[60] Since he did not receive such support, the attack on Ethiopia was justified as an example of Italian power and idealism, which easily tore down the decadent, lazy and cowardly democracy, especially the one which supported the Barbarians and was against "the mother of civilizations".[61] It is clear that the aggression of Ethiopia to Mussolini was just cause for confrontation with democratic systems in Europe and the USA (the same as Hitler in Germany) to promote his arrangement as successful and to suspend democracy. Populist politics was she which gave him fuel in his aggressive rule, in whichthe war in Ethiopia was greeted by the people with one of the most impressive ceremonies in fascist Italy, called the initiative "Gold for the Fatherland" in which citizens donated gold jewelry, even wedding rings in exchange for a metal bracelet on which the words "Gold for the Fatherland" were engraved. The collected donated gold was used to finance the war in Ethiopia.[62]

Before starting his triumphant march expansionist policy in the eastern Mediterranean and later in Africa, Mussolini managed to strengthen positions in the internal political struggle with brutal clashes with other political representatives, primarily with the Socialists and Communists. Fascists, led by one of the most trusted men of Mussolini, Dino Grandi, formed armed squads of war veterans called "Balck Shirts" (squadrists), in order to restore order to the streets of Italy with a firm hand. The "Balck Shirts" collided with communists, socialists and anarchists at parades and demonstrations. The government rarely interfered in the actions of the "Black Shirts", which was due in part to the threat and widespread fear of

---

[59]Ibid
[60]Cannistraro, P. V. (April 1972). "Mussolini's Cultural Revolution: Fascist or Nationalist?". Journal of Contemporary History (SAGE Journals Online) 7 (3)
[61]Smith, Denis Mack, Mussolini's Roman Empire, p 71
[62]Brendon, Piers, The Dark Valley: A Panorama of the 1930s, p322-3

communist revolution. Socialism was convicted, especially its international forms and socialist sympathizers were imprisoned as "Russian army".[63] A pro-fascist newspaper editor, fearing that Fascist violence will be condemned by the women, convinced them that the killings were necessary to save Italy from the "Bolshevik beast."[64]

In his first speech as a member of Parliament, Mussolini stated that there was no chance for an agreement between communists and fascists although he was willing to cooperate.[65] The later Spanish civil war was also presented in the Italian fascist propaganda as a "crusade war against communism". In a totalitarian country the presence of foreign cultures (as in Germany) was also a target of attacks. "Americanism" was the subject of organized propaganda because it conquered as "greasy stain that spreading across the entire area of European life".[66] French and Russian literature were also accused of polluting the youth, and British literature was used to be presented as decadent, just as was the French. The low birth rate in these countries was mocked and it was propagated that Italy saved Britain and France in the First World War.[67]

All propaganda activities were concentrated and implemented by one press center, until in 1937 Ministry of National Culture was established.[68] A separate Ministry of Propaganda was founded in 1935 with main aim to tell the truth about Fascism, refuting the lies of its enemies, as well as to clarify ambiguities that could be expected in such a large and dynamic movement.[69] The main theme in the propaganda was to present Mussolini as superior, even mythical creature with superhuman nature (news were placed on how Mussolini managed to stop the leak of lava from the volcano Etna or that he caused rain in the dry Sahara, during his visit to Libya). Newspapers were divided into pro -fascist, who were awarded large financial subsidies, and the others, which were usually banned on charges of publishing false information in order to spread hatred among the

---

[63] Bosworth, R. J. B., Mussolini's Italy, p134
[64] Ibid
[65] Gallo, Max, Mussolini's Italy, p122 Macmillian Publishing Co. Inc., 1973 New York
[66] Smith, Denis Mack, Mussolini's Roman Empire, p 28
[67] Ibid
[68] Rhodes, Anthony, Propaganda: The art of persuasion: World War II, p70-1 1976, Chelsea House Publishers, New York
[69] Smith, Denis Mack, Mussolini's Roman Empire, p 85

population and to discredit the government. In 1926 a decision was brought on the necessity of government permission to allow anyone to deal with publishing or publishing a paper.[70]

Besides newspapers, the radio was also widely used for popularization of the fascist propaganda and defamation of political opponents. Mussolini especially used the radio to transmit his speeches and as a tool for indoctrination of the youth with fascism.[71] Film was not massively used for propaganda because the Italian public was not particularly interested in "serious" films produced by the government, so the strategy for the seventh art was more related to censorship of unwanted film materials. Therefore, a government body was established to produce documentary films in order to explain to the population the achievements of fascism.[72]

Many of the leading Italian graphic artists accepted to draw fascist posters. To oppose the British pamphlets, their posters showed that the rule in Britain would be worse than bombing and that barbarism would occurr. Americans were presented as robbing the the wealth of Italy.

Parallel to these propaganda activities, another process took place: italisation of street names and monuments in Slavic and German language regions of Italy, there were also legal prohibition for the teaching in schools to be conducted in a language other than Italian. Teaching programs in schools were adjusted for fascist objectives (manner which the Nazis later admitted they imitatated), so primary schools spent twenty percent of their time for teaching on teaching children to be good fascists. Those teachers who resisted were removed, and textbooks were required to have an explicit content about the "fascist soul".[73] Back in 1926, a law ordered to itallianize the surnames of the Slavic population.

---

[70]Rhodes, Anthony, Propaganda: The art of persuasion: World War II, p80-1 1976, Chelsea House Publishers, New York
[71]Ibid
[72]Ibid
[73]Gallo, Max, Mussolini's Italy, p220 Macmillian Publishing Co. Inc., 1973 New York

Racial policy in fascist Italy

Regarding the racial question, Mussolini claimed that the world is divided according to a hierarchy of races (stirpe), which was based more on cultural than biological basis, and that history is nothing more than a Darwinian struggle for power and territory between the different "racial masses". The mere fact that Italy suffered from overcrowding was taken as evidence of the cultural and spiritual vitality of the Italians, who sought with a reason to colonize countries that Mussolini claimed belonged to Italy as a successor of the Roman Empire on historical basis.. According to Mussolini, demography was fateful; nations with increased population were destined to conquer, and nations with reduced populations have reduced power and therefore deserve to die. Hence, the importance of birth rate for Mussolini was crucial, because only by increasing the Italian birth rate Italy could, in the future as a great power, secure the conquered spazio vitale. For Mussolini, the Italian population had to reach 60 million to be able to fight a major war and therefore he had ruthless demands of Italian women to have more children in order to reach the magic number of 60 million.[74] His dream was to create an Italian nation which will be big, respected, and feared from Europe and the whole world. In his statement in 1928, he emphasized the importance of the vitality of the race:

> *When the city dies, the nation deprived of the young blood of the new generations is created by people who are old and degenerate and cannot defend themselves from the young people who begin to attack the undefended borders [...]. This will happen not only in the cities and among the nations, but also on a much larger scale: the entire white race, the western race can be submerged by other colored races which are multiplying at a rate unknown to our race.*[75]

Although Italian fascism has changed the official position to race from 1920 to 1934, however, in its ideology it initially did not discriminate Italian Jews. Even Mussolini acknowledged that a small contingent of Jews lived there "since the days of the kings of Rome" and should "remain

---

[74] Kallis, Aristotle. 2000. Fascist Ideology. London: Routledge.
[75] Griffen, Roger (ed.). Fascism. Oxford University Press, 1995. Pp. 59.

intact".[76] Curiously, there were some Jews in his National-Fascist party, as was Ettore Ovaca, who in 1935 founded the Jewish fascist party La Nostra Bandiera (Our Flag). But by 1938, Mussolini was heavily affected by Hitler, which became apparent with the introduction of the so-called Manifesto of the Race. The manifesto, which was modeled on the Nazi Nuremberg laws was a set of laws adopted in fascist Italy during July 1938. The laws were considered anti-Semitic and they took from the Jews thier Italian citizenship. With racial laws, marriages between Italians and Jews were annulled, the Jews were removed from positions in banking, government, and education, and their properties were confiscated. The Manifesto of the Race declared Italians descendants of the Aryan race, and as its title implies, it pointed out the races that are seen as inferior. These laws also were targeted towards African races. Among the 42 signatories of the Manifesto of the Race, there were two doctors, an anthropologist, a zoologist and a statistician. With this manifesto, Mussolini decided to adjust to the National Socialists with the introduction of anti-Semitic laws in Italy as proof of his loyalty to the alliance between Italy and Germany. This shift towards racism caused some nationalists to approach the latent biologism, by which Fascist regime changed from anti-racism into a racial anti-Semitism of German type.[77] The German influence on Italian politics disrupted the established balance in Fascist Italy and proved to be very unpopular to most Italians, so that the Pope Pius XII sent a letter to Mussolini in which he protested against the new laws.

Historians widely speculated on the reason for Mussolini to adopt the Manifesto of the Race in 1938 and agreed that it was just a tactical game in order to strengthen the relations of Italy with Germany on the eve of World War II. In an interview in December 1943, Mussolini, expressed remorse for adopting the Manifesto of the Race:

> *The Manifesto could have been avoided. It dealt with scientifically vague thought of a few professors and journalists and a German essay, which was translated into bad Italian. It is incompatible with what I have*

---

[76]Hollander, Ethan J (1997) (PDF). Italian Fascism and the Jews. University of California.
[77]Gregor, A. James; The Search for Neofascism, New York, Cambridge University Press (2006).

> *said, written and signed on this topic. (...) For these reasons, I am far from accepting the myth of Alfred Rosenberg*[78]

Mussolini also referred to the Muslims in his empire and most of the Arab countries in the Middle East. In 1937, Muslims from Libya presented to Mussolini the "Sword of Islam" while Fascist propaganda presented it as the "Protector of Islam."[79] He once said that "Islam is perhaps more effective religion from Christianity". Mussolini expressed a fierce attack against Christianity and the Catholic Church. He believed that the Socialists who were Christians or who have accepted the church marriage should be expelled from the party. He accused the Catholic church of "its authoritarianism and its refusal to allow freedom of thought".[80] Despite such attacks, Mussolini was aware that he needed to maintain popularity among the population in which the Catholics dominated. Therefore, he fast reterred and took more measures with which he managed to get closer to the Catholic Church and the Vatican. Such wooing policy towards the clergy brought him the privilege to be praised by the Pope Pius XI and the official Catholic newspaper wrote that "Italy has been restored to God and God to Italy."[81] However, since 1938, Mussolini returned again to his anti-clericalism. He could once in a while say for himself that he is a "complete infidel," and that "the papacy is a malignant tumor in the body of Italy which must be eradicated once and for all, because there is no place in Rome for the Pope and for him."[82]

The turbulent political scene in Italy, until the collapse of fascism in 1943, is characterized by a system that covered every area of the public and private life of the population and represented a totalitarian system of the most brutal kind. The proclaimed fascist ideology and the prohibition of a different opinion led to a complete suspension of freedom of speech. In such a setting, the political discourse of the fascists had unrestricted ability

---

[78] Gillette, Aaron (2002). Racial Theories in Fascist Italy. Routledge. p. 95.
[79] Arielli, Nir (9 June 2010). Fascist Italy and the Middle East, 1933–40. Palgrave Macmillan.
[80] Smith, Denis Mack. 1982. Mussolini: A biography, Borzoi Book published by Alfred A. Knopf, Inc.
[81] Roberts, Jeremy (2006). Benito Mussolini. Minneapolis, MN: Twenty-First Century Books, p. 60.
[82] Smith, Denis Mack. 1982. Mussolini: A biography, Borzoi Book published by Alfred A. Knopf, Inc.

to inspire (un)official dealings with political opponents who were guided in parallel with meaningful campaigns, propaganda and liquidations. The propaganda was led in popularizing the ideology of superiority of the Italian nation, but also in spreading of hatred towards the "inferior" peoples. The vocation of Mussolini as a writer and journalist only has only been his advantage from the very beginning of his political career, to use the power of media and public speech for stronger promotion of his ideas, which represented, according to current notions, hate speech with political, religious, ethnic, gender and racial character. But above all, they had utilitarian nature, motivated by the desire for longer and more comfortable retention of power, unlike German National Socialism, which had strong ideological and theoretical foundation and was systematically implemented.

Hate speech in post-war Europe - from condemnation to controversy

The end of the Second World War and the traumatic experience of National Socialism, led to the development of awareness in Europe to a level that would never again allow to enable creating a setting in which you can systematically develop hatred towards an entire people and for it to represent preparation for its physical liquidation. The numerous regulations, conventions, recommendations and declarations adopted in the years following the war, will only fram this attitude and formalize it in regulations that prohibit and condemn hate speech.

Below we will look at several characteristic cases that describe the situation in post-war Europe, which, in some cases, was on the verge of controversy between hate speech and free speech.

It is understandable for the public in Germany to be most sensitive to the cases of hate speech, and there the regulation shall most rigorously treat such cases because the effects of hate speech not only determines the current social situation, but also the historical experience as well as the cultural and political values and norms. Therefore in Germany after the Second World War any public expression of anti-Semitism leads, because of the National Socialist past, to strong reactions not only from the small but influential Jewish community, but also from the general public. The criteria for defining what antisemitic statements are, are very low and most such statements, as well as any denial of the Nazi crimes (in the form of so-called Auschwitzlüge - lies about Auschwitz) is subject to criminal prosecution. A good example of such a mechanism is the scandal of the Christian Democratic politician Martin Hochman, Member of the German Federal Parliament. In a speech to a small audience on the Day of German Reunification, on October 3, 2003, accidentally discovered by a journalist online, Hochman presented the thesis that "the Jewish people in recent history has its dark side, because the Bolshevik movement in Russia was 'led by Jews'. Therefore, Jews may be called 'people blamed' (Tätervolk). And because Jewish Bolsheviks have also given up Christianity as National Socialists, neither Germans nor Jews are a nation of balmed ". Under strong public pressure, even before the criminal charges against Hochman by the Jewish community in Germany even enter the procedure, the Christian Democratic Party was forced to exclude its representative from the parliamentary club, as well as from the Parliament. To which extent was the whole affair politically explosive shows also the fact that the chief of the special unit of the German army was fired only two and a half hours after the information leaked to the public that he congratulated Hochman for "remarkable speech".[83]

In the review of the state of hate speech in Europe since the Second World War, the most striking and spectacular is the case of the writer Salman Rushdie and his novel "The Satanic Verses" (The Satanic Verses), published in 1989. Rushdie's novel was received in the West with enthusiasm, and the author was recognized as one of "the most original and most talented writers of our time", while the then Iranian government, based on the opinion of religious experts estimated that Rushdie had "insulted the Prophet Muhammad in the fundamental principles of Islam" and therefore the author was sentenced to death in the form of a fatwa. In the non-Muslim world public that act was deemed "an act of political terrorism" and in the Muslim world prevailed the view that Rushdie has "offended the religious feelings of millions of Muslims" and that, therefore, he deserved some kind of punishment (although not necessarily death).

---

[83]Beham, Mira. 2004: "Govor mržnje u politici i medijima". Objavljeno u Vacic, Z. (ur.) 2004 Etika javne rijeci u medijima i politici, Centar za liberalno demokratske studije, Beograd, 2004.

Italian journalist Orijana Fallaci caused a storm of protests in Europe because of her attitude expressed in the book "The Rage and The Pride", in which, among other things, she says that Muslims "multiply like rats and spend the day with buttocks raise in the air, praying five times a day". Fallaci's passionate polemic on Islam ("The only difference between modern and radical Islam is the beard") and opposition to European and Arab anti-Semitism, was the subject to legal debate in France, where non-governmental human rights organizations filed criminal charges for hate speech and demanded the book be withdrawn from the French market. Orijana Fallaci was acquitted of all charges, and the book became a million bestseller, especially in countries with large Muslim communities such as Italy, Germany and France. Fallaci was not punished, although in France there are laws that sanction hate speech.[84]

In contrast, Great Britain after World War follows the American model of wider freedom of speech, so, many British media are known for their uncontrolled vocabulary referred to different (social) groups. Especially when it comes to the Germans, the British newspaper headlines often use comparisons with Nazis or Prussian militarists, who, according to statements by a former German ambassador in London, constantly fed negative stereotypes and cause physical attacks. Thus, according to the diplomat, the title before the football match Germany - England, We want to beat Fritz! ("We want to beat Fritz" - and Fritz is an allusion to the last German emperor), led to incidents in which German children were beaten in England. Newspapers, of course, were not punished because there were no public protests.[85]

That in liberal democracies open insults without sanctions, but also without serious consequences for social relations are possible, shows the media war that broke out in 2003 between England and America, on the one hand, and France, on the other hand, due to opposition of the French to the military campaign against Iraq. Top-selling English daily newspaper "The Sun" published several special editions in which the French President Chirac is represented as a worm and, among other things, was called "Sadam's whore". French public felt extremely offended and in the war of

---

[84]Ibid
[85]Ibid

words, largely returned to old stereotypes of the long Anglo-French hostility.[86]

This review would be incomplete if it did not mention the case of the "Mohammed cartoons" published in the Danish newspaper "Jyllands-Posten" on 30.09.2005 in which the Prophet is presented in a derogatory manner that cause a severe reaction among Muslims around the world. Such a reaction has forced the Danish newspaper to send an open letter to Muslims in which it gave explanation that the illustrations were not intended to offend anyone and that it is sorry about the inconvenience incurred. However, apology was not expressed because the cartoonists defended with the freedom of speech.

The chronological overview shall be finished with our region, starting with the civil war in Yugoslavia at the beginning of the nineties of the last century. As assessed by Beham, analysis of the communication process in the breakup of former Yugoslavia shows that the media in the vacuum of the overpolitical state, when the old political system died off, and the new was still not established and in circumstances of economic crisis played an important role in the antagonisation of people. An atmosphere of fear and uncertainty was created in which "others" were guilty of "our" misfortune and the attitude towards the "others" was defined historicaly, economicaly, religiously and nationaly. Under such assumptions even the simplest national historical review, for example, published in the newspapers, or the mere display of one's ethnicity to could be interpreted by the "others" as abusive, or even as hate speech. However the emotional mobilization of Yugoslav peoples according to political interests of national leaders was performed through aggressive speech which in wars, often became open hate speech and sustaining violence. The media here became instruments of war propaganda that actually happens even in democratic societies. One of the more recent explanations of this phenomenon was given by Jamie Shea, a former spokesman for the NATO alliance, in which he explained the role of the Western media in the NATO bombing of Yugoslavia: "The journalists were our soldiers in the sense that they had to explain to the population why was that war necessary."[87]

---

[86] Ibid
[87] Ibid

Even in the new millennium the region of Southeast Europe is not isolated of occurrences of hate speech in political speech and in the media. The space could be divided into two sub-regions. One is states of former Yugoslavia, while the other the remaining states. Because of the recent bloody wars in the dissolution of the joint state, the emerging countries, similar to post-war Germany, are very sensitive to manifestation of hate speech, especially if it is motivated by ethnic hatred. Ten years after the last bloody conflicts on the area of former Yugoslavia, the Independent Association of Journalists in Serbia has initiated investigation of journalists who during the war contributed to inciting hatred and war through their articles that practiced hate speech. Within this initiative, the Serbian prosecutor's office should issue a report on the media picture in Serbia during the last decade of the last century and what the prosecution discovered in the pre-trial proceedings. With this the prosecutor investigates the suspicions that some media personalities have committed crime "organizing and inciting commission of genocide and war crimes" of the Criminal Code of former Yugoslavia. According to Judge Vladimir Vukchevikj in the criminal legislation during the 90s of the last century, there was a crime - spread of racial and religious hatred. But when it comes to the nineties, according to him it is an outdated crime, although stimulating speeches took to the front thousands of people and awakened in them a motive for serious crimes.[88] However, many lawyers agree that proving someone's guilt that through hate speech he incited hatred and murder is practically a battle lost in advance because such a charge cannot generally be related to a journalist and his text or attachment, if the executor of the crime is not found and he admits that he commited the crime exactly motivated by specific journalistic work.[89] This situation can to a large extent be reflected on the situation in Bosnia and Croatia.

---

[88] Radoja, Žarka, „Uloga medija u ratnim sukobima na prostoru bivše SFRJ, Kako kazniti ratno huškanje?"

[89] In addition to this goes the fact that from World War II until today there are only two cases in which journalists were processed due to the use of hate speech. The first is at the Nuremberg Trials, when Julius Steicher, founder and editor of the anti-Semitic magazine Der Sturmer was sentenced for inciting murder and extermination. The second case is before the International Criminal Tribunal for Rwanda, in which cases against four founders and journalists of Radio Television Libre des Milles Collines were processed. They are convicted because their reports published names of Tutsis and

In the case of Macedonia, explicit expression of hate speech can be found during the military conflict in 2001. In those few months of military crisis, some (semi legal) radio stations in Albanian language played songs with extremely abusive text and called for killings (chorus "Kaur head will roll from the Citadel"). Similar chorus had the Macedonian side, with songs in a negative context for "Albanians, Muslims, mosquees". Fortunately, such events were of short time period and disappeared with the resolution of the conflict. However, in recent years, according to the estimates of influential international organizations and domestic observers, hate speech is massively present in the Macedonian media, especially on the social networks.

Although EU members, the issue of hate speech exists in Bulgaria and Greece. The judiciary tolerates the party ATAKA for years, With the leader Volen Siderov and ITS members who clearly use hate speech in their public speeches. When talking about Roma from parliamentary pulpit they call them gypsies, collectively prescribe criminal tendencies to them and accusing them of "gypsy terror". The Turkish minority, due to the high birth rate and its religious buildings, is treated as a threat to the future of the Bulgarian state and nation. This party is directly connected with television "SKAT" which through skillful manipulation with old and uneducated interlocutors from rural parts, pulls out of context statements that cause ethnic hatred and call for war between the Bulgarian and Turkish population. These occurences are repeatedly noted in the annual reports of the Bulgarian Helsinki Committee on Human Rights and other organizations.[90]

In Greece an exemplary case of promoting hate speech was spotted on the parade of their special military forces in March 2010, of which cried out for death of Turks, Macedonians and Albanians. Although the scandal received weight because hatred was promoted by a state institution(the

---

incited them to murder, as well as publishing locations where some refugees were hiding and calling for their retrieval and destruction.
[90] See more on: http://www.osce.org/documents/odihr/2005/11/16836_bg.pdf, http://www.mediatimesreview.com/september05/ataka.php, http://www.bghelsinki.org/index.php?module=news&id=1312, http://www.vbox7.com/play:a258eb80

Army), the government in Athens presented the case as isolated and announced investigation.[91]

Of these cases one gets the impression that the post-war experience in Europe, although highly sensitive to hate speech, still did not react the same way in all cases. The historical weight that the Holocaust carries on the one hand, and the religious diversity, on the other hand, make the practice full of controversies in which different actions and reactions were taken in seemingly similar cases in which the qualifications of hate speech or freedom speech, in some cases, were given under controversial circumstances. But that issue will be addressed in more detail in the following chapters.

AMERICA

Twenties of the 20th century - a decade of intolerance

Although the ideas of National Socialism and Fascism were characteristic for Europe, in the USA the presence of hate speech in public discourse also had a stormy development in the 20th century. Changes that shoke the oldest continent in the first decades of the last century have did not lose their influence and reflection on American soil also. European trends in interaction with authentic American centuries long racist and discriminatory experience, even from the time of colonialism and the extermination of the indigenous Indian tribes, as well as the later treatment of African-American slaves, created the conditions for aggressive presence of hate speech. More to it, in combination with (for European legal and political thought) the controversial relationship between hate speech and freedom of speech, based on the First Amendment of the US Constitution, they created a dynamic social scene full of different experiences. Virtually every decade of the 20th century was filled with dramatic developments in

---

[91] „Утрински весник", 29.03.2010, Скопје,
http://www.utrinski.com.mk/default.asp?ItemID=67A15FD461B23542AA2175032D63B79F
„Дневник", 12.03.2007, Скопје,
http://www.dnevnik.com.mk/default.asp?ItemID=45876693D08A064FA7427B03864CF212

the field of interethnic relations and interracist relations, which makes this review chronologically very important, without the right to be overridden for a longer period. But let's follow the order.

The twenties of the last century in the USA were known as the decade of intolerance. Fanaticism was the symbol of the period of prohibition, progressive women and flourish of the stock. It was a period when the organization which supported the discrimination of black people for the first time - the Ku Klux Klan - mass paraded in the capital city. Another important event occurred in 1921 when the Congress, for the first time in American history, limited immigration, which drastically reduced the influx of Catholics and Jews from southern and eastern Europe, and the universities in the country introduced quotas to limit the number of Jewish students. The case "Soko" and "Vanzetti", in which two Italian-American anarchists were executed for robbery and murder in a very vague procedure is one of the symbols of the anti-immigrant mood of the time.[92] However, as assessed by Samuel Walker, unfortunately the twenties were not the most fanatic period in American history because there is considerable competition for that title. A hallmarks of racism is present throughout the entire American history, and religious prejudices also have equally long history. The movement of large number of migrant Catholics in the thirties and forties an incented the ugly prejudice against Catholics which is still ongoing. The difference is that in the twenties prejudice could most openly be expressed than ever earlier and it was very likely for them to be written down as a law. But beneath the surface new movements also appeared - the victims were returning the kick back. For the first time in American history, blacks, Jews and Catholics have made organized and sometimes successful efforts to combat discrimination - concludes Walker.[93]

The most famous in the world for its innovative mechanical solutions in the automotive industry, Henry Ford had a dark spot in his biography. For the American public he has never been known as the worst anti-Semite in the USA, but of course he was the richest and most famous. The creator of the famous Model T and the inventor of modern production line for cars,

---

[92]Perrett, Geoffrey, America in the Twenties: A History (New York: Simon and Schuster, 1982)
[93]Walker, Samuel, Hate speech: the history of an American controversy, University of Nebraska Press, 1994

Ford was a national hero in the twenties. He was also a fierce anti-Semite who had financial resources that enabled him to widely share their views. His personal newspaper "The Independent" (Independent), had a circulation of over 600,000 copies and Ford asked the distributors to sell it as an official product of the company. Anti-Semitism was one of the main elements of the newspaper. "Independent" published the notorious "Protocols of the elders of Zion", a long series of articles about the alleged evils of the Jewish people. Also, Ford first published again the first eighty articles in the form of a book "The International Jew - The World's Foremost Problem" (The International Jew - The World's Foremost Problem) and it sold in more than 500,000 copies.[94]

The headline in another newspaper, "The Saturday press", which provoked a procedure before the US Supreme Court, was filled with anti-Semitic outbursts as sharp as everything else that was published in the Journal of Henry Ford. The views of the authors as "There are too many people in this city, especially those involved in public life, that exercise orders and recommendations by Jewish gangsters" or "Virtually every supplier of whiskey, every owner of a distribution network, each gangster with the face of a snake and every thief in Minneapolis and Saint Paul is a Jew" were characteristic for this newspaper. Editor Jay M. Nir insisted that he did not want to stigmatize all Jews and that the rats among them have done that.[95]

A characteristic of this period was that the main problems with the regulation of hate speech were still not evident, nor were they a subject of debate in the 20s of the last century. The most important question that still emerged was the question of the role of the First Amendment. What is the scope of the freedom of speech and to which extent it protected the offensive forms of expression? The dominant vision of the American society in the 20's was aggressive Anglo-Saxon Americanism. The real American either a born Anglo-Saxon or the one who had assigned Anglo-Saxon habits and values (at least so it was understood by most Americans). It was a time of continuous racist thinking, even among the most educated

---

[94]Lee, Albert, Henry Ford and the Jews (New York: Stein and Day, 1980)
[95]Walker, Samuel, Hate speech: the history of an American controversy, University of Nebraska Press, 1994

members of society. Politicians talked with ease about "the English race" while historians and politicologues were writing scientific papers that demonstrated the virtues of the democratic institutions English. English parliamentary democracy was seen as the culmination of the centuries-long process of political development. As millions of immigrants came from Eastern and Central Europe (reaching nearly one million per year before World War I), the Anglo-Saxon elitists turned on the alarms about the dangers of suicide of the race from the enormous tide of emigration. President Theodore Roosevelt advised the Americans with Northern European ancestry to have larger families and not to allow to be exceeded in number by the newcomers. Similarly as in Nazi Germany, the scientific research on the nature of human intelligence were trying to prove that Nordic nations are more evolved than whites from the South and East of Europe or Asians.[96] Anti-Semitism in the Journal of Henry Ford and the one presented by Jay Ner, as well as the hatred towards Catholics among the Ku Klux Klan were only rough versions of the ideas that were more elegantly expressed by the educated elite.[97]

In order to provide preserve the Anglo-Saxon values, the civic leaders staged a mass American movement. Immigrants should be assimilated into the cultural norms of Anglo-Saxon America, and the habits of the old world, in their view, should not and could not continue. Public education was the primary tool for achieving this goal, and the knowledge of English language was mandatory. The movement for Americanization was forcible and often violent. Conservative business interests led this movement and defined the unions, anarchists and after 1917, the communists as foreign imported ideas. hey sought to limit immigration, deportation of foreign-born radicals and banning radical political ideas by criminalizing syndicalism. In many respects, the movement for Americanization was similar to the culture wars in the 80s and 90s of the 20th century. In both periods the cultural elite felt that it is under threat from changes in the demographic profile of the country and the requirements for inclusion of historical victims in creating prejudice and discrimination.[98]

---

[96]Gould, Stephen Jay, The Mismeasure of Man (New York: Norton, 1981)
[97]Higham, Strangers in the Land, chap. 6, "Toward Racism: The History of an Idea".
[98]Berman, Paul, Debating PC (New York: Dell, 1992)

The moderate or liberal response to the new American demography was expressed in the concept of the "melting pot". The idea was that, instead of imposing Anglo-Saxon culture of the newcomers, to form a completely new form of culture of the mixture of different ethnic groups, religions and cultures. The idea of the melting pot was more liberal than the idea of the movement for Americanization and it did not completely disclaim the contribution of the non- Anglo-Saxon groups. But they did not fully respect the cultural autonomy of the immigrant groups and considered that the habits of the old world were inappropriate for America and should be changed.[99]

The answer of the newcomers was the struggle for acceptance and equality which was led by a group of civil rights organizations which began to emerge even before the First World War. The American Jewish Committee was established in 1906, followed by the establishment of the National Association for the Advancement of Colored People (NAACP)) in 1909 and the Anti-Defamation League (ADL) in 1913. However, there was no Catholic organization for the protection of civil rights which would it look like the NAACP or ADL. To a certain degree American Catholics did not need such a thing because with their number and political control in urban areas, they had considerable political power. In the 1930s, the Catholic Church had a significant impact on public policy on a national level for issues like censorship and contraception.[100] After the anti-Catholic attacks on the presidential candidate from the Democrats - Al Smith in 1928, the National Conference of Christians and Jews (NCCJ) was established to promote religious tolerance.[101]

The Thirties and the impact of National Socialism

According to Walker, in the battle to prove who belongs to America and under what conditions, the First Amendment of the Constitution, finally, played a central role. The result was slightly visible in the 20s of

---

[99] Walker, Samuel, Hate speech: the history of an American controversy, University of Nebraska Press, 1994
[100] Walker, Samuel, In Defense of American Liberties: A History of the ACLU (New York: Oxford University Press, 1990)
[101] Encyclopedia of Associations, 26th ed. (Detroit: Gale Research, 1992)

the last century. The issue of hate speech only been open through the first attempts to control the prejudice and discrimination. Hate speech distinguished as a national and international issue in the mid 30s. After the triumph of the Nazis in Germany in 1933, Nazi groups began to parade in the USA, calling themselves Silver Shirts, White Shirts, Brown Shirts etc. A reporter counted 300 paramilitary groups. The leader of the Silver Shirts called President Roosevelt "Dutch Jew" and the election of the 31 US President Herbert Hoover was characterized as meeting the desire of some English Jews. Violence accompanyied the rallies of the association Friends of New Germany and speculation spread that the Silver Shirts received money from the German government. Suddenly, a new kind of aggressive, militaristic and anti-democratic political movement arose in the states. The Brown Shirts were often engaged in deliberate provocative tactics, parading in uniforms near Jewish settlements. It initiated the most difficult issues related to First Amendment: whether the organizations which were committed to destroying democracy were entitled to use constitutional freedoms to achieve their goal? This was not an academic question in the early 30s because the tactic of Nazi Germany was to provoke disorder as a way to discredit the Weimar Republic as well as the principles of democracy. The fact that such tactics worked the Nazis threw new light on the issue of freedom of speech and freedom of assembly in the United States.[102] The result was a statement titled "Shall we defend free speech for Nazis in America?"- published in 1934.[103]

Shall we? – the answer was affirmative and thereby declared that the First Amendment protects the freedom of speech, press and assembly as for the Nazis and the other anti-democratic groups. This statement of 1934 has contained the basic elements of what would later become the American public policy. For critics of such a response, Nazism was so brutal regime that it does not deserve any tolerance. The Nazis had already had suppressed civil liberties in Germany and they would do the same in America if they are given a chance.[104]

---

[102]Walker, Samuel, Hate speech: the history of an American controversy, University of Nebraska Press, 1994
[103]ACLU, Shall We Defend?
[104]Walker, Samuel, Hate speech: the history of an American controversy, University of Nebraska Press, 1994

As the thirties passed, the situation in Europe is slowly becoming worse. Despite frequent attacks on German Jews, Hitler became increasingly violent in his plans to conquer territories. Many people were convinced that the Second World War is inevitable and saw the Spanish Civil War as a testing ground for German military tactics. These developments have intensified the calls for limiting the American Nazi groups and European experience supported the need to stop the fascist movement before they become strong. Almost every European country adopted laws that restricted the anti-democratic groups and Americans who supported the appropriate response to fascism, examined these laws with great interest. However, it is important to note that the debate over how to respond to domestic fascism included a very small circle of people. The majority of Americans, in varying degrees, were isolationists, indifferent to the fate of European Jews, or even attracted to some aspects of German Nazism and Italian Fascism. An opinion poll from 1938 showed that 58% of the Americans believed that European Jews are fully or partly responsible for their persecution.[105] The United States with their national policies were also extremely indifferent to the fate of European Jews, even to refugees from the Nazis who sought entry in the states.[106] The alarm about the threat of the Nazis was limited to part of the Liberals, most of the organized left-oriented and the American Jewish community, concludes Walker. According to him, the most important aspect of the US response to domestic fascism was quite a bit of action were taken. The state of New Jersey adopted a Law on Racial Hatred in 1934 which was supplemented after four years with the Law Against Wearing Military Uniforms. The legislature in New York debated on a similar law, but it was denied. Even the American Jewish Committee opposed the law, believing that "intolerance is fed from pressure". However, the state successfully persecuted the German-American Alliance in 1939, with the same law that used to prosecute the Ku Klux Klan because it was not registered. The most important anti-Fascist measure taken in the USA was that of House Committee on Un-American Activities in the Congress (HUAC)), which,

---

[105] Centril, Hadley, ed., Public Opinion, 1935-1946, (Westport, Conn.: Greenwood Press, 1978)
[106] Wyman, David S., Paper Walls: America and the Refugee Crisis, 1938-1941 (New York: Pantheon Books, 1985)

paradoxically, in particular, was directed against communist subversion and give pretty little importance to fascist groups.[107]

The ACLU also kept its position against restrictions on political expression and strongly opposed the anti-fascist laws implemented in Europe. Public display of flags, signs and uniforms was protected with the First Amendment. The Executive Director of the ACLU, Roger Baldwin, believed that the swastika had as much right to be flying as American stars or any other flag. However, the ACLU allowed some restrictions on freedom of assembly. They referred to the ban on parading with masks. Several US states adopted such laws in the twenties in response to the Ku Klux Klan and the ACLU agreed that these prohibitions shall not conflict with the First Amendment.[108] Considering the violent record of the clan parading with masks was considered a form of provocation and insult.[109]

Finally, only one law on hate speech was adopted in the thirties, and that was the mentioned Law on Racial Hatred from New Jersey which forbade racial propaganda. The battle over the Law demonstratted the three important points on the issue of hate speech: the relative weakness in the support for such laws, the dangers of selective application and, lastly, the growing commitment to the values of the First Amendment (Walker). The New Jersey law was a direct result of violent clashes between supporters of the Nazis and anti-Nazi groups. Friends of New Germany, at their meeting of October 16, 1933, clashed with thousands of anti-Nazi protesters and the conflict grew into a full riot. In response to the event, the authorities in several cities in New Jersey banned rallies organized by the Friends of New Germany.[110] The Law on Racial Hatred was based on the fundamental principle that ensuring the rights of most Americans called for certain restrictions on the rights of other smaller groups. It introduced criminal sanctions for anyone spreading "propaganda or statements which create or have the purpose to create prejudice, hostility, ridicule, disrespect of people etc., because of their race, color or belief or way of practicing religion" It was also illegal to spread propaganda "in any meeting of two or more

---

[107]Walker, Samuel, Hate speech: the history of an American controversy, University of Nebraska Press, 1994
[108]Ibid
[109]ACLU, Shall We Defend? (1934)
[110]Glaser, "German American Bund"

people on any parade, public or private," including the use of "any flag, symbol, emblem, image, photograph". Possession of propaganda literature intended for its dissemination was also illegal. Finally, it was illegal for an owner to rent a place from which the propaganda shall be spread.[111]

The application of the Law Against Racial Hatred in New Jersey, as assessed by Walker was most harmful for the law itself. The most important point was that the law was hardly applied. For six years there was no prosecution of any anti-Semitic or group. The first and the only reported case eferred to the Jehovah's Witnesses who had been accused of distributing anti-Catholic literature. In 1940 a procedure was started for checking the constitutionality of the law of New Jersey, in times when Europe was at war, and the US were bound to intervene in it.

In its assessment of the thirties Walker thought they finished with pretty little action against domestic Nazis in the USA. In retrospect one could confidently say that the German-American Alliance, the Silver Shirts or any other paramilitary group represented a real threat to American democracy. Finally, the political system was able to prove its viability. Economic reforms in the New Deal (New Deal) and the adoption of the regulation of the economy by the Government, convinced most Americans that the established political system was able to respond to major crises and thereby suppress radical groups.[112] The Law Against Racial Hatred of New Jersey, from 1934, was finally rejected by the Supreme Court of the State on the basis on a violation of the First Amendment. The decision was one of the main pillars for the development of US policy.[113]

Creating a national policy on hate speech in the forties

In the early forties a national policy on hate speech began to appear in the United States and its central goal was wide commitment to protecting from offensive speech based on the First Amendment. The US response to

---

[111] Walker, Samuel, Hate speech: the history of an American controversy, University of Nebraska Press, 1994
[112] Brinkley. Voices of Protest
[113] Walker, Samuel, Hate speech: the history of an American controversy, University of Nebraska Press, 1994

the then war and the Holocaust differed because of different domestic circumstances. The most important result was the birth of the modern civil rights movement as a broad interrace coalition. The persecution of European Jews raised the awareness about the racism that existed in America. On the other hand, the leaders of African Americans took up more militant stance because they were asked to fight for justice abroad and they were seeking freedom in the country. The leader of the black people Philip Randolph threatened to march to Washington to demand "fair federal practices in employment" - militant expression that could not be imagined just a few years earlier.[114] Series of racist riots in 1943 prompted many white Americans to understand that racial discrimination was not only contrary to the ideal of equality, but it also threatened the efforts in war. However, on the issue of hate speech, Americans learned another lesson from the experience with the Nazis. Primarily, it underlined their awareness of the importance of the constitutional protection of persecuted minorities. Largely, the US thinking on constitutional rights was stimulated by the examples of totalitarianism abroad, primarily in Germany and the Soviet Union.[115]

The single and most important event, with great influence on US attitudes, law and policy on the issue of hate speech was a unique domestic case: the national crisis on Jehovah's Witnesses. As a small, but very offensive and aggressive group, Jehovah's Witnesses raised the issue of hate speech in a way that had special significance for American constitutional law: how should a society react to offensive religious propaganda when the source of such propaganda is a religious minority? This caused the use of freedom of belief and the practice of faith from the First Amendment and expedited the development of a specific law derived from the First Amendment.[116] Recapitulating the case of Jehovah's Witnesses, Walker notes that the fact that Jehovah's Witnesses were the cause of national crisis in the thirties and forties, today surprises most Americans. As described by Walker, Jehovah's Witnesses today are a

---

[114] Garfinkel, Herbert, When Negroes March (Glencoe, Ill.: Free Press, 1959)
[115] Walker, Samuel, In Defense of American Liberties: A History of the ACLU (New York: Oxford University Press, 1990)
[116] Walker, Samuel, Hate speech: the history of an American controversy, University of Nebraska Press, 1994

subtle and passive group that is recognized by their big temples and occasionally preaching from door to door. They are the least intrusive of all evangelical religious groups in the USA. Still, in the past, more than a decade, they were almost a hated group in America, target of legal restrictions and violence. Growing public confrontation finally exploded in violence in 1940, in the place Maine, when a group of 2500 people burned a temple of Jehovah's Witnesses and started to attack their personal homes. According to some reports, the entire adult population of the city of Lichfield, Illinois, was mobilized to attack a group of Jehovah's Witnesses. At the same time, in Nebraska, a member of the sect was snatched and neutered. Long before this surge of violence, the Witnesses were target of countless state and local laws, made to stop their preaching on religious conversion.[117]

Persecution of the Witnesses caused long series of cases before the Supreme Court; a scientist listed the fifty court cases from the thirties to the eighties, and the Witnesses won almost all.[118] With the possible exception of African-Americans, not a single other group in American history had made a greater contribution to constitutional law as Jehovah's Witnesses, by which they extended the protection of individual rights in a number of important areas.[119] How did that happen? Jehovah's Witnesses were a religious sect were which hated and organized violent attacks on other faiths, especially the Roman Catholic Church. According to their paranoid worldview, the Satan was everywhere, in business, in politics and in faith. Most of all, he manifested himself in organized religious groups. Because the Witnesses believed that they are the real people of God, logically any other groups that were "intruders" or " hustlers" - their favorite epithets for these presumed agents of the Satan. Since the Catholic church was the oldest and largest Christian denomination, it was understandable for them that it was the biggest hustler of all.[120] The leader of the Witnesses Joseph Franklin Rutherford devoted an entire book entitled "Enemies of the evil

---

[117]Ibid
[118]Abraham, Henry J. Freedom and the Court, 5th. Ed. (New York: Oxford University Press, 1988)
[119]Kalven, Harry, Jr., The Negro and the First Amendment, Phoenix ed. (Chicago: Univeristy of Chicago Press, 1966)
[120]Walker, Samuel, Hate speech: the history of an American controversy, University of Nebraska Press, 1994

done by the Catholic Church" calling the Catholic Church "old ' prostitute' with long 'and inquisitorial and awful' past."[121] To a lesser extent, the Witnesses also attacked Jews for who they once believed had a special relationship with Jehovah, but in their new aggressive stance they relied on their claim that they are the chosen people of God and denied the similar views of Jews.[122] However, it should be noted that the hostility of the Witnesses towards Jews was different from the famous anti-Semitism and it was not as dominant theme in their hatred.

In terms of doctrine, the Witnesses have pointed out, as we said, the status of people chosen by God and each member was considered a priest with the task to extend their faith. Tactically, they began an aggressive campaign for conversion that spread their message in the world and with which they recruited new members. This effort was incredibly successful, with membership increased from 400,000 at the end of the twenties to over four million at the beginning of the forties of the last century.[123] They went door to door, interacted with people on the street and to them that was known as "testimony on the corner." Even if their message was not insulting, many people considered their activities are exaggerated. The attacks of hatred against Catholics and other religions have caused angry and violent response because Jehovah's tactics were intentionally provocative, similar to those of domestic Nazi groups: they deliberately went to neighborhoods inhabited by Catholics, faced with people face to face with the message for which they were aware that offends the religion of the listener. By doing that the Witnesses caused hostile response from the one that was for the Nazi groups because they attacked the persuasion of the Americans on a higher level. The result was a massive confrontation with the authorities across the USA. Additionally the local communities also sought limitation of the Witnesses by law.[124]

---

[121] Rutherford, Joseph F., Enemies (Brooklyn, N.Y. : Watchtower Bible and Tract Society, 1937)
[122] Penton, M. James, Apocalypse Delayed: The Story of the Jehovah's Witnesses (Toronto: Univeristy of Toronto Press, 1985)
[123] Beckford, James A., The Univeristy of Prophecy: A Sociological Study of Jehovah's Witnesses (Oxford: Basil Blackwell, 1975)
[124] Walker, Samuel, Hate speech: the history of an American controversy, University of Nebraska Press, 1994

In chronological view, as the most important event in the forties in American history of hate speech, Walker analyzes the most famous controversy about Jehovah's Witnesses, remembered to this day, and refers to their opposition to greet the flag of the United States. The background of "Barnett case" (Brown v. Board of Education) was the interpretation by the Witnesses of a section of the Exodus 20: 3-5: "You shall not have other Gods before me" and "You shall not create idols, nor worship or serve them. " Jehovah's Witnesses believed that this passage forbade them to greet the flag that led the family Barnett in an awkward situation with the local authorities.[125] The Barnett family refused to adapt to such practices that led to the initiation of complex litigation that resulted in one of the most elocutionary constitutional defense of the freedom of personal conviction. The Court found that forcing to greet a flag is not a reasonable method to teach citizenship and that the refusal by children did not jeopardize public safety. More importantly, their compulsion to utter an oath of loyalty in a way that violates their sincere religious beliefs was a totalitarian idea. Judge Robert H. Jackson famously wrote an opinion on the "Barnett case" and it was often quoted: "If there is a fixed star in our constitutional constellation, it is that no authority, lower or higher, cannot determine what is acceptable in politics, nationalism, religion or other matters of opinion and cannot force citizens to confirm it by word or deeds."[126]

With its activities in the forties, Jehovah's Witnesses have given special contribution to the issue of hate speech that referred to the principle of inclusiveness and tolerance for the small and offendable minorities and that meant tolerance of hate speech. The cases with the Witnesses marked the beginning of the formation of national policy on hate speech.[127]

---

[125] To understand the case, it should be viewed in a broader spcial context that dominated at the time in the United States. Then international events (World War II) had an impact on the behavior of local authorities. The world went to global conflict and many Americans fetl the need to confirm patriotism and moral values among the population. The most appropriate method was to get all the students to greet the flag, recite the oath of loyalty and pray every morning.
[126] Ibid
[127] According to Walker, the hearing from 1944 year marked the highest point in the effort to secure federal law on hate speech. Both houses of Congress were dominated by Southern Democrats who were inclined to segregation and who because of their age

The post war period - victory for freedom of speech

From the fifties to the mid-seventies, the USA developed a national policy on hate speech. That policy protected the offensive forms of expression and was part of the wider development of the rights from the First Amendment, by which a strong national commitment to the principle that debate on public issues should be smooth, comprehensive and open was reflected.[128] This period roughly began in the years after the Second World War and ended with the controversies in Skokie in 1978. Several general features are inherent in this period. First, protecting from offensive speech was really a national policy in terms thatit was based on decisions related to the First Amendment, and brought by the Supreme Court. As Archibald Cox would say, no political issue that was initiated, was transformed into a legal issue and taken to court to be decided.[129] The result were set of national standards for religion in schools, police interrogations, profanity and offensive language. In terms of offensive speech, the trend was to prohibit any restrictions on content.

The emergence of the Supreme Court as the creator of a national policy was one of the greatest changes that have occurred in modern American history. The policies and practices of public institutions have been radically altered. Questions whether public schools should conduct daily prayers and in what way, if the police can interogate suspected crimes were catapulted into national policies and presidential candidates claimed they would change the judicial decisions on the rights of suspects, school prayers and pornography.[130]

Second, as the protection of offensive expression became increasingly broader and more clearly defined, the contrast between American law and

---

controlled key Committees. It is important to know that the southern block prevented the adoption of a federal law against lynching in the thirties and has prevented the adoption of any reasonable civil rights bill until 1964. They believed that any prohibition or restriction of hate literature would threaten the segregationist thought. After a surge of activity in the forties, proposals for federal laws restricting hate speech slowly disappeared and almost died in the early fifties. (Walker, Samuel, Hate speech: the history of an American controversy, University of Nebraska Press, 1994)
[128]New York Times Co. v. Sullivan, 376 U.S. 254 (1964)
[129]Cox, Archibald, The Warren Court (Cambridge: Harvard University Press, 1968)
[130]Lasser, Williams, The Limits of Judical Power: The Supreme Court in American Politics (Chapter Hill: University of North Carolina Press, 1988)

policy and those of the rest of the world also intensified. International developments were moving towards more explicit condemnation of racist and religious propaganda, while the USA actually went for integration of hate speech as an integral part of public discourse and freedom of expression based on the First Amendment. Third, and perhaps most important aspect of this period was the issue of civil rights. The mid sixties have labeled the highest point of the civil rights movements in America with what it defined itself as a broad interrace coalition committed to racial equality and to halting all forms of discrimination. The issue of civil rights has become central to US policy in the mid-fifties, and thus covered the national hysteria about domestic communism. One historian called the period "the era of civil rights".[131] For Walker, the achievements of the movement were really impressive and the end of legal segregation in public schools and in the public space, then the end of systematic racial discrimination in voting and commitment to equal opportunities as a national policy, were inserted in numerous laws and regulations. These were events with truly historic dimensions, even if in the eighties some African Americans liked to emphasize that there was lack of progress - concludes Walker.

The agenda of the then civil rights movements is the key to understanding the direction of the issue of hate speech. At first glance, there is an apparent paradox: civil rights groups as part of their broad attack on discrimination, chose one of their goals not to be limiting hate speech. That is, they refused this potential remedy even when their equivalents in other countries decided on such a step. They decided that because their greatest success came from legal disputes in matters related to personal freedoms. Therefore, the promotion of the rights of minority groups was required by court decisions based on personal rights to equal protection, timely trial, freedom of speech and association. Any restrictions on personal rights were perceived as a threat to the entire set of constitutional rights. Therefore, the laws of group insult, which restricted freedom of

---

[131]Graham, Hugh Davis, The Civil Rights Era (New York: Oxford Univeristy ress, 1990)

expression, were perceived as a threat and not as a remedy for racial injustice.[132]

As Walker claims another matter related to the First Amendment was raised in situations when there was no threat to public order, but the speech insulted the feelings of the public. The feelings of the public were reviewed in the sixties, and one of the many offerings of this turbulent decade was creating new standards for public discourse in American life. The intense emotions that were raised by the civil rights movement, the Vietnam War, and, later, the controversy over abortion, resulting in the most extreme forms of defamation. Words full of emotion were a key part of the strategy to raise the audience by introducing basic moral issues in the debate. The word fuck entered into political discourse, especially wits its variant motherfucker version and in a particular case fuck the draft ("fuck the draft version"). The change of standards in the political arena was transfused in the general discourse, and thus brought the public words that were previously reserved for military barracks or male wardrobes only. Already in the eighties teenagers regularly used terms such as fuck, suck, dick. Two popular slogans used for T-shirts and labels were "Shit happen" and "Life sucks". Numerous comedians, including Richard Prajor Eddie Murphy as the most striking, made the word fuck a central element in their shows. In previous years, public uttering of such words had been unthinkable and would most probably lead to immediate arrest.[133]

---

[132] Walker, Samuel, Hate speech: the history of an American controversy, University of Nebraska Press, 1994

[133] In the late fifties and early sixties, the deliberate offensiveness comedian had direct political implications. Comedian Lenny Bruce became famous through his joke that attacked the hypocrisy of the then society. His goals were Puritanism about sex, racism, anticommunism organized religion, stupidity of self-proclaimed liberals and so on. Insulting almost every group, he inevitably collided with the law and is considered to have been arrested 19 times. Bruce was loved by his fans and many professional comedians as it significantly increased the range of comedy.Sex, politics and religion became permissible topics largely because of his pioneering work. In the hands of Bruce, comedy was a tool for social change, especially in the field of human rights and sexual freedom. His usual comic attacks, along with many jokes were made against Jews and African-Americans. He had started a sketch with the question: "Are there any Spaniards (used the offensive word: Spics), some Jews (derogatory word: Kikes) or blacks (derogatory word: Nigger)?". According to the columnist Net Hentof audience remained striking. But his goal soon became apparent: to bring taboos to light so they then break. One of these taboos was racism and to prove his point, he used traditional

The word fuck got to the Supreme Court in a series of cases in the seventies, including its variations like fuck, motherfucker, white motherfucker. The first and most important arose from a protest against the war in Vietnam. Paul Robert Cohen was arrested and convicted of disturbing the public peace becausehe wore a jacket with the words "Fuck the Draft!" in court in Los Angeles.The Supreme Court overturned his conviction and in the opinion of the conservative judge John Marshall Harlan, set new protection for offensive speech. Harlan emphasized that Cohen's conviction was based only on the content of his offensive speech or the offensiveness of the word fuck. His behavior was motivated by the fact that he like to communicate with other people in the court, and the words were not directed at specific people and the charge did not allege that someone in the courtroom was violently hurt by the writing on his coat. This also helped to eliminate the argument of the excited audience, that people were forced to endure the offensive word against their will. In short, the case (Cohen v. California) was based on alleged offensiveness of the word fuck. The most important part of the opinion of Harlan was his discussion on the nature of this communication. He considered that much of the linguistic expression served dual functions. Although the words have special meanings, regardless of their use in a given context, they also constitute emotions that are expressed differently. Words are often chosen because of their emotional power, not only because of their cognitive significance. Recognising the role of the emotional aspects of verbal communication, he found that they have enormous implications on the issue of hate speech. Many of the political conflicts of the sixties onwards were hiding in extreme moral values. First, the civil rights movements, then the war in Vietnam, women's movements, and the controversy of abortion were considered great moral battles. In the Cohen case, the obvious strength of Cohen's opposition to the Vietnam War and the proposal would not be the same if his coat wouldn't read "Fuck the draft" or "I don't like the draft". The same way, the use of the words "killer" or "killer of babies"

---

terms and stereotypes. (Free Speech for Me - But Not for Thee: How the American Left and Right Relentlessly Censor Each Other)

by protesters against abortion, although seemed offensive to the audience, carried with it the idea that abortion is a crime.[134]

The Cohen case was quickly followed by other cases in the use of offensive words. In 1972 the court overturned the conviction of another anti-war protester, who told the local police, "I'll kill you white bastard" and "You, bastard, I'll strangle you to death". He was convicted under the Law of Georgia, according to which it was offensive to use any insulting words in order to disturb the peace. He was not charged with endangering the life of a police officer, which would be a completely different issue. The court overturned the verdict because the Law was too broad.[135]

For chroniclers of eh cases of hate speech, the sixties were a difficult decade, not only because of the increase of racist and derogatory religious speech, but for the simple reason that white racist anti-Semites were not worried about being arrested. What was new in the sixties was that black militants began using derogatory terms against whites, the government or against the fanatics and the Catholic Church. While the Senator of Mississippi Theodore Bilbo, could address an African-American with "niger" without fear of arrest, black militants on the streets in the sixties and seventies had reason to fear arrest because of the use of abusive words. Such words were justified when the police had to arrest a black man because of indecent behavior or any similar charges.[136]

Hate speech in the 80s and 90s of the last century - crisis in university campuses

To the surprise of most experts on the issue of the First Amendment, the controversy with hate speech appeared againin the eighties. In the USA, universities adopted "codes of conduct" containing provisions that restricted the offending speech. The policy of the University of Michigan, for example, forbade any behavior, verbal or physical, that stigmatized or terrorized the individual based on race, ethnicity, religion, gender, sexual

---

[134] Walker, Samuel, Hate speech: the history of an American controversy, University of Nebraska Press, 1994
[135] Ibid
[136] Ibid

orientation, belief, national origin, age, civil status, disability or status of veteran from Vietnam.

The movement for codes on campuses was successful for a few years. The "Carnegie Fund" on improving learning assumed that until 1990 60 percent of all universities had some policy against fanaticism or religious harassment, while 11 percent were planning such policies.[137] All these codes did not bann hate speech, but many of them had hidden provisions on discrimination. Moreover, the limitations of offensive speech were widespread and a number of codes of students were adopted by leading universities in the states: Michigan, Wisconsin, Stanford, Emory and others. Dissemination of codes of speech on campuses was unprecedented: never before has there been such widespread support for punishing offensive speech. Compared with the support of the laws on group insult in the mid-forties, this support was very weak and produced quite little in the form of visible regulation. The movement for codes of campuses enjoyed the support of broad coalitions of students, supported by the academic community. This attack on hate speech was a response to the new political and legal developments in the eighties, in the campus and outside of them. Racism reappeared or, at least, racist sentiment was publicly expressed on university campuses. Meanwhile, the supporters on limiting hate speech, offered new creative legal arguments in addition to their proposal. The most powerful argument was that prohibiting hate speech is allowed and perhaps even an obligation under the Fourteenth Amendment of the Constitution of the United States (which protected from any kind of discrimination). This argument served as counter thesis in the opposition based on the First Amendment. As indicated by a law professor, the Fourteenth Amendment is a smaller part of the Constitution than the First Amendment.[138] Referring to the new doctrine on sexual harassment in the workplace, supporters argued that hate speech created a hostile atmosphere which interfered with the constitutional right to equal access to education. Campaigners against the codes shown great concern because they considered them the biggest threat to freedom of speech and academic freedom. They wondered whether it would be possible to discuss sensitive

---

[137]Carnegie Fund for the Advancement of Teaching, Campus Life (New York, 1990)
[138]Gale, Mary Ellen, "On Curbing Racial Speech", Responsive Community 1 (Winter 1990-91)

issues related to race or sex if fear is present that someone may be offended and because of that someone else would have to face disciplinary measures.[139]

Contrary to these academic debates about freedom of speech in search of answers for various controversial topics of life, however, speech codes on campus were the product of scary growth of racist incidents in universities which reached their peak in 1986 and 1987. Several of the more grotesque won national publicity and were regularly used as an argument to justify the codes. In 1986 a fight between drunk people at the "Massachusetts" University evolved into a brawl between fans of Boston "Red Sox", who were white, and fans of "New York Mets", who were blacks. According to the reports, a crowd of three thousand white men chased and beat all the Blacks they ran into. The boiled atmosphere began to line up incidents of racial basis: Thr fraternity "Zeta Beta Tau" of the University of Wisconsin held an imitation of an auction with slaves. African student at the College "Smith" found a note under her door on which was written: "African monkey, do you like bananas? Return to the jungle!" Another African-American student at the "Brown" University found a note under his door reading: "This is a room only for colored." Someone wrote on the blackboard of the "Michigan" University: "It's a pity to looseyour mind - especially for a Niger". Astudent at the "Perdue" University found - "Die nigger!"written on the door of his room. In one of the longest and most published series events the conservative college students of the "Darmut" College started a campaign against the African American music teacher William Cole. In that incident, after classes, four white students physically opposed the professor in an apparent attempt to provoke a fight. The National Institute Against Prejudice and Violence listed a total of 250 incidents of fanaticism on campuses in the period 1986 to 1989. It is impossible to say with certainty whether there was a real increase in in the racist events on campuses or just more of them were published, since there is no systematic data on such cases. However, it was not relevant whether there was a real growth because the reported incidents were themselves shocking and so direct that caused fear. In those years, colored students thought that on some campuses had to be aware

---

[139]Hentoff, Free Speech for Me but Not For Thee (New York: Harper Collins, 1992)

from university administrators as well as from anonymous students - fanatics.[140] In September, 1992, after the attack on elderly woman by a suspected black, the authorities from the State University of New York delivered to the police its list of names of all African-American and Hispanic students on campus. The police then questioned the students - members of minoritis student in their dormitories, their jobs, even in the shower. On a formal legal basis, giving the list of names violated the federal law on privacy, but on a wider basis, it confirmed the conviction of minority students that university campuses are hostile to them.[141]

The movement for codes of university campuses was the most successful effort to limit hate speech in American history. The basis of this success was obvious - unlike previous legislative proposals for group insult, it had the support of well-organized supporters. The nature of that group and the reasons because its various members supported the limitations on hate speech are key to understanding the movement. The first important factor was the new demographic and political profile of American higher education. African American students as group were more numerous and better organized than ever before. Enrollment of Hispano Americans drastically increased from 472 000 in 1980 to 758 000 in 1990, while the number of Asians increased from 286 000 to 555.000 in eighties.[142] Feminism emerged as a powerful force on campuses. Parallel to the increase of Women's Studies programs of, professors feminists had a strong presence in many faculties. Many politically active students agreed with the idea preached by some lawyers, that the protection of pornography by the First Amendment violated their rights as women.[143] This skepticism towards the First Amendment encouraged them to seek restriction of hate

---

[140]Although in gathering materials for this study no empirical data or specific cases were found, possible assumption is that this atmosphere on the universities in the US, where even today, under the protection of freedom of expression abusive speech and hate speech is practiced among students, it also contributes to frequent mass killings of hostages and hostage dramas. In many cases these are ethnic minorities (black, yellow, Hispano Americans) or frustrated white students who were previously subject to fierce verbal insults or ridicule from the rest of the student population - note-auth.
[141]"Anger over List of Names Divides Black from Their College Town", New York Times, September 27, 1992
[142]Cronicle of Higher Education, August 26, 1992
[143]MacKinnon, Catherine, "Pornography, Civil Rights and Speech", Harvard Civil Rights-Civil Libertis Law Review 20 (1985)

speech directed toward women. Gay students also had the active participation on many campuses.

Despite rapid empowerment of minority groups, rising racial tensions, as assessed by Walker, were the result of a complex mix of economic factors, crime and changed the agenda the civil rights movements. Since the mid-seventies until the nineties, the poor become even poorer, while the rich were even richer, the middle class remained at the same place. The increase of the misery of the lowest layers produced a new name for them - subclass. The worst of it was the violence between gangs linked twith drugs, so that entire districts were grounded by drugs and gangs. Gang violence caused the death of many bystanders, including small children. Because of the drug that was used by injection, AIDS grew into an epidemy and had a disproportionate effect on the poor. Previous profile of a typical HIV positive man moved from white-professional to a poor black gay drug user. But all Americans suffered from changing economic trends. The increase of misery in the poorest was in parallel with the growth of the black middle class. In the eighties, the difference between poor black and middle class black families was significantly increased and the income of black families with two employees almost leveled with equivalent among whites. However, the problem of whites and blacks was the reduction in the percentage of stable wages for families. The majority of middle-class whites who worked made no economic progress between the seventies and the nineties (unlike the black middle class) and in many respects they have seen their outlook worsened as well as the future of their children. In the context of their reduced economic opportunities, crime to blacks became a trap in the request for a person to blame for them not having a personal perspective. Certainly university students were not immune to such temptation. These new economic, social and legal factors together contributed to the increase in racism among white students at universities in the eighties, Walker concludes.

Hate speech in the new millennium

Hate speech as an institutionalized social phenomenon received significant attention in the United States in the new millennium. The terrorist attacks of September 11, 2001 increased the already great number of cases of hate speech and hate crimes against Muslims and Arabs - or those that are considered to be Muslims or Arabs. Prejudices against this population are present in American daily life of most banal episodes as paranoid vigilance at airports and public transport, to open and (un) deliberate statements of insult in the media directed at Muslims. Slowly, but surely, in the first decade on 21 century Muslims and Arabs have taken over primacy from blacks and Hispano Americans as a target group for hate speech of white Americans. On the other hand, the uprising of Palestinians from the West Bank and in Gaza Strip, characterizes itself by deadly cycle of suicide, which is followed by a fierce retaliation from the Israeli army. This retaliation caused organization of demonstrations against Israel and expressing solidarity with Palestine in the USA. Many protesters carry banners which are addressed to all Jews and condemning Israel and anyone who supports Israel. Anti-Semitic slogans were shouted and displayed in the streets and public walls.

Neo-Nazis and thugs also expanded their hatred. Demonstrations and propaganda of the Ku Klux Klan openly invited people to violence. The Internet has become an important driving force of free speech. On the internet opinions publicly expressed, discussions are led, activities are published and communication is enabled. The number of websites with hatred skyrocketed, encouraged violence, rejecting the existence of the Holocaust and celebrating the idea of Nazism. Although such web pages are prohibited or subject to criminal monitoring in many European countries, they are legal in the United States.[144] Hate speech towards the LGBT population, is also infuriated. Such hate speech stems from racist thugs and other marginalized thugs, but also from established social elites. Filled with hate speech are texts of rap music of Eminem and some homophobic "gangsta" rap performers. Incidents on religious ceremonies also occur such as, for example, that on the funeral of Matthew Wayne Shepard[145] when cleric from the Baptist Church and its followers shouted insults and carried banners such as "Matthew burn in hell" and "AIDS

---

[144]Cortese, Anthony Joseph Paul, Opposing hate speech, Westport, Conn. : Praeger Publishers, 2006.
[145]Famous case of hate crime in the USA from 1998 when a boy was tortured and killed just for being gay.

cures gays".[146] Other religious fanatics, under the pretext of freedom of speech, announce that they will burn the Koran publicly, in front of TV cameras, which disturbs the Muslim community not only in the US but worldwide.

Hate speech against immigrants is also growing. In the 90s, according to the Census Bureau United States, there was a record number of immigrants in the United States. The majority of these migrants were from Central America, Asia and Mexico, and to a lesser, but also large numbers from South America and Africa. Accordingly, most of the greatest portion of colored people and the trend of emigration is known as the "Browning of America".[147] ociological analyzes show that hate speech against immigrants has been growing for three reasons: (1) because of their record number, (2) because of their race and ethnicity (they look like Euro-American majority) and (3) due to the imagined or real competition for resources - newcomers have decent and affordable housing (not already ghettoized), have stable employment (no longer manual workers, but successful managers and IT technicians) have social welfare and access to quality schools (Ivy League universities provide scholarships for talented students from poor countries).

But not only in the USA but also in other western European countries, such as Germany, Holland, Belgium, Great Britain and France, which have increased growth of colored immigrants from the third world. Expansion of antiemigrant movements in host countries, including the United States, following the immigration influx, which certainly suggests a turbulent and dynamic discussion on hate speech during the 21st century.

3. INTERNATIONAL DOCUMENTS AND NATIONAL LAWS RELATED TO HATE SPEECH

As we saw in the previous chapter, when the idea of penalizing group offending by the American political scene began to disappear so the movements in the rest of the world happened in the opposite direction.

---

[146]Cortese, Anthony Joseph Paul, Opposing hate speech, Westport, Conn. : Praeger Publishers, 2006.
[147]McLemore, S., and H. Romo. 2005. Racial and Ethnic Relations in America. 7th ed. Boston: Allyn and Bacon

World War II because of the Holocaust is the key point of reversal. In response to the genocidal policy in which more than six million Jews suffered, immediately after the war international movement was triggered that would ensure that in the future never similar crimeswould never be repeated. The Holocaust together with the struggle against colonialism, whose intensity increased after World War II, initiated international commitment to make the human rights and the fight against racism a priority, which had a decisive influence on the formation of the European case law on hate speech. This commitment was in the form of a series of declarations, conventions, charters, recommendations and agreements on human rights, so that from the end of the Second World War until the eighties of the last century more than forty declarations were made: twenty-one United Nations documents, ten Declarations of the International Labour Organization, four European conventions, three related to Latin America and four concerning Africa and Asia. All of them are addressing the issue of freedom of speech, but among those who have come across this issue, the tendency was for more explicit calls for limiting racist and religious forms of expression. In all international documents dealing with human rights and freedoms, including the fight against racism and racial discrimination, talk about the need to prevent hate speech that advocates, justifies or glorifies discrimination based on race, ethnicity, sex, religion, language or any other distinction. As Mary Ann Glenda says, characteristic of the human rights movements after World War II is that the discourse of human rights has spread worldwide.[148] The movements for international protection of human rights have become numerous and one commentator has called them "revolution" in international law.[149] Until then, traditionally, international law was concerned only with relations between states, and internal issues remained in the sphere under the sovereignty of each state. However, human rights movements after World War II emphasized the standards that should prevail in each state. The human rights treaties that followed, included more specific prohibitions on

---

[148] Glendon, Mary Ann, Rights Talk (New York: Free Press, 1991)
[149] Driscoll, Dennis J., "The Development of Human Rights in International Law", in the Human Rights Readers, rev ed. Walter Laqueur and barry Rubin, eds., (New York: New American Library, 1989).

insulting, racist and religious speech[150] and were codified by similar provisions of the European anti-fascist laws before the war.

International documents

In terms of hate speech, various international declarations on human rights have accepted the concept of group insult. All of them support the freedom of speech of individuals, but also limit the same to preserve the common good. Most of the declarations contain a specific prohibition on offending racist and religious propaganda. Laws that prohibit hate speech or generally known as racist speech or religious propaganda were adopted in several countries.[151] These laws were consistent with the mandate of various international declarations on human rights adopted after the war. The initial mandate of protection of human rights was set out in Article 55 of the Charter of the United Nations, which declared that the United Nations would "promote universal respect and observation of human rights and fundamental freedoms for all without distinction as to race, sex, language or religion". This general mandate was elaborated in a series of subsequent documents. It is not necessary to consider all those here and for our purposes we will look at some of the most relevant as:

- Universal Declaration of Human Rights, adopted on December 10, 1948;
- International Covenant on Civil and Political Rights from 1966; and
- International Convention on the Elimination of All Forms of Racial Discrimination, also from 1966.

The Universal Declaration of Human Rights is the most important document in the field of international human rights. It includes extensive support for freedom of expression and belief. Article 18 states: "Everyone has the right to freedom of thought, conscience and religion; this right includes freedom to change his religion or belief, and freedom, either alone or in community with others and in public or private, to manifest his

---

[150]Brownile, Ian, ed., Basic Documents on Human Rights (Oxford: Clarendon Press, 1981)
[151]Coliver, Sandra, ed.., Striking a Balance: Hate Speech, Freedom of Expression and Non-discrimination (London:Article 19, 1992)

religion or belief in teaching, practice, worship and observance." Article 19 states: "Everyone has the right to freedom of opinion and expression; this right includes freedom to hold opinions without interference and to seek, receive and impart information and ideas through any media and regardless of frontiers." Universal Declaration continues by stating that not one of the rights here is absolute.[152] Article 29, paragraph 2 defines the scope of allowed limitations: "In the exercise of his rights and freedoms, everyone shall be subject only to such limitations as are determined by law solely for the purpose of securing due recognition and respect for the rights and freedoms of others and of meeting the just requirements of morality, public order and the general welfare in a democratic society". Article 30 states: "Nothing in this Declaration may be interpreted as implying for any State, group or person any right to engage in any activity or to perform any act aimed at the destruction of any of the rights and freedoms set forth herein." The Universal Declaration does not contain specific restrictions on hate speech, but the exceptions provided for in Articles 29 and 30 clearly imply that such restrictions are permissible if required. Successive declarations of human rights have explained the intention through detailed definition of the types of restrictions on individual rights that are allowable. These limitations include specific prohibitions on insulting racist and religious speech.

The International Covenant on Civil and Political Rights defines specific requirements for limiting the freedom of speech. Article 18 confirms the freedom of speech and belief, stating that "everyone shall have the right to freedom of thought, conscience and religion". In the second paragraph of Article 19 it is stipulated that "everyone shall have the right to freedom of expression". However, paragraph three states that the right to freedom of expression carries with it special duties and responsibilities. It may, if necessary, be limited under the following conditions: a) For respect of the rights or reputations of others, b) For the protection of national security or of public order or of public health or morals. The second paragraph of Article 20 is even more specific - any advocacy of national, racial or religious hatred that constitutes incitement

---

[152]Brownile, Ian, ed.., Basic Documents on Human Rights, 2d ed. (Oxford: Clarendon Press, 1980);

to discrimination, hostility or violence shall be prohibited by law. The Human Rights Committee of UN has issued an interpretation of this paragraph which compels the signatory countries to adopt legal prohibitions on hate speech, although such laws must not contain penalties. Other suitable penalties are also acceptable.[153]

The provisions of the International Covenant and other human rights declarations are not binding for the signatory countries. The countries can ratify them as other agreements, but they can also express reservations, understandings and declarations (sometimes referred to as RUD). By the spring of 1992, six of the 105 countries that have ratified the International Covenant on Civil and Political Rights had expressed reservations about the second paragraph of Article 20 (8 others expressed reservations in respect of Article 1: Prohibition of war propaganda). The six countries were: Australia, Belgium, Luxemburg, Malta, New Zeland and the United Kingdom. The USA finally ratified the Convenant in April 1992 and expressed their reserves concerning that the United States has no commitment to the provisions which are contrary to the First Amendment of the US Constitution.[154]

The Covenant is not the only action taken by the United Nations in relation to hate speech. In March the same year, the UN opened the process for signing the International Convention on the Elimination of All Forms of Racial Discrimination. Article 4 of the Convention provides that "States Parties condemn all propaganda and all organizations which are based on ideas or theories of superiority of one race or group of persons of one colour or ethnic origin, or which attempt to justify or promote racial hatred and discrimination in any form, and undertake to adopt immediate and positive measures designed to eradicate all incitement to, or acts of, such discrimination". To this end, with due regard to the principles embodied in the Universal Declaration of Human Rights and the rights expressly set forth in article 5 of this Convention, inter alia:

---

[153] Boerefijn, Ineke and Oyediran, Joanna, "Article 20 of the International Covenant on Civil and Political Rights", in Coliver, Striking a balance
[154] Coliver, Striking a balance, "Annexe B: Reservation and Declaration concerning Racist Speech and Advocacy of Racial and Religious Hatred"

(a) Shall declare an offence punishable by law all dissemination of ideas based on racial superiority or hatred, incitement to racial discrimination, as well as all acts of violence or incitement to such acts against any race or group of persons of another colour or ethnic origin, and also the provision of any assistance to racist activities, including the financing thereof;

(b) Shall declare illegal and prohibit organizations, and also organized and all other propaganda activities, which promote and incite racial discrimination, and shall recognize participation in such organizations or activities as an offence punishable by law;

(c) Shall not permit public authorities or public institutions, national or local, to promote or incite racial discrimination.

Articles 6 and 7 of the Convention require states to provide effective protection against racial discrimination and take effective measures to combat prejudices and promote understanding and tolerance.

Restrictions on the offensive racist and religious speech are also contained in other human rights declarations. The Convention on the Prevention and Punishment of the Crime of Genocide (1948) prohibits "direct and public incitement to genocide". The draft text on the Convention on the Elimination of All Forms of Religious Intolerance 1967 calls for "equal protection before the law against promotion or incitement of religious intolerance or discrimination" (Article 9). The Committee on the Elimination of Racial Discrimination in its General Recommendation on Discrimination recommended that countries "take action against any tendency of targeting, vilification, creating a stereotype or profile, on the basis of race, color, descent or national or ethnic origin of the members of civic groups (...) especially by politicians, officials, employees in education and the media, the Internet or other electronic communication networks and in society in general" (paragraph 12).

Although not included in the group of international conventions that we focused on, it is important to mention the Statute of the ad hoc International Criminal Tribunal of former Yugoslavia (ICTY) and Rwanda (ICTR) and the Statute of the permanent International Criminal Court (ICC), which also provided "lawful punishment of incitement - including verbal – for some of the crimes over which courts have jurisdiction". Thus Article 4 of the Statute of the ICTY consideres an offense "a direct and public incitement to genocide crime", while the Statute of the ICC for individual considers a criminal responsibility "any ordering, facilitating, solicitation or inducement to (such) a crime which happened or was planned" (Article 25). Article 2 of the Statute of the Rwandan Court considers an offense "any publicly and direct reference to genocide." Guided by this provision, this Court for the first time, after the trial for Nazi war crimes at Nuremberg, convicted hate speech as a war crime when three journalists/anchors were sentenced to life imprisonment because through their daily media they incited genocide.

European documents

European Convention for the Protection of Human Rights and Fundamental Freedoms of the Council of Europe (ECHR) from 1950 is most referent European document which guarantees the right to freedom of expression, but envisages its limiting, which is necessary in a democratic society for the protection of, inter alia, the reputation or rights of others.

According to Article 10 of the ECHR, 'everyone has the right to freedom of expression, which includes freedom to hold opinions and to receive and impart information and ideas without interference by public authority and regardless of frontiers'. The exercise of these freedoms, since it carries with it responsibilities, may be subject to such formalities, conditions, restrictions or penalties as are prescribed by law and are necessary in a democratic society in the interests of national security, territorial integrity or public safety, for the protection of disorder or crime, health or morals, reputation or rights of others, for preventing the disclosure of confidential information or for maintaining the authority and impartiality of the judiciary.

Consequently, the restriction of the freedom of expression is allowed when each element of the triple test of the ECHR is met, which means that the limitation should:

- be foreseen in a national law;

- aim to protect the rights and interests mentioned in ECHR;
- match the requirement of "necessity in a democratic society".

Article 17 of the ECHR states: "Nothing in this Convention may be interpreted as implying for any State, group or person any right to engage in any activity or perform any act aimed at the destruction of any of the rights and freedoms set forth herein or at their limitation to a greater extent than is provided for in the Convention". This provision not only addresses the states, but all groups and individuals. It is not a further restriction of the rights of the Convention, but, on the contrary, the aim of Article 17 is to ensure the permanent maintenance of the system of democratic values emphasized in the Convention. This article noticeably, aims to prevent totalitarian groups to use the principles set by the Convention for their own interests.[155]

Although the European Convention on Human Rights and, in particular, its Article 10, which guarantees freedom of expression remains an indisputable reference, there are other non-binding text, agreements or instruments adopted by the Council of Europe which deserve to be mentioned. In 1997, the Council of Ministers of the Council of Europe, noting the resurgence of racism, xenophobia and anti-Semitism, but also taking into account the importance of freedom of expression, issued several recommendations and instruments of the governments of the member states to "to take measures to combat hate speech".

- Recommendation (97) 20 on "hate speech" adopted by the Committee of Ministers on October 30, 1997 gives a definition of "hate speech" denouncing all forms of expression which incite racial hatred, xenophobia, anti-Semitism and all forms of intolerance. In this document it is stated that such forms of expression may have a greater and more damaging impact when shared through the media. However, the text says that national jurisdictions and practice should clearly distinguish the responsibility of the author of the term "hate speech" and that of the media for their expansion as part of the mission to communicate information and ideas on matters of public interest.

---

[155] Manual on hate speech, Anne Weber, Council of Europe Publishing, 2009

- The Declaration of the Committee of Ministers on freedom of political debate in the media adopted on 12 February 2004 stresses that the freedom of political debate does not include freedom to express racist opinions or opinions which are an incentive to hatred, xenophobia, anti-Semitism and all forms of intolerance. It also stresses that defamation or insult by the media should not lead to custody unless the sentence is not strictly necessary and proportionate to the seriousness of the violation of the rights or reputation of others, especially where fundamental rights are seriously violated by statements of libel or insult in the media such as "hate speech".
- In Recommendation 1805 (2007) on blasphemy, religious insults and "hate speech" against persons based on their religion, adopted on 29 June 2007, the Parliamentary Assembly reaffirms the need to punish statements in which a person or group of people are the target of hatred, discrimination or violence on religious grounds.
- In General Policy Recommendation no.7, the European Commission against Racism and Intolerance (ECRI) defines racism as "the belief that the foundation such as race, color, language, religion, nationality or national or ethnic origin justifies the contempt for a person or group of people, or a sense of superiority of a person or group of people" and addresses the issue of racist speech:
  - General Policy Recommendation No. 7 on national legislation to combat racism and racial discrimination requires the adoption of solutions from criminal law to combat racist statements from the various member states of the Council of Europe.: Such statements refer to "public incitement to violence, hatred or discrimination, public insults and defamation or threats against a person or group of people based on their race, color, language, religion, nationality or national or ethnic origin. Public expression with a racist aim of racist ideology or public denial with a racist aim, crime, genocide or crimes against humanity or a war crime, should also be punishable by law. Finally, by public spreading with racist aim or racist material containing racist expressions should also be a target for criminal sanctions.

ECRI insists that such solutions from the Criminal Code should provide "effective, proportionate and dissuasive sanctions as well as secondary and alternative sentences". Although this framework decision has no direct impact on the EU member-states and although the European Commission has taken the decision not to act as an executive body this decision, however, requires member-states to adopt legislation against various forms of hate speech, mostly against speech that "publicly forgives, denies or trivializes the crimes defined by the Nuremberg Tribunal".

Moreover, ECRI reports for each country clearly reveal that there is consensus in Europe on the need to combat racist expressions by punishing crime. However, ECRI has in recent years increasingly faced with arguments that call for freedom of expression in an attempt to justify the lack of activities, particularly through punitive measures. ECRI considers that the right to freedom of expression should be limited to fighting against racism, particularly when related to the rights and reputation of others and to protect the human dignity of the victims of racism. According to the European Court of Human Rights such restrictions should respect the conditions set out in Article 10 of the European Convention on Human Rights. ECRI, however, stresses the importance of freedom of expression as one of the main foundations of democratic societies and the need to keep all human rights and to maintain a balance between the conflicting rights.

Seeing that racist speech is far from disappearing and actually increased in the past few years, particularly in political discourse, ECRI adopted the Declaration on the use of racist, antisemitic and xenophobic elements in political discourse on 17 March 2005: "ECRI condemns the use of such elements in the political discourse and considers such use of 'ethically unacceptable'". ECRI also published a Declaration on combating racism in football on May 13, 2008 on the occasion of the European Football Championship EURO 2008.[156]

The European Social Charter in the fields of economic and social rights, and the Framework Convention for the Protection of National Minorities, also contain measures aimed at protection against all forms of discrimination. The Revised European Social Charter "prohibits any

---

[156] Manual on hate speech, Anne Weber, Council of Europe Publishing, 2009

discrimination based on race, color, religion or national origin in the enjoyment of those rights recognized".

Also, the European Parliament stresses in its Resolution on the right to freedom of expression and respect for religious beliefs, adopted on February 16, 2006, that "freedom of expression should always be enjoyed within the limits of the law and should coexist with responsibility and with honors towards human rights, religious feelings and beliefs, whether associated with Islam, Christianity, Judaism or any other religion".

A few efforts of the countries participating in the Organization for Security and Cooperation in Europe (OSCE) are also directly relevant to the fight against hate speech. Not only have the member-states recognized the primary nature of the right to freedom of expression on several occasions, but they have also expressed their firm commitment against hate speech and other expressions of aggressive nationalism, racism, chauvinism, xenophobia, anti-Semitism and violent extremism, as well as discrimination based on religion or belief, and stressed that promoting tolerance and non-discrimination can contribute to reducing the grounds for hate speech.

The European Court of Human Rights (ECHR) in establishing the relationship between freedom of expression and its possible limitations, expressed the following:

- "Freedom of expression is one of the basic principles that build democratic society and one of the main conditions for its progress and for the development of every person. It applies not only to 'information' or 'ideas' that find favorable reception or are deemed as abusive, offensive or accepted with indifference, but also to those that offend, shock or disturb the state or any other part of the population. Such are the demands of pluralism and tolerance without which a democratic society could not be called as such".

According to the practice of the ECHR among the exceptions to freedom of expression is the restriction of the so called "hate speech".[157]

---

[157] "Реч на омразата в медиите на България и Македония: прояви, фактори, решения", available on http://osi.bg/downloads/File/HateSpeech_Report_BG.pdf

The internet and hate speech

A specific and new problem for (criminal) prosecution of hate speech and combating discrimination is the medium known as Internet which has accelerated multiplied and globalized the communication process. Literally limitless possibilities of the Internet to spread obscene information and each individual having the same free access to all information, are deemed as the greatest achievement in the history of mankind when it comes to freedom of thought. However, it was quickly realized that the free space and cyberspace are legal enclave I which it can be uncontrollably acted, therefore the Council of Europe already in 1989 began preparing regulations against digital criminal offenses that would punish hackers, theft of intellectual property and use of computer fraud. Adopted as a Convention on Cybercrime[158] in November 2001, these rules have proved insufficient and a ratified amendment was formulated in November 2002 that puts hate speech via the Internet in a separate sentence. The ban on spreading misinformation encompassed "any material, any image or any other form of presentation of ideas or theories that advocate, promote or incite hatred, discrimination or violence against any individual or any group of individuals based on race, color, national or ethnic origin or religion".

The amendment of the Convention is made under the influence of national and international laws on hate speech and, simply put, it means: what is forbidden offline, is also forbidden and online. This opened the old dilemmas, but also opened some new. For example, the USA, which have an observer status in the Council of Europe, supported the Convention, but not the amendment because, according to their understanding of things, it restricts freedom of speech in an unacceptable extent. Like other regulations and laws concerning the punishment of hate speech the amendment on hate speech on the Internet also leaves room for broad interpretation, which for some media and NGOs was a reason to suspect that the amendment could be used to introduce hidden censorship of Internet content that are not politically acceptable. On the other hand, the structure of Internet communication causes other, new problems to governments and courts. The huge number of pages and the inconsistency

---

[158] http://www.coe.int/t/dghl/standardsetting/t-cy/ETS%20185%20macedonian.pdf

of the Internet makes it practically impossible for consistent and comprehensive implementation of the criminal prosecution because if you abolish any illegal page, it may appear with other providers. Providers, on the other hand, refuse to be guardians of the content spread by their domains because, as they say, it is impossible to control the flow and volume of information so that such self-regulation is virtually inapplicable. Logically, their authors and owners are responsible for the pages, and they can sit on an island in the Pacific Ocean, whose government does not even know about the laws for Internet communication or are in liberal America, which is a kind of "digital paradise" illegal space when it comes to hate speech and the content of the flow is without any control and sanctions. Therefore, because of the lack of international cooperation and global harmonization of criminal prosecution of hate speech on the internet, this medium still remains the freest communication space, with all the advantages and dangers that freedom of speech carries with it.[159]

The Additional Protocol to the Convention on Cybercrime associated with the investigation of the crimes with racist or xenophobic nature through computer systems, adopted on 28 January 2003 and entered into force on March 1, 2006, is of particular importance because it concerns the spreading of hate messages over the Internet. Countries participating in this Protocol are obliged in their domestic law to adopt legal and other measures required for procuring the following acts as criminal offenses, in situations when committed internationally and unlawfully:

- distribution or any kind of provision of racist and xenophobic material to the public through a computer system;
- threats through a computer system by running a serious criminal offense as defined in domestic law;
- distributing or providing public material that denies significantly reduces, approves or justifies acts that constitute genocide or crimes against humanity as defined in international law and recognized as final and binding decision of the International Military Tribunal, established by the London Agreement of 8 August 1945 or any other

---

[159] Beham, Mira. 2004: "Govor mržnje u politici i medijima". Objavljeno u Vacic, Z. (ur.) 2004 Etika javne rijeci u medijima i politici, Centar za liberalno demokratske studije, Beograd, 2004.

international court established by relevant international instruments whose jurisdiction is recognized by that member and all that through the computer system.

This general position, after six years was followed by the Protocol against the spread of racism through computer systems and it is stated that "each signatory country shall adopt regulations and other measures necessary to proclaim the acts as spread of racist and xenophobic material to the public through computer systems and criminal offenses no mater whether these offenses are made in the country or abroad". Protocol does not require such acts to be criminalized if domestic law has already established legal equivalent of this. Also, there is a legal practice in other countries in which the legal restriction of hate speech is accepted.[160]

However, countries are increasingly dealing with the issue of hate speech originating outside their borders, and only virtually located in their country. Spain has asked internet providers to block websites that violate the Spanish Law on Hate Speech. France went even further and accused the server "Yahoo" from the United States for violations of French laws on hate speech. Although this server is based in the USA, in addition to its website it also maintains websites specific to certain countries, including France. This case was interrupted by the service for auction of products offered on "Yahoo", which included 1000 products that have been characterized to be associated with the Nazis and the Third Reich. Because these products were available to residents of France, either through yahoo.com or via the French site yahoo.fr, a French court ruled that "Yahoo" has violated French laws that prohibit the display and sale of Nazi propaganda materials and objects. The court asked "Yahoo" to prohibit access to these products for the people of France. Although the "Yahoo" was technically able to comply with the court's order for its French site, it claimed that it was impossible to stay away from French residents access to materials on its main website. French court, unsatisfied with the answer, ordered "Yahoo" to comply with the order and fined it with 100,000 francs for each day of non-compliance. The Court also ordered that the sentence refers to yahoo.com, not the site "Yahoo" for France. Certainly this was not

---

[160] Saunders, Kevin W., Degradation What the History of Obscenity Tells Us about Hate Speech, New York University Press, 2011

the end of the case. Because "Yahoo" is a US company, it asked the courts in the United States to confirm that such declarative sentence is void and that the sentence cannot be enforced by the courts in the USA. The US court ruled that France had the right to enforce its laws within its territory, but it also determined that the First Amendment would preclude the application of such penalties in the United States. The case was later rejected by the Appellate Court because of jurisdiction, and the arguments regarding the First Amendment were not refuted.[161]

Polish authorities became interested in the website redwatch.com which is set in the US, but is also available in Polish several years ago. Blacklists from this website have caused many incidents involving violence (setting bombs and attacks with a knife). For the rest of the world it is incomprehensible how the USA can not close these servers, and a victim from Redwatch, England asked how a country, because the First Amendment, is not sufficiently powerful to shut down servers that set pedophile materials.[162] In an article in the Chicago Tribune from 2007 it was stated that "Thousands of websites in foreign languages in the world ... use US servers in in order to avoid domestic laws which prohibit Holocaust denial or spread racist or anti-Semitic ideas. Because servers are located in the USA, they remain outside the competence of prosecutors in Europe, Canada and other countries".[163]

Having regard to what has been previously said, I have concluded that previous experience with the Internet shows that the USA, although considered proponents of free expression and no restriction on various topics for public discussion and debate, from a European perspective, are in danger of being recognized as a host of hate speech.

---

[161] Yahoo! Inc. v. La Ligue Contre le Racisme et L'antisemitisme, 433 F.3d 1199 (9th Cir.) (en banc), cert. denied, 547 U.S. 1163 (2006).
[162] Working, Russell, "Illegal Abroad, Hate Web Sites Thrive Here: 1st Amendment Lets Fringe Groups Use U.S. Sites to Spread Their Message around the World," Chicago Tribune A1 (Nov. 13, 2007), available at 2007 WLNR 22413864.
[163] Ibid

Sexist and homophobic speech

Initially we mentioned that any offensive speech is not hate speech, but any hate speech is in its semantic basis, offensive speech. The same is true of profane or vulgar speech, which is usually not considered hate speech, but rather a stylistic feature of one's personal discourse and as such gives the impression of the morality and (un)education the one who uses it. On the other hand, application of vulgarity in different artistic expression can also represent promotion of hate speech. Pornographic film is considered a driving force of hate speech against women in the ideologies of women haters and is associated with the degradation of women in such films. Therefore, the interest of society to regulate hate speech mostly derives from his offensive nature and although vulgarity in pornographic films refers to sex as an act (a highly intimate act of human nature, given public exposure and meaning), and hate speech refers to the degradation of women (represented as an object of humiliation in such sexual intercourse). Both segments of the pornographic film represent forms of offensive speech.

However, as assessed by Kevin Saunders, international agreements on hate speech do not apply to sexist speech that is offensive speech by gender affiliation. To him the reason for that derived as a result of the history and because the Holocaust was directed towards an ethnic and religious group, and not gender, and because in history there are no analogous cases of so widespread hatred that was based on gender.[164] Still, from the practice, it is clear that there is a speech that expresses, if not hatred, then degradation of gender affiliation and some of the definitions presented in international treaties can apply to this type of speech. The recommendations for hate speech from the Council of Ministers of the Council of Europe from 1997 include in its definition of "forms of expression which spread hatred expressed through discrimination or hostility towards minorities". The European protocol to the Convention against Cybercrime concerning racism spread through computers, says speech that is directed is the speech that "advocates, promotes and supports discrimination".

---

[164] Saunders, Kevin W., Degradation What the History of Obscenity Tells Us about Hate Speech, New York University Press New York and London, 2011

In his explanation, Saunders says that he chose to selectively quote parts of all definitions in a way that he defocuses of hatred, while focusing on the prohibition of speech that supports discrimination or hostility, because some of the definitions can be closer to sexist speech that expresses the inferiority or superiority and encourages discrimination. That way, although international treaties do not apply to the sexist speech, the same concerns about the harmful speech are involved in the agreements related to racial hatred. If international sentiment includes bans on sexist speech, there is a pattern to define speech which could be included. There are also inclusions of sexism in some laws on hate speech. Cases led according to the Civil Rights Act in the United States do not apply only to race. Under this act many of the cases of discrimination shall be based on gender and it is clear that sexist language can be a hostile environment for which the employer would be responsible. Therefore, employers have an incentive to take measures not only against employees who express hate speech on race, but also for those who express sexist sentiment.[165]

Homophobic speech is also not included in the definitions given in international treaties. Historically there is no difference. Homosexuals have also been victims of the Holocaust, and hate speech directed at them raises historical concern similar to that which occurs in hate speech in terms of race. The same pattern of definitions of hate speech shows that it can also be used for homophobic speech and there is no need to reduce the emphasis on the part of hate because this speech is an expression of inferiority. Considering that there is a growing recognition of the rights of homosexuals and wide acceptance of homosexuals as another minority, perhaps it is only a matter of time when laws will also apply to homophobic speech. Even more because at least one country has included hate speech against homosexuals in its law.[166] The Norwegian Criminal Code in Article 135a provides that "everyone is responsible and punished by a fine or imprisonment up to 2 years if he expresses or otherwise communicates, including through symbols, publicly or widely distributes an insult or hatred towards a person or group of persons based on origin, race, color, or national or ethnic origin. The same applies to any offensive

---

[165]Ibid
[166]Ibid

behavior towards a group or groups because of their homosexual preference or lifestyle"[167]. That way, homophobic speech is included in other forms of hate speech in Norway and taking into account the changes in attitudes toward homosexuality, this can be extended to other laws and international agreements. Much of the world believes that hate speech, at least on the basis of race and ethnicity, should be regulated, but perhaps there is a growing belief that hate speech on grounds of sex or sexual orientation should be treated similarly. The experience of Nazi Germany demonstrated that the effects of hate speech can be large.[168]

On the other hand, as we have seen, the conclusion in the USA is that the cost of free expression is not high in order to tolerate speech that degradeS people to under-human level but not on the basis of what have they done, but what they are. The positions of US laws does not follow the international example. As we have seen, freedom of expression so far enjoyed strong protection in the USA and the result is accepting, at least in the laws of speech that degrades others on the basis of their characteristics. Still, even in the USA such speech is not always protected. The American Convention on Human Rights, (1969) (Article 13, paragraph 5), explicitly prohibits advocacy of national, racial or religious hatred at regional level. Article 13 of the American Convention expressly prohibits "any propaganda for war and any advocacy of national, racial or religious hatred, which is an integral part of encouraging lawless violence or any other similar action against any person or group of people on any basis, including race, color, religion, language or national origin". This is the space where LGBT minorities should seek its protection from homophobic speech, concludes Saunders.

So, together with the Norwegian Criminal Code the American Convention on Human Rights is also one of most referent international models that are available to other countries when they decide to regulate sanctioning homophobic speech in their own legislation.

---

[167] Bjornar, Borvik, The Norwegian Approach to Protection of Personality Rights: With a Special Emphasis on the Protection of Honour and Reputation 133 (Bergen, Norway: Fagbokforlaget, 2004) (translating the Penal Code of May 22, 1909, No. 10, Art. 135a.).
[168] Saunders, Kevin W., Degradation What the History of Obscenity Tells Us about Hate Speech, NEW YORK UNIVERSITY PRESS, 2011

National laws and hate speech

In many European countries, legislation to prevent the use of hate speech is implemented in practice, thus contributing to the eradication of racism and stabilizing these societies. So for example, the constitution, criminal and other laws of Germany, Italy, France and Great Britain sanction various forms of hate speech; membership in neo-Nazi organizations, the use of symbols and other materials and desecration of the memory of victims of the Nazi genocide to the ban of racist cheerleading in the United Kingdom. Other countries follow the mandate of the international declarations on human rights; so, India has adopted the Law on Hate Speech in 1973, Brazil in 1985 and Argentina in 1988. The prohibition of hate speech represented a global movement which reached its peak in the seventies and eighties of the 20th century.[169] The countries that adopted laws that criminalize hate speech are Austria, Belgium, Brazil, Canada, Cyprus, England, France, Germany, India, Israel, Italy, the Netherlands and Switzerland".

On the initiative of the European Commission against racism and intolerance, many European countries have established specialized bodies to combat racism and discrimination at the state level. Such bodies – parliamentary committees or trustees, government offices, ombudsman or commissions that deal with helping victims of discrimination, monitoring and implementation of national laws as well as combat racism by educational measures and media – are up until now implemented in Belgium, Finland Denmark, Hungary, Netherlands, Norway, Sweden, Switzerland and the UK.

In terms of the legal sanctioning of hate speech, I would like to make a small review of several countries. In Germany in the Criminal Law there are three Articles that sanction hate speech. They sanction only those speeches that disrupt public order and cause violent action. The article that refers to a group defamation allows slanders that are "considered that disrupt public order" to be punished. In the Constitution, Article 5 (1) determines very clearly that "every person has the right to freely express and share their opinions through speech, text and images and to

---

[169] Coliver, Sandra, ed., Striking a balance: Hate Speech, Freedom of Expression and Non-discrimination (London: Article 19, 1992), chaps. 27, 28, 29.

communicate without restrictions from generally accessible sources. Freedom of the press and freedom of reporting is guaranteed There is no censorship". But as in other countries, with clear guarantees established for the freedom of expression, other provisions limit this right. Article 5, section 2 states that "these rights are limited by the provisions of general law, with provisions to protect the rights of youth and personal dignity". Perhaps the most important, and almost regularly urged by the court is the provision for limiting the expression in Article 1, which states that "human dignity is inviolable. Its protection and respect is the duty of every state institution". Thus, the German constitution has set a hierarchy of values. Ronald Krotoszynski says: "Freedom of speech is simply not the most important constitutional value in the German legal system. Instead, human dignity has this position. Hence, in case of conflict between human dignity and freedom of speech, freedom of speech usually relents.[170] The motivation for displaying dignity comes from the German experience at the time of Nazism. Expression of anti-Semitic feelings deserves protection and neo-Nazi parties are banned. Concerns about anti-Semitism and the Nazis goes as far as banning denial of the Holocaust and the Nazi apparatus. A special provision in the German Criminal Law prohibits so-called Auschwitzlüge ("Lies about Auschwitz"), is a provision that permits impunity those who dispute or minimize the Holocaust. Under German law, which sanctions hate speech, spreading propaganda material of "unconstitutional" organizations (mostly refers to neo-Nazi associations), the use of symbols such organizations, reference to hatred and violence against segments of the population is also punishable. Also in Germany there is a permanent phone line on which citizens can report attacks by neo-Nazi groups, as well as constant surveillance of websites with racist content.

In another country with historical experience with fascism, Italy, legal measures to combat racism and discrimination are not included in the Criminal Law, but are distributed in several separate laws, that re-establishment of a fascist party is prohibited by the Constitution. These separate laws prohibit spreading ideas based on racial superiority and

---

[170]Krotoszynski, Ronald J., "A Comparative Perspective on the First Amendment: Free Speech, Militant Democracy, and the Primacy of Dignity as a Preferred Constitutional Value in Germany," 78 Tulane L. Rev. 1549 (2004).

hatred, the reference to racial, ethnic and other violence or provocation, groups and organizations with such purposes, the use of their symbols of sporting events, as well as justification of fascism genocide. However, some political parties, the Northern League, openly use racist propaganda means, especially when talking about immigrants from non-EU countries so that the European Commission against Racism and Intolerance recommended to use existing and introduce some ad hoc measures, which would prevent such parties to use hate speech for political purposes.

In the UK, although it does not have a specifically written Constitution as a fundamental legal document, there are several laws governing hate speech and other forms of racism. British courts have accepted the superiority of the Parliament and are hesitant when they need to declare acts adopted by Parliament invalid. The lack of written guarantees of individual rights IS in part overcome by the Human Rights Act from 1998. The purpose of this regulation is to ensure the insertion of the European Convention for the protection of human rights and fundamental freedoms in British law. The Public Order Act prohibits verbal or any other expression of materials that incite racial hatred, printing and distribution of such material, including music and movies. The Footbal Offences Act prohibits racist cheering. In response to its growing racist problems England brought the Race Relations Act in 1965, and it prohibits "knowingly and unwittingly giving racist statements justifying discrimination" and prohibits publications that can incite hatred based on color, race, ethnic or national origin.

France is another country with rigorous legal measures to prevent hate speech and it has adopted a Law on Hate Speech as early as 1972. Besides discrimination, hatred and violence based on origin beeing punitive, justifying the crimes against humanity, and wearing an uniform and carrying emblems reminiscent of "persons responsible for crimes against humanity" are also punitive. Unlike other countries, in France "not public incitement to discrimination, hatred or racial violence" (meaning conspiracy militant groups) is also prohibited and it is punishable by confiscation of weapons and materials used for committing offenses, and referral to voluntary work.

The Canadian Charter of Rights and Freedom protects the right to free expression. In its second part, the Charter states: " Everyone has these basic freedoms: a) freedom of conscience and religion; b) freedom of thought, belief, opinion and expression, including freedom of the press and other media of communication; c) freedom of peaceful assembly; and d) freedom of association". Still, the Canadian Charter explicitly indicates that the freedoms and rights it protects are not fully protected. The first part of the Charter states: "The Canadian Charter of Rights and Freedoms guarantees the rights and freedoms only to reasonable limits set by law and in a manner that could be justified in a free and democratic society".

The Constitution of the Russian Federation "guarantees each person freedom of speech and idea" while prohibiting advertising of any social, racial, national, religious or linguistic superiority.

Legislation in the countries of Southeast Europe also treats hate speech on several levels. Despite the Constitution and the Criminal Laws in some states, and the Public Information Law, the Law on Public Broadcasting Service and the General Codex of Journalists also exist, as well as the specialized codex of journalists working in print, electronic or new media. In all these documents hate speech is not allowed.

From this review it is clear that European reality much more sensitively approaches the problem of hate speech than the American liberal tradition, for which it could be said that it has build a cult of freedom of speech in the second half of the twentieth century.

4. HATE SPEECH AND/OR FREEDOM OF EXPRESSION

Introduction

There is no democratic country, which in its constitution and legislation does not include provisions that prohibit discrimination on racial, gender, religious, ethnic and other grounds. Those provisions in the national legislation are based on universal and several internationally adopted documents, which, as we have seen previously, except that relating to protecting people from discrimination and prohibition of racism, also apply to the right to freedom of expression as one of the fundamental human rights. The relationship established between freedom of expression and hate speech in the functioning of any democracy opens the polemic question whether such a relationship is placed in imminent conflict and whether the right to freedom of expression means freedom to offend the other? On the other hand, does the ability of the state to ban hate speech mean implementation of state censorship and the suspension of the right to publicly express different opinions and attitudes. The question is complex and there is no simple answer. The polarization is maximal: one the one hand is the American approach, which allows a wide interpretation of the right to freedom of expression, which often includes hate speech and that becomes evident as early as the First Amendment of the US Constitution, adopted in 1787, which guarantees that the Congress will not pass laws that will limit the freedom of expression and the press. On the other hand, European experience with fascism and National Socialism makes the continent intolerant towards any kind of promotion of racial, ethnic and other discriminatory ideas and attitudes in the public discourse. If we afford ourselves to generalize, we could conclude that the USA allow hate speech almost absolutly, while European and international law prohibit and punish it in numerous cases.

Modern liberal approach encompasses these two ideally-typical models. However, although this division is most evident, the question of the relationship between freedom of expression and hate speech is not black and white dichotomy, so that no hate speech is consistently allowed in the USA nor always banned in Europe.[171] There is no doubt that every democratic government will use many means, including legislation, to ensure citizens' freedom of expression. But freedom of expression does not mean that everyone can say or shout what he wants in public, at a price to insults the other. The strongest argument for this is that if speech is aggressive and offensive may jeopardize the freedom of the other. For Foucault discourse on freedom of expression is at the top of government discourses as it sets the rules for all further discourses – which speech will be allowed, and which not, by the individuals and the state. His theory of power gives the key point that power is not apparent physical coercive

---

[171] Brugger, Winfried, Ban On or Protection of Hate Speech? Some Observations Based on German and American Law, 17 TUL. EUR. & CIV. L.F. 1 (2002);

force used by the state, but is something that is subtly steered through language. If, as claimed by Foucault, power in society comes from the use of language, then the danger of abuse of language can consequently lead to abuse of power.[172] That is, we saw in the case of National Socialists and fascists which made their social supremacy by promoting the racial theory and hatred towards the opponents in the public discourse, in which the media were a powerful tool in the dissemination of what we today call hate speech. There are views that if the former country promptly intervened to prevent this kind of speech the consequences would probably have also been prevented. Hence, the restriction of hate speech also allows restriction of expression of those who, using exactly this right would have abolished the right of others. The key sentence that supports this view is "No freedom for the enemies of freedom," which means that speech cannot be used freely in order to hurt the other. In the end, such an attitude can be a justification for the introduction of so-called "militant democracy" and measures that threaten the fundamental constitutional and civil rights and freedoms of individuals or specific groups.[173] The most ardent advocate of militant democracy was Karlo Lowestein, who was led by the fact that democratic societies have the right to self-preservation and obligation to dampen anti-democratic movements that threaten democracy. As a result of his research on the state of democratic states before World War II, he came to the conclusion that the fundamental weakness of democracy was, in fact, its most glorious value, which made it vulnerable to the aggressive tactics of fascist and other anti-democratic groups. The problem was tolerance: democracy and democratic tolerance were used for its destruction. He argued that European fascist movements were very successful in exploiting the exceptional conditions offered by the democratic institutions. According to him, excessive "formalism in the rule of law" opened the possibility for the fascists to destroy democracy. Therefore, an alternative to excessive formalism in the rule of law, according Lowestein was in "militant democracy". Suppression of anti-democratic movements was needed only as a measure of self-defense. Lowestein was unwavering for

---

[172]Levin, Abigail, The Cost of Free Speech Pornography, Hate Speech, and their Challenge to Liberalism, Niagara University, New York, 2010
[173]Beham, Mira. 2004: "Govor mržnje u politici i medijima". Objavljeno u Vacic, Z. (ur.) 2004 Etika javne rijeci u medijima i politici, Centar za liberalno demokratske studije, Beograd, 2004.

this argument. Democracies should exercise some of the measures of fascists: "The political technique could be defeated only in its field and with its methods, or more simply -" you should be fighting fire with fire".[174] Later, the judge of the Supreme Court of the United States, Robert Jackson, put the argument even more directly emphasizing that the law of freedom is not a "suicide pact" and that the preservation of freedom requires some restrictions to preserve order. Judge Jackson was very aware of the Nazi tactics, because he was the chief American prosecutor at the trials of Nazi leaders in Nuremberg. "I had the opportunity to learn how insidious abuse of our freedom of expression can break a society, brutalized to its main elements, prosecute, sometimes even execute whole minorities"[175] - he commented.

After the war, in an attempt to prevent the revitalization of the Nazi movement, after the war the Constitution of West Germany was conceived according to the so-called militant democracy, just as the trend throughout Europe has been a tendency to restrict freedom of expression, if the right to protection from discrimination is questioned. The theoretical basis was that there must be a balance between individual rights and collective welfare, and the human right to promote hate speech must be assessed together with the common good of society.

Compared to democratic societies in Western Europe, the United States have a different approach to the conflict between freedom of expression and equal treatment.[176] One of the stronger arguments for broad protection of (hate) speech is the fact that freedom of expression has traditionally been important for minorities to express opinions which seem absurd or even offensive to the majority. Many thinkers believed that protecting offensive speech is a moral duty. For example, the famous representative of the French Enlightenment, the philosopher and writer Voltaire, sublimated his opinion in an often quoted sentence: "I disapprove of what you say, but I will defend to the death your right to say it" For the

---

[174]Lowenstein, Karlo, "Militant Democracy and Fundamental Rights, I", American Political Science Review 31 (June 1937).
[175]Walker, Samuel, Hate speech: the history of an American controversy, University of Nebraska Press, 1994
[176]For more see: Boyle, Kevin, 2001, "Hate Speech-The United States Versus the Rest of the World?", Maine Law Review

English philosopher John Stuart Mill, who is the father of the liberal thought, the public sense arises from smooth competition of different viewpoints. In his work "On Liberty", first published in London in 1859, he gives the classic defense of free speech:

- First, if any opinion is compelled to silence, that opinion may be true. To deny this is to assume our own infallibility.
- Secondly, though the silenced opinion be an error, it may, and very commonly does, contain a portion of truth; and since the general or prevailing opinion on any subject is rarely or never the whole truth, it is only by the collision of adverse opinions, that the remainder of the truth has any chance of being supplied.
- Thirdly, even if the received opinion be not only true, but the whole truth; unless it is suffered to be, and actually is, vigorously and earnestly contested, it will, by most of those who receive it, be held in the manner of a prejudice, with little comprehension or feeling of its rational grounds.
- And fourthly, the meaning of the doctrine itself will be in danger of being lost, or enfeebled, and deprived of its vital effect on the character and conduct: the dogma becoming a mere formal profession, inefficacious for good, but cumbering the ground, and preventing the growth of any real and heartfelt conviction, from reason or personal experience.[177]

More recently, the British philosopher Bertrand Russell formed a hypothesis, according to which democracy requires the highest degree of tolerance: "it is an essential part of democracy, that substantial groups, even majorities, should extend toleration to dissentient groups with different opinions, however small and however much their sentiments may be outraged. In a democracy it is necessary that people should learn to endure having their sentiments outraged". These and similar arguments are used by those who advocate mostly for approving position on hate speech. The US constitutional law protects hate speech, almost always, although it requires a great price for the dignity, honor and equality of the attacked or the civilization of public debate and public order. The reason for this is that

---

[177] Heuman, Milton & Church, Thomas W., Hate Speech On Campus 6-7 (Northeastern University Press 1997).

the constitutional law of the United States when it comes to hate speech, primarily in the phenomenon sees "speech" (not hate) which, in turn, compared with the competing values, in almost all cases is considered a "priority right". To the speech which offends one should respond with counter-speech rather than with state regulation. In contrast, other major countries, such as Germany, Canada and members of the European Council and international law see in the hate speech hate more than speech and do not give the freedom of expression priority over other values such as dignity, honor, equality, courtesy or public order.[178]

In general, the ratio of legal state and international law towards hate speech cannot be narrowed down to the fact that the speech is "always protected" or "never protected". Rather it can be said that the right sometimes helps hate speech, and sometimes not.[179] We will consider the variations in more details below, referring to the European and American concept in view of the conflict between freedom of expression and hate speech.

Europe: dignity of the other before the freedom of expression

The atrocities of the Nazis and the Holocaust quite influenced the shaping of European case law on hate speech. Postwar legislation in Europe excluded any possibility of promoting speech that expresses discrimination or hatred based on racial grounds. The fact that a historic event acted motivationally for European jurisprudence, coincides with the far-reaching view of Foucault in order to clearly see the relationships of power in a situation, it is extremely important to understand its historical background. European countries as well as internationally the European Union, a symbol of activist liberal states explicitly prioritize the human dignity over freedom of expression. This privilege of dignity is conceptually synonymous to the fundamental liberal idea that all citizens should be treated with equal care and respect. The fundamental right to

---

[178] Beham, Mira. 2004: "Govor mržnje u politici i medijima". Objavljeno u Vacic, Z. (ur.) 2004 Etika javne rijeci u medijima i politici, Centar za liberalno demokratske studije, Beograd, 2004.

[179] Brugger, Winfried, Ban On or Protection of Hate Speech? Some Observations Based on German and American Law, 17 TUL. EUR. & CIV. L.F. 1 (2002);

freedom of expression is recognized in each European country as a matter of human rights. However, states are receptive to the content regulation of that right in the case of hate speech. Because, as much as the area of freedom of expression is primarily , some restrictions on the exercise of this right are necessary in certain circumstances. Unlike the right to freedom of thought (inner conviction or forum internum), the right to freedom of expression (external manifestation or forum externum) is not an absolute right. The enjoyment of this freedom carries with it certain duties and responsibilities and is subject to certain restrictions (as stated in Article 10 of the European Convention for the Protection of Human Rights and Fundamental Freedoms of the Council of Europe), especially for those speeches concerning the protection of the rights of others. Therefore it considered necessary in certain situations for the democratic societies to punish or even prevent all forms of expression which spread, incite, promote or justify hatred based on intolerance. The challenge that democratic governments must face is finding the right balance between the conflicting rights and interests concerned. The EU and its member states have taken the approach of balancing the rights in their law on rights and restrictions in which the EU is placed as a base for egalitarian activist decisions under these laws.

The key for international and European level is that the ideology of freedom of expression is not an imperative that can overlap other human rights and certain social values. According to Michael Rosenfeld, "collective concerns and other values such as honor and dignity lie at the heart of the conceptions of free speech that originate in international covenants or in the constitutional jurisprudence of other Western democracies".[180] There, hate speech is largely is prohibited and is subject to criminal sanctions. To Tarla Mekgonagl freedom of speech is not allowed to suppress equality or non-discrimination. Actually, freedom of expression is a right that is more or less shaded, and is an advantage over other, competing rights.[181] Mentioned in the ECHR, the right to freedom of expression is subject to restrictions necessary in a democratic society,

---

[180]Rosenfeld, Michel, Hate Speech in Constitutional Jurisprudence: A Comparative Analysis, Cardozo Law Review (Vol. 24:4), 2003.
[181]McGonagle, Tarlach, "Wrestling (Racial) Equality from Tolerance of Hate Speech", Dublin University Law Journal (ns) 21, 2001.

which requires that this right must be limited when it interferes with the rights or reputation of others and show that there is a balance between the right to freedom of expression and other rights. The ECHR exists despite legislation on hate speech and strongly demonstrates that hate speech is considered a case in which the rights or reputation of others justify restricting the freedom of expression. Here it is obvious that the EU sees the rights as general interest, and according to Raz rights must be limited to protect the rights and freedoms of others.[182] In multicultural societies, which are characterized by a diversity of cultures, religions and lifestyles, sometimes, it is necessary to align freedom of expression with other rights such as the right to free thought, conscience and religion or the right to be free from discrimination. Such is its place in the system of rights guaranteed by the already mentioned Universal Declaration of Human Rights, the International Covenant on Civil and Political Rights, the Convention on the Elimination of All Forms of Racial Discrimination.

In national legislation, most strikingly seen in the German case, where Article 5 of the Constitutional Law of Germany states that "every individual has the right to freedom of expression, but these rights are limited when it comes to ... right personal honor". Article 1 states that human dignity is the highest value and Article 18 allows reduction of other rights when the right to dignity is violated. These ideas of honor and dignity coincide with the requirement of Dworkin that every citizen should have the right to equal care and respect, and given that in practice they are regarded as trump cards against hate speech, they show that Germany acts in the framework of balancing rights.[183] Furthermore, the German use of words such as "honor" and "dignity" coincide with the comments of the critical race theorists: minority understand hate speech as an attack on their dignity and German legislation seeks to recognize and protect this dignity.[184]

---

[182]Raz, Joseph (1992) Rights and Individual Well-Being. Ratio Juris 5, 2 (July): 127–42.
[183]Dworkin, Ronald (2005) Taking Rights Seriously. Cambridge, MA: Harvard University Press.
[184]Levin, Abigail, The Cost of Free Speech Pornography, Hate Speech, and their Challenge to Liberalism, Niagara University, New York, 2010

With a brief consideration of European jurisprudence in cases of hate speech on national and international level, it becomes clear that the EU and its member-states, notably Germany, serve as top examples of activist liberal state in the service of equality.

For the first time, the European Commission of Human Rights has availed Article 17 in the context of the Cold War, in its decision on the Communist Party against the Federal Court in Germany, considering that the creation of communist social order by means of a proletarian revolution and the dictatorship of the proletariat is opposed to the Convention. Although political activities conducted by this party at the time of the lawsuit were constitutional, the Commission concluded that the Party had not given up their revolutionary goals.[185]

In the following decades, Strasbourg had to face the new challenges faced by democracies in Europe. The fear of a revival of National Socialism as a totalitarian ideology contrary to the Convention, has led the Commission and the Court frequently to apply Article 17. The Commission continually asserts:

- "National Socialism is a totalitarian doctrine incompatible with democracy and human rights, and its supporters undoubtedly follow the objectives as described in Article 17. Therefore, any activity inspired by Nazism would be considered incompatible with the Convention".

Article 17 shall apply to prevent freedom of expression to be used to promote revisionist or denial statements. Denial is a special category for racist comments because it constitutes denial of crimes against humanity, thinking here of the Nazi Holocaust and inciting hatred against the Jewish community. This idea of damnation, which contained not only expressions which constitute waiver or excuse for the crime, but also expressions advocating racial and religious discrimination, appeared gradually. An example can be seen in the decision of the European Commission in the case Honsik v. Austria:

---

[185] Communist Party (KPD) v. the Federal Republic of Germany, decision of 20 July 1957, Yearbook 1, p. 222

- "According to he circumstances in this case, the Commission notes that the findings of the Court of Asizes and the Supreme Court that the posts of the applicant, which are biased and polemical, are far from any scientific objectivity and deny the systematic killing of Jews in Nazi concentration camps using poisonous gas. The Commission previously considered that statements such as those of the applicant are contrary to the basic ideas of the Convention as outlined in its preambles - namely, justice and peace and further rejection of racial and religious discrimination".[186]

On the topic, in its decision on the case Lehideux and Isorni, the European Court added that "like any other remark directed against prominent values of the Convention ..., the pro-Nazi policy could it be allowed to enjoy the protection of Article 10".[187] Therefore there is a "category of clearly established historical facts - such as the Holocaust - whose negation or revision would be excluded from the protection of Article 10 by Article 17".

The case of Garaudy v France[188] is a turning point in the use of Article 17 because the Court clearly applied the principles outlined above to show the inadmissability of the application, confirming that:

- "Denial of a crime against humanity is one of the most serious forms of racial defamation of Jews and inciting hatred towards them. Denial of this type of historical fact undermines the values on which the fight against racism and anti-Semitism is based and represents a serious threat to public order. Such acts are incompatible with democracy and human rights because they violate the rights of others. Their supporters undoubtedly had concepts that fall into the category of aims prohibited by Article 17 of the Convention".

---

[186] Hinsik versus Austria no. 25962/94, Commission decision from October 18, 1995 DR 83, pp. 77-85, also Marais versus France no. 31159/96 Commission Decision from 24 June 1996 DR 86, p. It refers to the publication, but the real aim of the applicant, hidden behind a scientific demonstration, was to question whether gas chambers existed and whether they were used for genocide.

[187] Lehideux and Isorni v. France [GC], judgment of 23 September 1998, Reports of Judgments and Decisions 1998-VII, para. 53.

[188] European Court of Human Rights, (Application No. 65831/01), 24 June 2003

The European Court also had the recourse of Article 17 when the right to freedom of expression was applied to foster hatred or racial discrimination and exceeded the limits of revisionism. First the European Commission of Human Rights, and then the European Court used Article 17 to challenge the applicants that gave open racist statements creating racist hate speech. In its decision for inadmissability in Glimmerveen and Hagenbeek v. the Netherlands[189], the Commission considered that the applicants who follow a policy that clearly involves elements of racial discrimination, cannot rely on Article 10. In this case, the applicants were convicted of possessing leaflets addressed to "white Dutch people", which meant that they had the tendency to ensure that anyone who is not white should leave the Netherlands.

In the case of Norwood v. the United Kingdom, the Court first applied the Article 17 in the event of a direct attack on the Muslim community. The applicant presented to the Court his conviction that he had publicly expressed through the window of his apartment on which he had hung a large poster of the BNP (British National Party) and photography with the Twin Towers in flames followed by the words "Islam out of Britain - Protect the British! "and a symbol of New Moon and star put in a banning traffic sign. The Court decided that "such a violent attack against a religious group, linking the entire group with a serious act of terrorism, is incompatible with the values guaranteed by the Convention on tolerance, social peace and non-discrimination. Showing a poster on the window, by the applicant, constitutes an offense under the meaning of Article 17 and therefore he does not enjoy the protection of Articles 10 and 14". As a result, the application was declared inadmissible by the Court because it was incompatible with the provisions of the Convention.

In the case of Pavel Ivanov v. Russia[190] the Court decided that the applicant could not be protected by Article 10 since the publication whose author he was and which led to his conviction by the domestic courts, were intended to encourage hatred toward Jews and are therefore inconsistent with the values of the Convention: tolerance, social peace and non-

---

[189]Glimmerveen and Hagenbeek v. the Netherlands, Nos. 8348/78 and 8406/78, decision of the Commission of 11 October 1979, D. R. 18, p. 187.
[190]Pavel Ivanov v. Russia (dec.), No. 35222/04, decision of 20 February 2007.

discrimination. Faced with a clear racist statement, the Court excluded him from the protection of Article 10 of the ECHR.

It should be borne in mind that once the judgments of the European Court are final and enforceable regarding the member States of the Council of Europe they are also binding for the state which was a party to the proceedings before the European Court. However, since the European Court has jurisdiction to decide on all matters pertaining to the interpretation and application of European conventions and protocols, the legal positions that the Court takes on certain issues in the cases for which it decides and which interpret the essence of the rights guaranteed by the European Convention are of great importance for all states, no matter if a particular decision does not refer to them as a party in the proceedings. Monitoring and implementation of the practice of the European Court, regardless which state the present case applies to, allows the member-states to identify and resolve the same or similar problems in their laws and practices, also by taking appropriate measures to prevent possible filing of applications to the European Court, thus condemning the violation of human rights and the payment of any damages.

Although adopted at the national level, interesting is the judgment in the case "Auschwitz lie" from 1994, which is a result of the protest planned by the National Democratic Party (NDP) in Munich, on which David Irving, revisionist historian and denier of the Holocaust from England was supposed to be a guest. The German government asked the party to take measures to ensure that the Holocaust will not be denied, or, otherwise, to be prepared for the protest to be banned. When the conditions for the protest were appealed by the NDP the Federal Constitutional Court concluded that there was no violation of Article 5 and the protection of freedom of expression provided for there. The Court made a distinction between opinion which expresses the personal relationship of the individual with any expression, which is not subject to proof of truthfulness or untruthfulness, and actual expressions concerning the objective link between reality and such statements. False statements and false information do not deserve protection, particularly in cases where they violate the dignity.

Unlike these cases, which were related to cases that can be perceived as hate speech, when it comes to the right to freedom of expression, the European Court noted that the media have an obligation to transmit to the public information and ideas on political issues, even those that are controversial, and that obligation goes along with the public's right to be informed. However, the European Court stated that in the case of a reference to violence and/or hatred national authorities have greater discretionary assessment in deciding on the need for an opinion on the right of freedom of expression. In many cases, the European Court ruled that the statements involved did not constitute an incitement to violence and that the opinion of the authorities about the freedom of expression of the individual is breached because it was disproportionate to the objective pursued. Thus, in the case Jersild v. Denmark the European Court has found violation of the right to freedom of expression, when the journalist was sentenced before the domestic courts because he did not permit the members of the extreme group of young people to express racist views in a television interview. However, the European Court held that the purpose of the interview was not a propaganda of racist ideas and opinions. Namely, The European Court pointed out that the methods of objective and balanced reporting may vary significantly, which, among other things, depends on the medium. Therefore it is not a task of the European Court or domestic courts with its opinion to substitute the opinion of the media on which technique of reporting will the reporter apply. Furthermore, the European Court held that "punishing journalists for assisting in the dissemination of statements by another person in an interview would seriously jeopardize the contribution of the media in debates on matters of public interest and should not be envisaged unless there are particularly strong reasons for doing so". However, it is interesting that in this case seven judges emphasized their opinion because they thought that by punishing the journalist would not have infringed the right to freedom of expression. In the separate opinions, inter alia, it is stated that, although the International Convention on the Elimination of All Forms of Racial Discrimination "probably does not require punishment of journalists for the TV show of this kind [...], the media also have a responsibility to take a clear position in relation to racial discrimination and hatred". So, the good intention of the journalist in such situations is not sufficient, especially when the journalist himself provoked racist statements. The following was also noticed: "They want to defend the program citing that it was supposed to encourage healthy reaction among viewers. It is a show of optimism that is, at least, contested by the experience. Many young people today, even much of the population, face the difficulties of life, unemployment and poverty and cannot wait to find "scapegoats" that someone carelessly offers the; the journalist responsible for the show. did not try in any way to challenge the views that had been presented, which was necessary in order to minimize the impact of such a statement, at least in terms of the audience".

In the case Sürek v Turkey (No. 2) 127, the Court found a violation of the right to freedom of expression, when the applicant was convicted for publishing the names of officials who were responsible for combating terrorism. Considering the seriousness of the offenses that were committed by these officials, the European Court concluded that the public had a legitimate interest to be informed not only on their behavior, but also on their identity. In any case, this information had already been published in another newspaper, therefore, in the opinion of the Court, the interest in protecting their identity was "significantly" reduced. Also, the European Court stated that the criminal conviction and sentence which was imposed might discourage media to contribute to opening debate on matters of public interest.

In countries that restrict freedom of speech also, in order to protect and defend the dignity of discrimination (especially in Germany), there is a wide scope for interpretation of hate speech and many decisions are discretionary. Thus, the German Constitutional Court abolished the decision of the Bavarian Higher Court, which convicted the journalist Regensburg for incitement to racial hatred (Volksverhetzung) since in the article of the division of functions in the new city government he wrote: "Minister of Culture - a Jew?". The German Constitutional Court held in its justification for rejecting the ruling that from the circumstances and context in the present case, it largely depends on whether the labeling of the other as a Jew can be understood as an information or discrimination. As far as stigmatization of Jews in the Third Reich was a call for discrimination and harassment, so much today it must be taken into account that it is not necessarily so. When it comes to the Minister of Culture, it may be of importance for the assessment whether he is a good choice for this function if you know that the candidate is Jewish (as he himself introduced). His relationship with the Jewish culture could be a benefit for the city.

The most interesting case, which referred to the use of Nazi symbols, showed not only that such symbols are banned, but that the Federal Constitutional Court of Germany is capable to draw the lines for application of this prohibition. In the case of the use of Nazi symbols from 1990, the Court changed the sentence for the use of these symbols. The use of these symbols in the context of T-shirts was obviously satirical. A T-shirt with the inscription "European Tour", had the character and the name of Hitler, the dates 1939 and 1945, the map of Europe and a list of European countries. Most countries were those that were occupied by Germany, but the list also included England and Crete, and the names of the two islands were crossed with a note "canceled". The second T-shirt also had the image of Hitler, but this time with a yo-yo, and commentary on "European yo-yo champion, 1939-1945". The Court stated that these T-shirts did not aim to promote the Nazi principles and anti-Semitism, but they were satirical and had to be protected as art.

The aforementioned book of Muslims by Oriana Fallaci, for example, also falls into that kind of freedom of speech as it is considered that it represents a provocation that leads to thinking. On the other hand, where there is an intention to propagate Nazism, restrictions remain. According to Krotoszynski "copies of 'My fight' cannot be sold in Germany or the German".[191] The French writer Michel Houellebecq was acquitted of an accusation of hate speech, although in an interview he said: "Islam is the dumbest religion. When you read the Koran you feel broken. The Bible least is at least beautifully written because the Jews had a terrific literary talent". Before the court, the author explained that he felt no hatred towards Islam, but contempt. And the verdict claimed that he did not hate Muslims, but only Islam. One of the fiercest public advocates of Michel Houellebecq, was Salman Rushdie in his article in the "Washington Post" upheld the acquittal because, according to him, the opposite would mean a blow to the

---

[191] Krotoszynski, Ronald J., "A Comparative Perspective on the First Amendment: Free Speech, Militant Democracy, and the Primacy of Dignity as a Preferred Constitutional Value in Germany," 78 Tulane L. Rev. 1549 (2004).

freedom of expression. Muslim organizations in France, who sued Houellebecq, protested and claimed that he would be convicted if the same thing he said about Islam, was said about the Jewish faith.[192]

The legally punishable offenses subject to limitation of freedom of expression include insult and defamation which primarily protect public figures. The legal practice has shown that laws against defamation and insult are very problematic, as they are usually used to silence the media and mainly by politicians and other public figures. It is worth mentioning that England, which is known for broad interpretation of the freedom of expression, has one of the strictest laws against defamation, which can be used in different ways. A remarkable example is the verdict that by which the small London newspaper "LM" (Living Marxism) was sentenced with millions of pounds in damages over an article in which the journalist Thomas Daichman showed in details how the team of the English television ITN in the summer of 1992, in Bosnia, in order to publish pictures of "concentration camps" entered in otherwise empty space enclosed by barbed wire and wire an d recorded people like they are in camp. The ITN journalists were recognized to have suffered defamation because Daichman claimed that they have done that intentionally, that is willfully deceived the world public, which, in the opinion of the Court, was not so. (The Court did not go into the question of truth and accuracy of Daichman's research, but only assessed the (no) intention to manipulate the viewers by television). The consequence of this decision was that no media in England was allowed to publish this story again.[193]

From what has been said so far it can be seen that the courts are the ones that must decide which speech is hate speech, and which will be understood as freedom of expression. Most of the cases are easy to recognize when heard. However, the difficulty for most of the speeches that have elements of hate speech, for the implementation of the doctrine of words that cause violence, is the lack of direct confrontation. Such are websites with hate speech which are confronted with their target groups, but not in a direct way. In many cases the websites from Europe confront

---

[192]Beham, Mira. 2004: "Govor mržnje u politici i medijima". Objavljeno u Vacic, Z. (ur.) 2004 Etika javne rijeci u medijima i politici, Centar za liberalno demokratske studije, Beograd, 2004.
[193]Ibid

their target groups who are an entire ocean away and when, as we have seen examples of hate speech online, the courts have shown their impotence in terms of world networking space. Especially when they confront with the American conception of freedom of expression.

USA: Hate speech as regulated speech

As in Europe, the attitude of society towards hate speech and freedom of expression in the United States is also based on direct historical experience, with the difference that the US approach has went in a completely opposite direction. The historical experience in the USA dates back to the War of Independence against Britain in the 18th century and that war partly constituted a war for rights that were limited by the British government, including the freedom of expression. Because of these historical reasons, free speech in the United States has supreme power as opposed to free speech in continental Europe.[194] This becomes evident as early as in the First Amendment of the US Constitution, adopted in 1787, which to this day today "protects freedom of expression and ensures that the Congress adopts no laws abridging the freedom of speech and the press"[195]. This provision makes the USA the only states that give broad constitutional protection to hate speech.

From a European perspective, quite properly the following questions can be asked: If it is clear that some words show hatred and cause pain, why aren't they prohibited by law? Why does the USA not punish anyone who publicly uses it with an intention to offend anyone? Other forms of harm are punishable, why not punish this one? The function of criminal law is to define the standards of a civilized society and to prescribe penalties for conduct that violates these standards. Almost all states prohibit hate speech directed against racial, religious or ethnic groups, so why is that not so in the USA?

The American legal doctrine is quite different and there laws allow a broad debate on a variety of topics in which the use of offensive words is

---

[194] Whitman, James Q., Enforcing Civility and Respect: Three Societies, 109 YALE L.J. 1279, 1281 (2000).
[195] http://www.usconstitution.net/xconst_Am1.html

allowed. The Constitution does not distinguish and protects the words that are important to people, but also the words that are offensive to them. The First Amendment guarantees freedom of expression of ideas that people appreciate, but also ideas they hate.[196] It means that many offensive things, or things that hurt can be said without fear of criminal prosecution. American experience shows that the best method to combat prejudice is by limiting discrimination, education on diversity and the free flow of ideas, but not by limiting expression. It is perceived as soon as you look at the cases from the beginning of the last century. When the US administration at the end of the First World War, by law declared illegal any "unfair" or "offensive" criticism of the government and began to confiscate anti-war pamphlets and mail from the opponents of the war, the National Civil Liberties Bureau was based which focused efforts to protect freedom of expression during war. The Bureau was transformed in the 1920s in American Civil Liberties Union, which most stubbornly remained in opposition to the restriction of freedom of expression. Although it never advocated that any speech cannot be banned, it defended the broad definition of freedom of expression. So, in the twenties of the last century the Union advocated for the survival of the anti-Semitic magazine published by Henry Ford. The trend of the US legislation and judiciary to restrict the First Amendment changed in the mid-twentieth century, in the direction of liberalization of the freedom of expression, including hate speech, which made the USA the states with the most far-reaching right to express opinion.[197] Since then, in all interpretations of the First Amendment by the courts in the USA, they usually protect hate speech and see it even as political speech.[198] As we have previously seen, although, according to a study in the eighties of the 20th century, hate speech almost reached the level of an epidemic in university campuses in America, so that 25% of all students were subjected to ethnic violence (threats or violence based on

---

[196]Walker, Samuel, Hate Speech: The History of an American Controversy 8 (University of Nebraska Press 1994).

[197]Beham, Mira. 2004: "Govor mržnje u politici i medijima". Objavljeno u Vacic, Z. (ur.) 2004 Etika javne rijeci u medijima i politici, Centar za liberalno demokratske studije, Beograd, 2004.

[198]Saunders, Kevin W., Degradation What the History of Obscenity Tells Us about Hate Speech, New York Universi t y Pre s s

race, gender, ethnicity, religion or sexual orientation)[199], the influential university elite was against introducing speech codes. They argued that academic freedom sometimes includes discussions on controversial topics such as gay marriage and evolution or giving advantage to minorities in employment. According to them, colleges and universities are known for intellectual exploration of controversial views and therefore they should not take any measures that may be interpreted as an academic censorship.

Theorists like Mark Greber, emphasized the importance of free speech as an individual right, which, like the right to property can not be violated unless it is closely linked to criminal activity.[200] Anthony Cortese says that these interpretations of hate speech are reflected in the attitudes that messages of hate, leaflets and graffiti are simply examples of the exercise of the constitutional right to free speech by individuals.[201] He adds that it is much easier to allow speech with which we agree than speech of which we abhorre, and freedom of speech means that all ideas should be heard, with people, and not the government, will decide what is true, what isn't. For Judge Delgado there is no doubt that the tyrants and fanatics should be applauded rather than feared from.[202]

However, in the legislation of the United States there are provisions that limit the freedom of expression. The First Amendment, which protects the public interest in free expression must be balanced with other interests in society with which it can clash. The first test of that balance is possible confrontation with the Fourteenth Amendment to the Constitution which guarantees equal protection for all under the law and prohibits discrimination.[203] However, according to Cortes, American case law is still far from "entrying to grips with" and "cutting" free speech (First Amendment rights) from freedom of discrimination (protected by the

---

[199]Schmitt, Richard. 2000. "Radical Philosophy: 'Philosophers Combating Racism' Conference", American Philosophy Association Newsletter 99(20
[200]Graber, Mark A., Transforming Free Speech: The Ambiguous Legacy of Civil Libertarianism, 1991,
[201]Cortese, Anthony Joseph Paul, Opposing hate speech, Westport, Conn.: Praeger Publishers, 2006.
[202]Delgado, Richard, "Hate Cannot be Tolerated", usatoday.com, March 3
[203]http://www.usconstitution.net/xconst_Am14.html

Fourteenth Amendment).[204] According to some critics, the right to equal protection means prohibition of offensive racist speech and the constitutional principle of equal protection applies to many other groups. That way, words that offend people based on their religion, ethnicity, gender, age, civil status, sexual orientation or physical ability, should also be limited. So, for example, certain forms of slander are considered criminal offenses, such as spreading some lies and inciting murder or violence. Legal innovation is a means to prohibit hate speech and provide protection against discrimination. The most explicit cases in American legal tradition, when free speech was protected, were the cases of "clear and present danger".[205] This doctrine comes from the judge of the Supreme Court of the United States, Oliver Wendell Holmes Jr., according to whom the speech should be protected only if it does not impose a "clear and present danger" to the people. He explained that with the question: "Can anyone can invoke freedom of expression if false, in a crowded movie theater, he shouts 'fire' and causes panic" !?[206] In Holms's instance, sane individuals are forced to act out of fear for their safety. So, according to the doctrine of "clear and present danger" what is important is whether the words are used in such circumstances and are of such a nature that create a clear and present danger that some basic evils will be achieved that Congress has a right to sanction because freedom of expression does not mean freedom to terrorize or arouse hatred.[207]

The few examples that follow are far from the ambition to be comprehensive, but they clearly show in which directions ranged American jurisprudence the two Amendments from the US Constitution needed to confront and when the right of free expression collided with what is seen as hate speech.

---

[204]Cortese, Anthony Joseph Paul, Opposing hate speech, Westport, Conn.: Praeger Publishers, 2006.
[205]Sandy Starr, „Understanding Hate Speech, Hate Speech on the Internet", December, 2004 http://www.osce.org/publications/rfm/2004/12/12239_94_en.pdf
[206]Schenk v. US, 249 U.S. 47, 1919, http://caselaw.lp.fi ndlaw.com
[207]Михајлова, Елена, „Говорот на омраза и културната различност", Темплум, 2010

In the precedent of 1969, i.e. in the case Brandenburg v. Ohio[208], the US Supreme Court upheld the right of a racist organization Ku Klux Klan to represent the idea of returning of all Jews in Israel and all the blacks in Africa on rallies. This decision privileged the freedom of the speakers to the detriment of the equality of those to whom the speech was intended. The court had the attitude that because this representation was not intended to cause direct action on the target groups - meaning it did not cause "violent words" that would be grounds for exclusion from the protection of the First Amendment – it had to be protected as political speech (the most protected class of speech in the First Amendment is precisely political speech). If, however, it contained content directly inciting of unrest, based on its goals, then that speech would not be protected. Accordingly, the case Brandenburg showed strict restriction of the US Court of "time, manner and circumstances" for political speeches, initially promoted by Mill, according to which the content should not be restricted, but only time, manner and circumstances of the utterance if these things pose a risk to the public, for example, if the words of interest are considered "violent" they may be subject to restrictions by the state. Such an approach, regardless of merit, certainly does not balance the right to freedom of expression with the imperative that all citizens shall be treated with equal care and respect, protected in the Fourteenth Amendment equal protection clause; or by considerations of how the words of the speakers undermine the speech of the target groups and thus infringe of target groups protected by the First Amendment. Moreover, the decision of Brandenburg failed to take into account the historical context of the statement: these statements were expressed during the culmination of the civil rights movement in the US and because of that this right was stronger. Therefore, Brandenburg must be understood as non-egalitarian decision, which privilege the freedom of the speakers at the detriment of the decision that would be in favor of equality that the state owes to all citizens. Although hate speech is political speech according to the Supreme Court of America, however it can, alternatively, be interpreted as "violent words" or words that can be said to

---

[208]Brandenburg v. Ohio, 395 U.S. 444 (1969).

incite violence and, in this case, to be considered not worthy of constitutional protection.[209]

The American commitment to the protection of hate speech reached its highest point in 1977-78 with the famous controversial case National Socialist Party of America v. Village of Skokie[210]. The case referred to the question whether a group of American neo-Nazis - members and supporters of the National Socialist Party of America had the right to demonstrate in a predominantly Jewish suburb of Chicago, Skokie, - even despite the strong opposition of the local Jewish community. The Council of Skokie passed three decrees to prevent Nazi protests, which later became key elements of a court case that followed. The first Rulebook, set condition for providing $ 300,000 from the organizer of the protest for public responsibility and additional $ 50,000 for any damage caused by the demonstrations. The Second, prohibited dissemination of any material inciting hatred against people based on their race, nationality or religion. And the third, banned public demonstrations of members of political groups if they wear military uniforms. Shortly after these Rulebooks appeared, the Court of Appeal of the seventh circle declared all three unconstitutional. The Court noted that while public demonstrations may be subject to reasonable restrictions in terms of time, place and manner, Skokie hasn't ever complained about it. The second and third Rulebook directly hit the content of the calls and symbols, so that the Court decided that censorship based on the content of an idea was forbidden by the First Amendment. The Court found that the Nazi symbols, and their support for the genocide, are not violent words because no personal contacts are expected, and people from Skokie indicated that there are no threats to reactive violence. The Court also referred to the argument that the proposed demonstration would cause psychological trauma for residents of Skokie who survived the Holocaust. The Court found that the individual people can file damage claims based on intentional infliction of emotional distress, but the First Amendment does not permit prohibition of activity due to such outcomes. For the Court there was no doubt that the Nazi march will upset some residents of Skokie, but this was not an excuse to ban a peaceful form of expression. In short, the

---

[209] Levin, Abigail, The Cost of Free Speech Pornography, Hate Speech, and their Challenge to Liberalism, Niagara University, New York, 2010
[210] National Socialist Party of America v. Village of Skokie, 432 U.S. 43 (1977)

sensitivity of the audience could not overcome the fundamental rights.[211] The court declared it was "perfectly clear that the state should not make criminal the peaceful expression of unpopular views ... and public intolerance and animosity cannot be grounds for restricting these fundamental freedoms".[212]

Fighters for civil rights welcomed the developments in Skokie as a great victory. Federal courts confirmed the First Amendment rights of potentially offensive group and thereby confirmed the commitment to unfettered, and volumous wide open speech on public issues. The decision confirmed the commitment to freedom of expression which developed in the decades that preceded it. The only judge who disagreed with the decision was Lee Bolinger, who pointed out that "it's as noone liked the result, but all felt confined by the First Amendment".[213]. The dissatisfied judge asked relevant question: "Are we enslaved by freedom? Do we have to do some things, for example, to protect hate speech, only because the First Amendment forces us?"The majority of judges from the Court of the seventh circle vehemently denied, claiming that the decision was dictated by the fundamental assumption that if these rights were valid for all, then they had to protect not only the advocates of the ideas that are affordable, but also those whose ideas are repulsive . The result in the Skokie case was dictated for the judges by choosing how to best protect civil rights. Most judges rejected the option of limiting hate speech because the interests of racial minorities and powerless groups are best defended by broadcasting and through speech.[214]

The Skokie case is important for American society for another reason: the longstanding national policy of Jewish organizations on placing in quarantine of all anti-Semitic speech collapsed. Up until then, the leaders of

---

[211] Walker, Samuel, Hate speech: the history of an American controversy, University of Nebraska Press, 1994
[212] Haupt, Claudia E., Regulating Hate Speech—Damned if You do and damned if You don't: Lessons Learned From Comparing The German And U.S. Approaches, Boston University International Law Journal [Vol. 23:299] 2005
[213] Bolinger, Lee, The Tolerant Society (New York: Oxford University Press, 1986)
[214] Walker, Samuel, Hate speech: the history of an American controversy, University of Nebraska Press, 1994

the Jewish community on national level, considered it is politically impossible to defend the rights of the Nazis by the First Amendment.[215]

The main exception in American jurisprudence, which limited freedom of expression, was the decision in the case Chaplinsky v. New Hampshire since from 1942, which created the doctrine of "violent words".[216] Same as in other cases of Jehovah's Witnesses, the face of Chaplinski who was a member of this religious community, along with several other Jehovah's Witnesses, defiantly appeared in the city of New Hampshire in order to convert some people from Catholics in their faith. As it often happened, then there was a confrontation with the local authorities. At one point, Chaplinski called an officer "damned racketeer" and "damned Fascist". He was arrested for this, according to the State law for the crime of insulting a person in public. "Racketeer" was a standard epithet used by Jehovah's Witnesses for the leaders of other religions, and Jehovah's Witnesses frequently also called their opponents fascists because as Jews, they were also hunted in Nazi Germany. In the context of World War II, the term fascist was very offensive to many Americans. The court upheld the conviction with an unanimous decision. Judge Frank Murphy, who was considered one of the strongest libertarians in the court, offered a two-layered analysis of the First Amendment. Although most of the speech was protected, according to him "there are a number of well-defined and narrowly limited classes of speech, whose prevention and punishment would never have caused problems with the constitution. These included indecent and vulgar words, defamatory and insulting, that is 'violent' words". Murphy further defined two types of violent words: words which when uttered cause injury and those who cause disruption of peace. Both parts of the definition of violent words, given by Murphy had an impact on the offensive racist and religious speech. The first category was wider. The category of words which with their uttering cause injury, potentially include almost any derogatory epithet, or evensome attitudes or opinions which are just embarrassing. Murphy did not define injury, but it could be interpreted as a psychological injury and damage to the reputation of a person or group of people. The second class of violent words are those

---

[215] American Jewish Congress, resolution, January 8, 1978
[216] Chaplinsky v. New Hampshire, 315 U.S. 568 (1942)

words that are intended to cause immediate disruption of peace and have a narrower, but still important implications for the issue of hate speech. Many of the acts of the controversial groups were and are being deliberately provocative. Nazi groups in the United States before World War II, paraded in predominantly Jewish neighborhoods, knowing very well that it could cause violent reactions. Jehovah's Witnesses deliberately appeared in Catholic neighborhoods to present their antikatolichka message. The following question is whether the right of a person to speak may be restricted because he threatens with violence to the audience?[217]

The two-layer definition of "violent words" set in the case Chaplinski appears to have given two options to restrict hate speech. The first referred to the words that can cause immediate disruption of peace, and the second to words which with their mere uttering inflict injury. The first possibility opened the door to situations when hostile audience, through threats of unrest, may force the speaker to be arrested and, thus, to stop talking. The second possibility is more related to hate speech, because any offensive statement toward someone because of race or religion can be defined as a violation.[218]

The decision on Chaplinski from 1942, found that "violent words" are not protected by the First Amendment. This included the words "which by their very utterance cause damage or immediate disruption of peace". Still, it is interesting that the Chaplinski case did not lead to the adoption of state or federal laws that would ban hate speech.

The second remarkable case, inwhich the right to freedom of expression was limited by the local court and then annulled by the Supreme Court, was the case of 1992. R.A.V. v. City of St. Paul[219]. In this case, a group of white teenagers were sanctioned by the local court, because they burned a cross in the yard of a black family. These offenders were charged on the basis of regulation of the city on hate crimes, which explicitly forbade displaying symbols "considered or for which there are reasonable reasons to cause anger, anxiety or dislike of certain people based on race,

---

[217] Walker, Samuel, Hate speech: the history of an American controversy, University of Nebraska Press, 1994
[218] Ibid
[219] R.A.V. v. City of St. Paul, 505 U.S. 377 (1992)

color, beliefs, religion or gender". Decree was directed towards hate speech to put it in the scope of the doctrine of unprotected "violent words" and not in the domain of judicial practice of protected political speech that allow restrictions on the time, manner and circumstances of political speech.[220]

In June 1992, the Supreme Court annuled the decision of St. Paul, Minnesota, which forbade the use of any symbol that causes anger, anxiety or rejection among others on the basis of race, color, ancestry, religion or gender. The Supreme Court ruled that even though the decree referred only to violent words and it is not comprehensive, the view prevalent in the decree is not neutral because it forbade speech to aim only certain groups and not all. Because specific prohibitions imposed by the decree, the Supreme Court ruled that the legislation imposed restrictions on the content of speech and that had to be discontinued.[221] The main factor was that the judges agreed that the burning of crosses is a protected form of expression under the First Amendment.[222]

Foucault's understanding of power as the creator of certain types of entities, depending on the historical situation and the discourse that acted in that situation, perhaps is best reflected in the decision in the case RAV v. City of St. Paul. According to Walker, the best way to make sense of the decision on the case R.A.V. is to say that the Supreme Court decided to protect the speech that will decontextualize history of cross burning and that those who do it will be presented as unpopular minority whose speeches must be protected by the court versus the state power of censorship. Those who burn crosses are shown as unpopular minority which the court must defend from the power of the state.[223] The logic of such reasoning is the altered reality - the reality of continued racism and exclusion is deleted and fanaticism is redefined as a majority condemnation of racist views. The powerful effect of burning crosses, attack, terror, have also been modified. Power was replaced and is in the hands of those who oppose racism; powerful antiracists captured the state and use the state to

---

[220]Levin, Abigail, The Cost of Free Speech Pornography, Hate Speech, and their Challenge to Liberalism, Niagara University, New York, 2010
[221]Ibid
[222]Walker, Samuel, Hate speech: the history of an American controversy, University of Nebraska Press, 1994
[223]Ibid

oppresse powerless racists.[224] To understand the change in the historical context of the burning crosses we will briefly return in the twenties of the last century. Burning crosses has always been an aggressive expression of racial hatred from the Ku Klux Klan and other white supremacists. The clan was founded in 1886 and used a mysterious language and incantations in their sacred rituals and tried to maintain the subordinate status of former black slaves. It also represented the idea of racial superiority of whites. The rituals burning crosses and dark warnings expressed during the night by people in costumes of white robe and hood were practiced . If these threats did not cause the wanted intimidation, the Clan switched to whipping, fires (burning houses), even sadistic and brutal murders of blacks. The Clan was strongest in the 20's and 30's of last century, with massive demonstrations in the capital and millions of members, including men, women, youth and children.[225]

In 1992, in the aforementioned RAV v. City of St. Paul case, a local court faced with such a potential scenario, but clearly changed position of power in favor of the anti-racists. Therefore, the Supreme Court wrote in its conclusion that "there should be no hesitation that the burning of a cross in the yard of a person is unacceptable, but Saint Paul has sufficient opportunities to prevent it without throwing the First Amendment into the fire."

If we consider the decisions of Brandenburg and R.A.V. together we will discover that in the case law in the United States dominates the view that hate speech as a political speech should not have any content restrictions. Furthermore, when political speech and violent words are next to each other, the rules for political speech - not to apply restrictions to the content - are applied in the doctrine of violent words in order to ensure that the doctrine of violent words can be used to protect minorities. In each case on freedom of expression, the court asks whether and to what extent the specified speech in question, shows the values that are important for the good functioning of democracy. Political speech, of course, is of great

---

[224]Matsuda, Mari J., Charles R. Lawrence III, Richard Delgado, and Kimberlè Williams Crenshaw (eds.) (1993) Words That Wound: Critical Race Theory, Assaultive Speech, and the First Amendment. Boulder, CO: Westview Press.
[225]Cortese, Anthony Joseph Paul, Opposing hate speech, Westport, Conn.: Praeger Publishers, 2006.

importance to democracy, and to what extent the speech shows the priority values, to that extent it must enjoy constitutional protection.[226] As Sumner states if you cannot explain that other than the right to freedom of expression other rights such as the right to equality is also an essential component of democracy, then this approach is unfinished.[227] When this is done, we need a way to arbitrage between rights. If all rights are in close relationship with democracy and if two rights in are in conflict in a particular case, how can we limit one because of the other without damaging the democracy itself? Neither for Brandenburg, nor for R.A.V. are these questions understood as a way of balancing the rights of freedom and equality, but were more concerned about whether hate speech should be placed in the category of protected speech as political speech.[228]

As can be seen from several major decisions on hate speech in the USA, instrumental approach that is aimed at balancing the rights can yield results that will support the main obligation of the liberal state to treat its citizens with equal care and respect. American legal history, in terms of hate speech, did not correspond to the treatment of the presentation of violence. Even in the more recent past attempts are made to limit such speech that particularly come to the fore in the 21st century and that will be discussed in more details in the following.

5. CRITICAL OBSERVATIONS OF THE EUROPEAN AND US APPROACH TO HATE SPEECH

Throughout the discussion so far, hate speech has been reviewed from European and American perspective, when we saw that each approach has its own specifics, features, and advantages and disadvantages. Of course, if you ask a European intellectual for his stance on this issue, he will most likely be more critical towards hate speech, while the expectation is that the American opponent will defend the right hate speech as part of free

---

[226] Levin, Abigail, The Cost of Free Speech Pornography, Hate Speech, and their Challenge to Liberalism, Niagara University, New York, 2010
[227] Sumner, L.W. (2004) The Hateful and the Obscene. Toronto: University of Toronto Press.
[228] Levin, Abigail, The Cost of Free Speech Pornography, Hate Speech, and their Challenge to Liberalism, Niagara University, New York, 2010

speech. Who is right, which is exactly what side should we take, to which approach should we lead to in building personal stance on hate speech? Is there a magic formula that can show us the right approach? How to avoid being unilateral - agree to the own right to freedom of expression, even be able to offend, and to condemn others about the same right? Does our geographical origin from Europe oblige us to stand behind the European concept, just as the American must apriori agree with the freedoms and rights of the First Amendment? As legalists and loyal citizens, of course we must recognize the laws of our own society, and through them the status that hate speech has. But as free thinking people, it is indisputable that we have the right to think freely, reason and a conclude as to which of these two concepts is closer to our worldview, principles, beliefs, sensibilities and personal philosophy.

In addition, not to take a side and suggest which position is right or wrong because it would be presumptuous for such a complex issue, which, as we have seen, in its development dynamics tends to transform as a result of societal changes. Therefore, we will only present different views, opinions and critical observations on both concepts, whereby leaving everyone to choose the preferred response in this pro et contra analysis of the European and US approach to hate speech.

Selectivity in the application of the prohibition

We will begin with a general observation that in every country specific (minority) groups are subject to discrimination and therefore European countries and the USA have a dialogue on the different treatment of these groups. The denial of the Holocaust is one of the central aspects in the European debate on hate speech and the uniqueness of the Holocaust could justify the hesitation whether it could be subjected to comparative analysis. It may turn out that the denial of the Holocaust is like no other form of hate speech. There is no doubt that the war and the Holocaust caused interest in the regulation of group insult. Anti-Semitism was exposed not only as an idea of hatred, but also as a source of the worst event in modern history. For some people it was conceivable that limiting ideas of hatred is appropriate for a civilized society. But the interesting question is why so few people in the USA have accepted such an argument.[229]

Unlike Europe and the Jewish suffering in World War II, in America slavery and segregation (racial separation) led to racial tensions which caused such a state among the non-white population in which enhanced protection from offensive or harmful speech was required. After World War II, the United States were radically different from the rest of the world on the issue of hate speech. As laws on group insult disappeared in this country, other countries introduced such restrictions, in accordance with the letter and spirit of various international declarations that have arisen after the war.[230] How and why did the United States differ on the issue of the standards in the rest of the world? The question is all more intriguing because "various international declarations were modeled on the US Bill of Rights" (Walker). As Walker argues, they are written charters of human rights, defined as personal rights, with special emphasis on the American concept of the rights to freedom of expression, press, association/gathering, trial within a reasonable time. Hence, it seems that the rest of the world took the US approach on the protection of personal rights, but went on a very different path on the issue of hate speech.[231]

Undoubtedly a number of lessons can be learned from the comparison between the two approaches mentioned in this paper. First, despite the cultural similarities between the western countries, in this case, first of all, we think of Germany and the United States, the legal basis regarding the value of free speech are quite different. Second, both systems are imperfect in their attempts to regulate hate speech. Third, the United States has a lot written about possible improvements to the regulation of hate speech, but most proposals ignore the limits of the First Amendment. Fourth, in Germany policy in the interest of protecting the Jewish population was

---

[229]Walker, Samuel, Hate speech: the history of an American controversy, University of Nebraska Press, 1994
[230]Brownlie, Ian, ed., Basis Documents on Human Rights, 2d ed. (Oxford: Clarendon Press, 1981)
[231]Walker, Samuel, Hate speech: the history of an American controversy, University of Nebraska Press, 1994

chosen, although the case law of the Constitutional Court is inconsistent in relation to other groups in German society.[232]

Both America and Germany have a written constitution which contains provisions that protect the freedom of speech. However, the value given to the speech in each constitutional framework is very different. The argument is that that not only were the two societies founded on different philosophical premises, but they offer different interpretations of historical events which have led to different results in the constitutional framework for the value of free speech. In the Charter of Human Rights in the US Constitution, freedom of expression has a prominent position, while Article 1 of the German Constitution talks about protecting human dignity. In America, individual values, especially freedom of expression, to promote "social interest in protecting 'the entire national collectivity', unless an individually, not so much social evil is shown".[233] In the context of the German constitution, all rights should be weighed to human dignity that takes precedence over all other values. The German approach is the approach of most Western democracies, but also access to international law (therefore we consider it in more details to – note -auth.) and all are identifiable as categorically "Kantianism" (Immanuel Kant); most of the traditions incorporated are classical liberalism, democratic socialism and Christian natural law thought. The German constitutional system is under the regulatory framework and therefore requires a balancing of rights and obligations by the state and by the citizens. The Kantian interpretation of the concept of human dignity is central to the postwar German constitutional law.[234] The Nazi Experience forced Germany to adopt the status of "militant democracy" (*wehrhafte Demokratie*), which means that democratic forces working against the order are not protected by it and that freedom of expression does not mean promoting the abolition of the existing constitutional order. Walker cites the aforementioned Karlo Lowestein, who describing the rise of National Socialism says: "Democracy and democratic tolerance were used for their own

---

[232] Haupt, Claudia E., Regulating Hate Speech—Damned if You do and damned if You don't: Lessons learned from comparing the German and U.S. approaches, Boston University International Law Journal [Vol. 23:299] 2005
[233] Ibid
[234] Ibid

destruction". The use of anti-democratic measures in order to preserve democracy is justified since established democracies could tolerate this compromise of the principle: "Where fundamental rights are institutionalized, their temporary suspension is justified". The opinion that prevails in Germany, as Brugger points out is expressed in the shouts "Never again!" (*Nie wieder!*) and "Destroy it in nascent!" (*Wehret den Anfängen!*).[235]

These differences led to several important consequences. Generally, the American tradition has greater confidence in the power of good opinions which compete with the bad and assumes that good ideas will prevail.[236] Offensive speech may have a beneficial effect, for example, in the struggle for civil rights in America, while its detrimental effect is what Germany and Europe are focused on, where it is viewed as a tool of oppression.[237] Because distrust in the government prevails in America, an opinion which is not often in Germany, there is a reluctance whether to allow the government to choose which are good and which are bad opinions.[238] Finally, the US courts tend to look for matters of public interest that may be over the element of hatred, and there is no such tendency in German judicial practice.[239] The provision on free speech in the German Constitution contains more words than the ten relevant words in the First Amendment, but that does not mean it is less vague. The comparison between the regulation of hate speech in the USA and Germany, gives us the main lesson which convinces that the approach of Germany is far from finding the answer to the question. The German court is embroiled in a balancing act that has not found a universal solution that can be applied to the dilemma of hate speech.[240] On the other hand, Haupt continues its argumentation, speech which is hostile towards the Nazis, the Communists or anti-Semites will not only be protected speech, but there will be no

---

[235] Brugger, Winfried, Ban On or Protection of Hate Speech? Some Observations Based on German and American Law, 17 TUL. EUR. & CIV. L.F. 1 (2002)
[236] Ibid
[237] Ibid
[238] Ibid
[239] Ibid
[240] Haupt, Claudia E., Regulating Hate Speech—Damned if You do and damned if You don't: Lessons learned from comparing the German and U.S. approaches, Boston University International Law Journal [Vol. 23:299] 2005

interest to compensate these groups. Directly speaking, the German Constitutional Court behaves more protective with respect to speech which in favor of the government's view of these problems than other types of speech. As for the other potential targets of hate speech it can be said that the legal prohibition is not universal and caution is reduced in the case of other groups such as Turks. As demonstrated by the case of "denial of the Holocaust," Germany's commitment to protect the Jewish sensitivity is considered incredibly far reaching. When we talk about other groups, the question is put on the individual, and not the group and it is not asked whether the uniform law of honor is violated. The law somewhat ensures equal protection against attacks by individualists. In fact, in the German doctrinal treatment if there is an attack on a group the attack is on every member of that group, according to the basis of group membership, rather than the group as such.[241] Compared with the treatment of other groups such as the Turks, it was shown that there is an obvious difference between German Jews and other foreigners or immigrants. Emphasizing unique belief of German Jews, leads to unconditional exception towards all other racial or religious minorities. The most significant aspect in the treatment of hate speech in German law is under discussion doubts about his flaws.[242]

Brugger locates the anomaly on the German model in another aspect, which is that hate speech is considered so large social problem in order for the criminal law to be applied against it. In a way, it's amazing to see that disobeying the free speech is based on previously exaggerated or too permissive criticized doctrine of free speech. As discussed earlier, the exclusiveness of the Holocaust is the only justification for the treatment of hate speech in German law. The exclusiveness of the Holocaust in the German and world history resulted in detailed prohibiting laws and long interpretations of the prohibition of lies in the case of the Holocaust.[243] Krotoszynski believes the German experience is not the best model. He says: "The German model, seems to fail on several key elements. The Constitution criminalizes hate speech that advocates for the demolition of the existing constitutional order, but the citizens, however, continue to join

---

[241] Ibid
[242] Ibid
[243] Brugger, Winfried, Ban On or Protection of Hate Speech? Some Observations Based on German and American Law, 17 TUL. EUR. & CIV. L.F. 1 (2002)

those organizations with such purpose. For more than fifty years censorship has failed to achieve its goal. Reports of anti-Semitism and violent events against ethnic minorities in Germany continue to concern (...) and the use of prohibition of hate speech, has failed to achieve its goal from an empirical aspect.[244] If a performance test is the complete elimination of anti-Semitism and violent incidents against minorities, then it is clear that the German approach is unsuccessful. But if we examine the reduction of anti-Semitism and ethnic violence, the continued presence of such acts shows failure. What would be necessary for empirical evidence is a comparison of the state of affairs on the restriction of hate speech and the situation in the absence of such restrictions. The best control, best comparative sample would be restrictions in Germany since the 1930s. Although there were other factors at the time, Nazis' speech caused more anti-Semitism and violence against minorities and more than that which can be noticed now. Maybe this is why Germany is not such a bad model for other democracies and even if Germany is not the model, there are many other democracies which have introduced limitations on hate speech and which can serve in that function - concludes Sanders.[245]

Hate speech as a weapon of the weaker

We have already seen that on American soil the main debate lead between experts is how to establish a balance between the First and Fourteenth Amendment, something that is (somewhat) absolved in Europe with Article 10 and Article 17 of the European Convention on Human Rights. Thus, Judge Richard Delgado frames the controversy about hate speech in terms of "constitutional provisions in collision", a conflict between the provisions of the First Amendment and the provision of equal protection to all (Fourteenth Amendment).[246] To Cortese such a balance in the USA does not exiast because hate speech violates constitutional rights

---

[244] Krotoszynski, Ronald J., "A Comparative Perspective on the First Amendment: Free Speech, Militant Democracy, and the Primacy of Dignity as a Preferred Constitutional Value in Germany," 78 Tulane L. Rev. 1549 (2004).
[245] Saunders, Kevin W., Degradation What the History of Obscenity Tells Us about Hate Speech, New York University Press, 2011
[246] Delgado, Richard, "Campus Anti-racism Rules: Constructional Narratives in Collision", Northwestern University Law Review 85 (1991)

because it is onthe other side of the equation. "Does the victim of hate speech not enjoy the constitutional right under the Fourteenth Amendment not to be marginalized, insulted and infamous only because of what he is? Then hate speech requires specific balancing of interests: in our society we value the right to say what we want. But we also value equality and we want the public and private law to reflect the privilege that gives the equal value of every citizen. When hate speech threatens this right, it requires sober thinking, and not an easy answer", argues Delgado.

In the United States you can hear the opinion that the best cure for bad speech is more speech. It can encourage the victim to use violent activity, instead of withdrawing into a hole or run to the authorities whenever he feels violated. In other cases, we may hear that hate speech is a corrective measure that serves as a way to expel pressure. Speaker "expels the anger from himself" and must be allowed to find a safe way out only in words. The suppression of anger, only means that later it is likely to occur in more dangerous form as physical violence. For the proponents of this thinking, free speech is not only recommended under the Constitution, but is also the surest way for minorities. The problem with this argument, as assessed by Delgado in the introduction of Cortese's work, that it simply is not consistent with what we know about human behavior. Reservoirs, pumps under pressure and other lifeless objects may be safer once the steam is released, but human beings are not. Research in the social sciences have shown that a speaker who uses hate speech is more, not less, prone to later do something violent. In addition, witnesses who see this it can also join him.[247]

Another argument in this American debate is that hate speech serves as a leader. It is better to have everything opened, rather than concealed, so you do not know when it will appear. It is true that the famous racist is less dangerous than one who is anonymous.[248] In the earliest discussion of this issue, in the twenties, Codman had argued taht ACLU had a paragraph on the freedom of expression and there was a clear distinction between words and deeds. Hidden crimes could be punished, but not forms of expression.

---

[247]Cortese, Anthony Joseph Paul, Opposing hate speech, Westport, Conn. : Praeger Publishers, 2006.
[248]Ibid

Public gathering is a form of political expression protected by the First Amendment.[249] Codman also raised the question of similar problems of vagueness and selective application. Pointing to the general pressure on the Communists and other radicals, according to the laws of criminal conspiracy, he argued that there was great disagreement over what constituted offensive speech. The ambiguous definition of what is permitted made the freedom of expression and gathering completely dependent on the opinion of the person who is currently in power.[250] For those who supported the ban on gatherings that could provoke unrest and violence, the complete answer is that no one can say in advance whether the rallies will cause them or not. Banning gatherings or rallies because some people think it may result in violence is only a pretext for arbitrary suppression of unpopular groups.[251] Prosecution of Nazi would only have made them victims and would only have caused an increase in the number of their supporters who would otherwise be neutral. The argument was that the best way to combat the Nazi propaganda is open through counter - propaganda, demonstrations etc. Once ramp is raised, the field is open to all. Even Jews who attacked the Nazis, could be punished under the general prohibition of offensive speech based on race or religion. This was an important point, given that there were many undercover cases of violence committed against the Nazis by anti – Nazi groups before World War II in the USA.[252]

Curley's arguments that legally allowed activity may be banned because of broader illegal objectives of the organization was especially present in the Cold War. Many anti-Communist measures were taken based on the thinking that the Communist Party constituted a criminal association rather than a legitimate political party and therefore they were not subject to protection from the First Amendment. The federal government and several US states adopted laws which instructed the Communist Party to register. Such requests were based on the opinion of the legislator that the

---

[249] Letter, Codman to Curley, October 11, 1923; Chafee Papers, box 30, HLS
[250] Walker, Samuel, Hate speech: the history of an American controversy, University of Nebraska Press, 1994
[251] The Rights to Advocate Violence (New York: ACLU, 1931)
[252] Walker, Samuel, Hate speech: the history of an American controversy, University of Nebraska Press, 1994

party represented a threat to national security.[253] It is important be noted that the decision was adopted at a time when few Americans and the Supreme Court were against such attempts to abuse the Communist Party. If the majority of Americans regarded the Communist Party subversive, in the same way the majority whites from southern USA (traditionally racially offensive towards blacks) regarded the NAACP as subversive to their lifestyle. Allowing the legislative majority to decide which ideas and groups are subversive or offensive opened the door to problems of uncertainties and selective application, concludes Walker.

The long battle in terms of hate speech during the 20th century (starting from the 30s), two arguments on limiting freedom of expression constantly occurred. The first is that a particular group is a special case and limited exception to the freedom of expression. The second argument is that free societies have the right, perhaps even an obligation to limit the activities of anti-democratic groups who intend to destroy freedom of expression and other democratic principles if they come to power. Supreme Court Justice Robert Jackson, in his position from 1949, a very said that in a very direct way: "Bill of Rights is not a suicide pact". The inclusion of the Fourteenth Amendment to the debate on hate speech was part of a much wider power, to which some lawyers and social critics belonged. For a number of different perspectives - feminist, left-oriented, African American, conservative and moderate liberal, a new critical thought was created which gave importance to the reduction of individual rights at the expense of the rights of communities or the interests of the society as a whole. The support for the restriction of hate speech came from the new movement that appeared on the scene in the eighties and was known as "communitarism".[254] Several organizations and activists began to argue that the rights revolution went too far in its emphasis on individual rights and that more attention should be paid to personal commitments and the needs of society as a whole. The Communitarians emphasized children and families, and thought that less emphasis should be put on the rights to happiness and self fulfillment because divorces happened very often, and, instead, the emphasis would be laid on the responsibilities of parents

---

[253] Ibid
[254] "A Communitarian Defense of Group Libel Laws", Harvard Law Review 101 (January 1988): 682-701

towards their children. Regarding hate speech, the communitarian platform supported freedom of expression, but invoked the personal restraint, even when you had the right to call someone by a name, you're supposed to use that right. For them, citizenship and the common good were more important than unlimited personal rights. In many respects communitarians gave life to the old "balancing test" which was the central point of the debate about the First Amendment in the late fifties and early sixties - the rights of the individual must be balanced with the interests of society as a whole.[255]

The sociologist and lawyer David Risman, as a supporter of Levestein's militant democracy, criticized the absolutist approach to the First Amendment and issues associated with it, as well as not having regard to the practical consequences of words. He offered the process of finding facts for disclosure of the nature and extent of harm in certain contexts. With the contextualized approach he held that the word has different meanings and effects depending on the time, place, the speaker and the audience. Identical words from the mouths of different people, according to Risman, carry a significantly different weight. He illustrated his point with the example of a political candidate from New York, who if he was anti-Semitic oriented, that would be fatal and a defamation under the law. In another city, where the Jewish voice is not as important, it would be less harmful and would not constitute an insult. To determine whether a particular event constitutes an insult continues Risman, the courts will have to engage sociologists to examine the sociological context. They could, for example, examine the reputation of the group in question, the power of the medium and so on. That way, if the fascists are considered universally undesirable in a certain community, references to someone as fascist would be an insult. Risman was open and straightforward in his basic position. He ended with a statement that "German experience" shows how laws can be a tool of the Nazis. There is no reason why it cannot also be a tool and democracy.[256]. In the middle of World War II and in the fight against totalitarianism in the Cold War, this was a powerful argument in USA.

---

[255] Walker, Samuel, Hate speech: the history of an American controversy, University of Nebraska Press, 1994
[256] Riesman, David, "Democracy and Defamation", Columbia Law Review 42 (1942):

Risman's contextualized approach to insult did not take an important place in American law which developed in completely the opposite direction, towards universal and neutral standards in terms of content, rather than the standard of details based on facts.[257] However, the arguments for contextualized approach reappeared in the eighties. Some supporters of the law on hate speech believed, for example, if a black person called a white *honkie*, it was less painful than a white man to call a black *nigger* and, consequently, the latter should be subject to prosecution. Other supporters of the law on hate speech thought that the offensiveness of the word "*zionist*" depends on whether it is spoken by a person under oppression, for example, a Palestinian or a member of a powerful group.[258] One of the most militant groups to protect gay rights was the organization called *Queer Nation*. The term *Queer* (Eng. abnormal, sick, unusual) is an old term that referred to the gay and it was banned as offensive in all campus according to the Codes of Conduct. Still, homosexuals' organizations in the seventies had accepted this their derogatory term as theirs.[259]. This showed that the meaning of words changed - terms indicating tribute yesterday, represented shame today and conversely - words that were offensive one day, were proudly used another day. How could the law on speech deal with such radical changes in the meaning and use of words? Could a word could be offensive when used by a person, and not offensive when used by aother? In the case of *Queer Nation*, the choice of words is deliberate. The word that denoted hatred became weapons.[260] This led the word *Queer* to no longer be perceived as offensive by the homosexual community. The same process occurred with the word "nigger". He was the most hated racist term for African Americans. Still, a few years ago rap group appeared on the music scene appointed *NWA - Niggers with attitude*. This group was very popular and sold several million copies of its album, without being played on major radio stations. The word

---

[257] Walker, Samuel, Hate speech: the history of an American controversy, University of Nebraska Press, 1994
[258] Matsuda, Mary J., "Public Response to Racist Speech: Considering the Victim's Story", Michigan Law Review 87 (August 1989): 2320-81, esp. p. 2364
[259] "Militants Back 'Queer', Shoving 'Gay' the Way of 'Negro'", New York Times, April 6, 1991
[260] Walker, Samuel, Hate speech: the history of an American controversy, University of Nebraska Press, 1994

beginning with "N" was echoed in the title of the album – *Niggasforlife*. In order to protect the feelings of readers and as a sign of understanding of the power of the word, the name of the album was written conversely. As with the word *Queer,* here also the most hated word was proudly taken over and transformed into a political weapon.[261]

Free debate in the public discourse, which included hate speech, in the US view has another quality. (Here we will give a brief commentary on the history of racial epithets in American political discourse). As it can be seen, all cases concerning the use of the word "F" were convicted: the opponent of the war in Vietnam (*Fuck the Draft*), the African American militant (*White motherfucker*) and the critic of the policies of the local school (*Motherfucker fascist pig cops*) were convicted. As an expert on the First Amendment, Kent Greenwalt held that it is no coincidence for those who are culturally less privileged or politically radical, to be more likely to use words or phrases that can be judged to have violated civil discourse.[262] According to him, "in the absence of real political power, extreme words, words full of emotion, etc., are the only weapons of the powerless to gain attention for an issue and to mobilize people to change. That is the main argument for the treatment of hate speech as free speech".

For Walker there was certainly a reason for such widespread acceptance of social policy dedicated to the unrestricted right to free speech. We have seen that the protection of the provocative and even offensive speech served the broader social and political needs. Especially provocative speech was the primary vehicle for the civil rights movement and the struggle for racial equality. By the leaders of these movements being committed to freedom of expression and that by the idea of banning hate speech remained without supporters, this idea was left an orphan in the political arena (Walker). The forces for civil rights came to the conclusion that so much controversy, as integration in schools in the South in the fifties, the struggle for racial justice in northern cities in the sixties and seventies, the success, if not the very survival of the activities for protection of civil rights, lay in protection of the provocative and

---

[261] Ibid
[262] Greenwalt, Kent, Speech, Crime, and the Uses of Language (New York: Oxford University Press, 1989) p.298

sometimes offensive language and hate speech. For the weak and excluded, speech was often the only resource available. The only hope was based, as told by Judge William Douglas, in words that cause, that offend, which introduce anxiety and create dissatisfaction with the status of things, even those who lead men to anger. On the same template, many cases in which Jehovah's Witnesses were protected in the late thirties and fourties it gave this religious group room for a maneuver with hatred. The broader message was that all these people are legitimate members of the American community and are entitled to rights and privileges as others. The message was a message of tolerance: it is the initial value communicated via the First Amendment.[263]

This critical review of the US experience with hate speech leads to a definite conclusion that protecting offensive speech is very important in the struggle for racial equality, together with the defense of other disabled groups, protesters against the war in Vietnam and others. The inclusion of the weak and the historical victims of discrimination is supported (but not fully achieved) through the broadest protection of offensive speech, regardless of its content. There is no doubt that freedom of speech is a fundamental principle of American democracy.[264] It allows all ideas to be heard and, thus, all people are free to choose how to behave. Freedom of expression is an essential element that allows all individuals to fully express their identity and also provides uniformity and guarantees that those in power will not be able to completely monopolize public discourse and prohibit some ideas.[265] <u>Here we can find the crucial difference with Europe: the poor and vulnerable groups in the USA have used hate speech to defend against more powerful and larger social groups and to improve their status in the community. In pre-war Europe it was conversely – the stronger usurped the institutional resources and abused the legitimate power of the state to deal with the weaker.</u>

---

[263]Bollinger, Lee, The Tolerant Society (New York: Oxford University Press, 1986), pp. 29-30
[264]Meiklejohn, Alexander, Free Speech and Its Relation to Self Government (New York: Harper and Row, 1948)
[265]Karst, Kenneth, "Equality as a Central Principle in the First Amendmant", University of Chicago Law Review 43 (1975)

Another American feature is their emphasis on individual rights. The habit of thinking in the framework of individual rights is so deeply embedded in American culture that most Americans are not aware of how unusual it is for the rest of the world. The emphasis on formal individual rights became particularly intense from the sixties onwards while most of the rest of the world preferred rights of the community. Hence, we can notice that the US courts can learn from the experience in other countries. Attorneys argue that limitation of hate speech, which can be seen as functioning successfully in many democracies, should lead to the conclusion that the USA may introduce restrictions on hate speech without any risk that it will penetrate into totalitarianism. Scientists see restrictions of hate speech as compatible with the freedom of expression necessary for the functioning of democracy. It has to be recognized that accepting restrictions in the United States would mean changing the law. Still, this change should be considered because the USA, although considered proponents of free expression are in danger of becoming the host nation of hate speech.[266] In particular, as we have seen, in the sphere of Internet.

On the other hand, in terms of hate speech, perhaps the most interesting issues surrounding international human rights declarations are various restrictions on personal freedoms they allow. To Walker, when an American would read these provisions he would read either with fear or ridicule. For him international human rights declarations open the issue of hate speech, but do not resolve it. The main issues, such as - when is offensive speech a protected form of political activity, and when it is a threat to public order - remain unanswered. The USA combat these problems by the First Amendment from 1919 and the result is a large number of court cases. The impression remains that the rest of the world has much to learn from the American experience when referring to the bitter issue of hate speech concludes Walker.

---

[266] Saunders, Kevin W., Degradation What the History of Obscenity Tells Us about Hate Speech, New York University Press, 2011

6. POSSIBLE TENDENCIES OF RAPPROCHEMENT BETWEEN THE TWO APPROACHES

The key from what has already been said is that the two approaches that treat the hate speech and freedom of expression - European and American - are diametrically apart from each other, representing two different concepts of the same problem. On how many different concepts are in question, we would round up the complete explication with the two most illustrative examples that can describe this diversity. In 1995, in the United States, some right-wing radio host said in his radio program that in practicing shooting firearms he used as targets drawings of the US President Bill Clinton and his wife Hillary and drawings with federal police agents. To him that was legally justified. In the same programme, he primed listeners when they defend their home from the police to "shoot twice in their body and if that is not enough to shoot in the abdomen". Although he was convicted by the critics for misplaced and shocking comments, however, from the National Association of Hosts of Radio Talk Show Programs he received the award for "freedom of expression" because of "the expressed courage".[267]

Ulrich Wicker, is a famous television journalist from Germany. In the fall of 2001, in one of his text he quoted the Indian writer Arundhati Roy, who compared the US President George W. Bush with the terrorist leader Osama Bin Laden by saying that they have the same fascist mindset. Although Wiciker conveyed this statement very carefully, it immediately led to violent reactions in the German (political) public. It was thought that it was offensive speech, not just for the American friends, but for all Germans who after all owed so much to America. Wicker avoided being fired by publicly apologizing for what he wrote.[268]

Observed through these two examples, however evident the difference between the two concepts is, still, it sounds unreal that the trends followed in the new millennium lead to the conclusion that there are opportunities to bring the two concepts together. This is particularly present after

---

[267]Day, Louis Alvin, „Ethics in Media Communications – Cases and Controversies".
[268]Beham, Mira. 2004: "Govor mržnje u politici i medijima". Objavljeno u Vacic, Z. (ur.) 2004 Etika javne rijeci u medijima i politici, Centar za liberalno demokratske studije, Beograd, 2004.

September 11, 2001, and the proclaimed global fight against terrorism. The reaction in the USA as a result of the attack on the World Trade Center led to the passing of the controversial so called Patriot laws, which for many lawyers and human rights activists are in direct collision with the human rights guaranteed in the Constitution. However, many influential voices today seek to amend the First Amendment, in order for the speech of hatred by radical Islamists could be declared unlawful.

This tendency of change is perhaps most precisely detected by the British writer of Indian origin, Kenan Malik in his book "From Fatwa To Jihad". In it he cites tan example from 1989, at the time when fierce discussions were led on the pronounced death sentence for the author of "Satanic Verses," Salman Rushdie. In such a public debate, organized by the Muslim Institute in Great Britain before the present TV cameras the institute's founder Kalim Siddiqui, publicly asked the audience how many of them supported the death penalty for Rushdie. Most of them raised their hand. On the next question, how many would be willing to carry out the sentence, he received roughly the same response from the attendees. A certain attorney addressed the International Board for the defense of Salman Rushdie with the suggestion to ask the British public prosecutor to bring charges against Siddiqui of inciting murder. The Board discussed the issue and came to the conclusion that Siddiqui's words, although they were shocking and repulsive, did not constitute incitement since neither he nor his followers were able to carry out threats in the case because they neither knew where Rushdie is nor they possessed weapons to do so.[269]

Eighteen years later, further writes Malik in 2007 a group of Muslims protested in front of the Danish Embassy in London due the offensive cartoons of Muhammad. The leader of the group, a certain Abdul Muhid, was spotted by the police as shouting "Bomb Great Briatin" and showing a banner with the slogan "Destroy those who insult Islam". Another protester shouted that the British troops should return from Iraq in coffins and that he wanted to see how their blood flowed in the streets of Baghdad. A third protester shouted "Let's bomb Denmark and the United States" and a fourth that Europe will pay in blood. To Malik it is clear that these protesters were

---

[269]Malik, Kenan, From Fatwa To Jihad: The Rushdie Affair And Its Legacy, Atlantic Books, 2009.

even less in a position to carry their threats into action than Kalim Siddiqui was in a position to kill Salman Rushdie, but despite this, the three loudest protesters were sentenced to six years in prison for inciting murder, while the fourth was sentenced to four years in prison for inciting racial hatred. The contrast between the treatment of anti-Rushdie protests and those who protested against the cartoons is an example of how the understanding of freedom of speech has changed in 20 years. Restriction of speech, supposedly to protect the culture and dignity of minority communities, is now used to breach the civil liberties of those same communities, concludes Malik. According to him, the law is now used for criminalization of not just speech that directly leads to injury, but speech that might indirectly lead to injury or one that is considered morally unacceptable. In other words, explains Malik, usually there is no direct relationship between words and deeds. How do people react to the words depends to a great extent on the individual. They are the ones who are responsible for the interpretation of words and their implementation into practice. Between the words and the deeds stands a human being, with his own mind, the ability to judge right and wrong and responsibility to face their own deeds.[270] For this writer there is no doubt that most people would agree that there is a difference between words and deeds. However, in post-Rushdie world, the law often acts as any space did not exist between the two. Aesop wrote – words are deeds. And it seems this is also so in the British law. Muslim protesters shout "Bomb Denmark" or "Death to those who insult Islam" may be idiotic and offensive, but the idea that they incite murder is equally idiotic and insulting to our intelligence. People do not react to words as robots. They think, rationally and act in accordance with their thoughts and judgments. Fanatical speeches certainly affect the avid fanatics, but fanatics must bear responsibility for the translation of the speech in deeds, concludes Malik.[271]

The tendency to restrict freedom of speech and the expansion of the area which encompasses hate speech, as the newspaper editor Brendan O'Neill writes in the journal "Spiked" the law in the UK recently put under the scrutiny the so called "mate speech" that two or more people informally

---

[270]Ibid
[271]Ibid

have with each other. According to O'Neill, intimate conversations are no longer between our interlocutor and us - if someone accidentally overheares our conversation and find it offensive to any other we automatically succumb under legal sanction. Never mind that the problematic phrase for us was completely meaningless, or even had the opposite meaning - what if a bystander hears it and tomorrow, because of it kills thousands of members of a minority!? "Welcome to the society without a sense of humor," ironically says O'Neill.[272]

We can be persuaded that this is not just a fictional sequence, as an allusion to Orwell's "1984", from the film of Michael Moore, "Ferenhait 9/11". In this film, the testimony given by a retiree from California, once he spoke with their friends about September 11, the war in Afghanistan, bin Laden and George Bush. In the conversation one of the participants said that Bin Laden is an idiot because of the death of many people. The retiree answered to that: "Exactly but he will never be a bigger idiot than Bush, who bombs around the world for oil companies to make profit". That evening the door FBI agents knocked on the door of his house, after a report of a friend. They came to question him because he publicly spoke about September 11, Afghanistan, Bin Laden, Bush and profits of oil companies.[273] As Walker explains, one should not be an expert on the First Amendment right to understand the national security, public order or public health and morals are extremely vague and elastic in the United States. After all, they are traditionally a justification for the restriction of individual rights in the USA in terms of political speech and association, public demonstrations, censorship of literature related to sex, access to contraception, abortion and so on.[274] To him, the trend in the US constitutional right is in narrowing the permitted uses of any of these restrictions. On the other hand, Senson anticipates in which direction might American society move: "Political discourses of the parties are filled with hatred because they are among the few remaining discourses where hate speech is protected. No one should be surprised if in the future, during an

---

[272] O'Neill, Brendan, "After Hate Speech, the war against 'Mate Speech'", Spiked, 13. 03. 2007, http://www.spiked-online.com/site/article/2953/
[273] Fahrenheit 9/11, http://www.youtube.com/watch?v=chj5R0Izt9s
[274] Walker, Samuel, Hate speech: the history of an American controversy, University of Nebraska Press, 1994

attack by a third, fourth or fifth party, the Republicans and Democrats unite and through bipartisanship approve a law that protects their representatives and members from hate speech."[275] According to his anticipations, criticizing the government will no longer be unpatriotic, but would constitute a criminal offense.

---

[275] "Hate Speech" in Political Discourse, 01.07.2004, http://karmalised.com/?p=549

7. CONCLUSION

From everything previously said about hate speech, it is clear that the legal systems of the USA and the European countries have different treatment of hate speech and its position in the space which belongs to freedom of expression. In the US legal system, hate speech is an integral part of free expression, while in Europe it represents an abuse of the basic human right to freedom of speech.

We have already asked the questions on which approach is correct and whether there is a limit to freedom of expression in a democracy and if there is, where should the line be drawn. Dilemmas are not easily solved and there is no universal answer: even the best intention to prevent the spread of hatred can easily deviate in totalitarian ban on different opinion and criticism; on the other hand, excessive openness in society on different views and attitudes can be deformed in the abuse of the right to free expression and losing the sense of responsibility towards public speech. Therefore, the greatest challenge in the legal sanctioning of hate speech is respect for freedom of expression as one of the fundamental rights of the citizen which is necessary for the functioning of any democratic society. However, unfortunately, the state has no universal "instrument" which would prove whether something is freedom of expression or its abuse. If such an instrument existed, the public could easily, for example in the Netherlands, determine and take a stand for situations like the one a few years ago, when a group of politicians colluded to have a public debate on the registration of a party that supported the legalization of pedophilia. Is this a legitimate political discussion or the peak of morally degraded public discourse in a liberal society?

In the absence of such an instrument, which are the opportunities that remain for us to properly position? The judiciary should, in terms of political extremism manifested through hate speech, take the place of a protector of the state, its democratic values and tolerance. But this is possible only if the judiciary is independent, politically neutral and competent to implement the laws that will restrict unacceptable public performances. At first glance, this task is not difficult. However, the problem arises in assessing the admissibility of certain behavior and in deciding whether a phenomenon is acceptable or unacceptable in a modern society. One of the ways to determine eligibility is whether the public performance is contrary to the interest of national security, territorial integrity, public safety, protection of health, morals, reputation or rights of others. So one level of protection from hate speech would be through direct implementation of the legal provisions and the use of repressive institutions (courts, police) which would work to prevent hate speech with strict legal penalties. However, the question remains how far should we go with the restrictive measures against hate speech, while not compromising the freedom of expression? We would say that repressive mechanisms in a healthy democratic society should be the final correcting measure that should be activated for the defense from such speech. The first level is supposed to be the democratic environment itself that is prevalent in the society and which would isolate hate speech as unacceptable phenomenon. If it has no followers and supporters it would represent an exception that would be marginalized. But to be truly marginalized, or even eliminated, hate speech must be attacked in the nascent because prevention is more effective and cheaper than the legal treatment. For this to be achieved, it is necessary in any society to popularize educational methods and generally accepted values, in order to prevent various prejudices that can lead to hate speech. If hate speech is a learned behavior, and not innate, and then we can forget it or, even better, not even learn it. According to psychology, the character of people is formed in the first five years of life, so the values and attitudes that are learnt in early socialization are the most effective "vaccination" against the prejudice virus of hate speech and it should start from an early age. Ethics in education can remove or, better still, prevent hate speech just as important the role the media is because they can offer ethical education and promotion of tolerance value system. The role of the media, public condemnation of political extremism and the majority valuable attitude that certain behaviors are unacceptable, often lead to a situation in which it is not necessary for the state to act repressively. The stronger is the reaction of society to unacceptable behaviors, the smaller the need of state repression and vice versa. In a healthy social environment in which the most undesirable political extremism would be isolated, the principle of freedom of expression would be met as well as the inconsequence of publicly stated opinions and the necessity of a small piece advocating extreme views that are unacceptable to the majority in every society. Experience has shown that a stable democratic society can withstand aggressive speech without serious consequences that would disturb the general peace. On the other hand, in an atmosphere of state or personal insecurity and fear, where the problem also is the unwillingness of the state to consistently implement the principle of the rule of law, law enforcement and promotion of human rights, then even the benign stereotypes can act extremely provocative, explosive and destabilizing. In such states hate speech will lead to political violence, discrimination, human rights abuses and, ultimately, to crimes. Therefore it is necessary to recognize this problem in any form in which it appears and to react until it is not too late.

It should also be cautious that hate speech (or its support) not always comes only from frustrated speeches and raigning of fanatical extremists on the margins of society, but also from the consent and approval of the ordinary, even respectable members of society. Although most people would not commit a hate crime, they also contribute to the creation of hate speech and prejudices with the passive sympathy towards it and sympathy towards those who promote hate crimes. The other layer are those peaceful observers of fanatic hate speech because they have economic or political benefits from the existing social constellations. Finally, there is one social layer, we would say the most numerous, which, although does not support hate speech, with his silence and absence of pro-active reaction (sometimes because of fear), avoids to publicly condemn hate speech. Although these people do not carry the virus of fanaticism or chauvinism inside, they still lack the courage to confront those who spread hate speech and propagate hate crimes. In such circumstances even the things which are not spoken are nothing short of those openly spoken. In other words, it is not only the speech of hatered (hate speech) that is important, but also "the silence of hatred" (hate silence). Perhaps the most illustrative description of this silent majority group and its political apathy is given in the song "First came" (Als die Nazis die Kommunisten holten...), by the German priest Martin Nimler in which he talks about the silence and lack of reaction of the German intellectuals to the rise of Nazism and the beginning of political purges directed against different social groups.

Except for socially marginalzed groups and the silent majority, hate speech can act seductively with the elite social strata, which was seen in the example of the upsurge of racism in American campuses in the eighties. Undoubtedly this was a multiple shock to American society since many of these incidents occurred in the most elite universities. Until then, Americans had strongly believed in the educated elite and in education as the best remedy for prejudice and that only uneducated lower classes could be disguised racists. Series of racist incidents among the most talented students in the states were enormous disappointment, which called for a response of the state through the adoption of codes of conduct because no one could assume when the speech could be transformed into action.

Our conclusion was that there must be a balance between individual rights and collective well-being which means that universal human rights and freedoms include both the individual and collective component and therefore the promotion of hate speech must always be evaluated together with the common good of society. Not accidentally in the Charter of UNESCO writes: "Since wars begin in the minds of men, it is in the minds of men that the defences of peace must be constructed".

CHAPTER TWO
POLITICAL DISCOURSE AND HATE SPEECH

1. DISCOURSE ANALYSIS

Introduction

As can be seen from the title, the subject of this study will be studying the political discourse, media and hate speech. Although each positioned for itself, they can represent an indigenous entity for research, however, their very holistic bringing in a relationship and getting into their complementarities will lead us to results for the full and comprehensive interdisciplinary analysis. In that synergies numerous are the elements that connect them and make them complementary. We continue in their detailed review and identification of the integrative elements, but at the beginning we would point out the main thing that connects them and without which each of the subjects of this research would be unworkable and could not be realized. That's – *language*. Language as a means of speech, communication and public way to manifest or materialize a mental activity. Language is the condition above all conditions which is necessary to exist in order to have speech of politicians, the media to have what to present to the citizens, and, finally, its content to be estimated, depending on the value judgments of the individual and society whether it is acceptable and affirmative (and represents freedom of speech) or it is disturbing and has a negative attitude (and represents hate speech).

The subject matter in this part of the study is certainly not a theoretical research on language. Our focus will be to analyze the language, but the one particularly used by politicians in their addresses to the public, so called political discourse and hate speech as one of the possible forms of public manifestation of political discourse. Certainly for their thorough study we will utilize the knowledge that linguistics gives us (especially semantics, which directly deals with the analysis of discourse), but in an interdisciplinary relationship with other sciences (communicology, psychology, law, sociology, politicology) .

Further in this chapter, in addition to discourse analysis, we will pay attention to the critical discourse analysis and political discourse as segments derived from discourse analysis.

Definition of discourse

In everyday life we often encounter the term discourse. Besides the already mentioned political discourse, we encounter scientific discourse, media discourse, medical discourse, technical discourse, military discourse, sports discourse and many other discourses. The first association from the semantics of the word discourse is that it is synonymous with the word speech/talk. By association we will conclude that, in fact, a political speech or a speech practiced by politicians; scientific speech which is used by professors of universities and researchers; media speech is the speech we meet in the newspapers or spoken by journalists who speak on radio and television; doctors have their own medical speech as well as computer scientists, engineers, technologists that have their own different technical speech. Military terminology is characteristic of soldiers in their speech, and sports speech is the speech of sports athletes. Certainly this division is not strictly determined and that there may be overlapping and combination of different ones. There could be a situation where a university professor uses scientific discourse in their lectures to students, but in combination with medical or technical discourse. Just as journalists can combine their media discourse with sports, military or political, depending on which area they follow their professional work.

Against this introductory, simplified attempt to explain the meaning of the word discourse, certainly there is a theoretical approach to its definition. The basic meaning of this term with various meanings is often defined as "linguistic structure and meaning greater than the level of the sentence". So, in order to able to talk about discourse, it should be greater than one sentence. Most often it is the paragraph, but also longer texts than it. Although correct, however, this is not the most precise definition of discourse. Because there are cases when in discourse analysis length of a text, i.e. elements that we analyze are not essential. Let's take for example the label that is attached to the entrance of the toilet - "Ladies," or as a designation of parking place the letter "P". This certainly is not a linguistic structure and has no meaning above the level of a sentence, but conveys certain meaning, some message. Therefore it is better to define discourse as language in use, rather than a linguistic structure above the level of a sentence. Some researchers who are interested in the written text, determine the unit of analysis that is big enough to determine the meaning. According to them that is the "paragraph".[276]

The most general definition of discourse is that it is a regulated manner of speech. To the French theorist Michel Foucault discourse refers to the language and practice and indicates the regulated production of knowledge, defining what can be said and what not. It is remarkable that in theory speech or discourse is differently defined according to the theoretical framework applied by the researcher. Thus, according to the definition of L. Bloom discourse means interconnected utterances successively uttered by one or more persons in a single speech event.[277] She uses the term statement to indicate that it is about meeting the communication, and not the grammatical need in a given voice interaction. However, we can also define the discourse as "a system of statements which connect the common meaning and value".[278] Thus, when we speak of "conservative discourse" in political discourse, we mean a set of conservative, traditional values and representing a position to maintain the existing relationships in society. For Witgenstein and Austin discourse is "language in use".[279] Based on their definition, poststructuralists and constructivists expanded the understanding of discourse as language in use, equating it with the process of creating meaning. Discourse is defined as "a set of meanings, metaphors, images, pictures, stories, statements which together produce a particular version of events".

---

[276] A paragraph is an independent unit of written discourse which is correlated with the theme, idea, a concept or an author. A paragraph contains one or more statements, and its completion marks the beginning of a new row.
[277] Bloom, L Language development: form and function in emerging grammars. (1970).
[278] Coates, Jennifer. Women, Men and Language. London: Longman, 2004 (3rd edition)
[279] Austin, J. Langshaw, How to do Things with Words: The William James Lectures delivered at Harvard University in 1955. Oxford: Clarendon, 1962.

There are linguistic interpretations which McHoul calls empirical-sociological[280], and which consider discourse exclusively oral or written interaction between the interlocutors and so the discourse is "linguistic communication understood as a transaction between the speaker and the listener, as interpersonal activity with a form which is determined by its social goals".[281] Broadly understood, discourse as language in use not only reflects social order, but also shapes the interaction of the individual with the world.[282]

The discourse can be written or spoken. Usually when we talk about written discourse we refer to "text" while the very notion of discourse often refers to "oral speech". Irrespective of how the discourse appears, studying it from different perspectives is possible by systematic application of different theoretical approaches. In this study it can be resorted to separating the discourse into parts. Semantic discipline that studies the major linguistic elements of the sentence in the written and spoken media is called "discourse analysis". Usually analysis refers to paragraphs or the entire text consisting several paragraphs which are interconnected. In such analysis the use of language is examined in conjunction with the context and nonverbal elements of language communication. Its concern is to explain the different elements of the nature of the conversation as a whole, because it is a product of several scientific disciplines interested to explain the linguistic activity (psychology, sociology, communicology, philosophy, anthropology). According to some views, discourse analysis is only a higher level of linguistic analysis of the sentence. For others, it is a separate approach to the language built by representatives of various disciplines including linguists. Because of this diverse research interest, it can be expected that the discourse analysis is not a homogenous approach to language, but the impacts of the disciplines from which the researchers originate can be felt.

---

[280] Mc Houl, A. (1994) Discourse. In: Asher, R.E. (ed.) The Encyclopedia of language and linguistics. Vol. 2. Oxford, New York, Seoul, Tokio.
[281] leech, G. N., Short, M.H. (1981) Style in Fiction. London and New York: Longman.
[282] Jaworski, A., Coupland, N. (1999) Introduction: Perspectives on Discourse Analysis. In: Jaworski, Coupland. (Eds.) The Discourse Reader. London, New York: Routledge.

The term discourse analysis was first used by the American linguist Zellig Haris.[283] His intent was to call attention to the necessity of research on the relationship between oral and written units.[284] Several years later, this commitment in the linguistic discipline was supported by research from other disciplines, in particular, by the anthropologist T.F. Mitchell.[285] In his work, he emphasizes that in the analysis of verbal behavior equal attention should be paid to the nonverbal data - gestures, situations and context in which the natural conversation takes place, given that they all affect the way verbal message is formed. This means that in the unit subject to discourse analysis verbal and nonverbal elements should be equally involved. To this author, the connected speech can be described only in relation to the context, which remained the basic and recognizable feature of discourse analysis for most researchers. Thereby it becomes increasingly apparent that units larger than a sentence can not be qualitatively explained only within the description of language structure.

For Pål Kolstø, the simple definition of discourse analysis is that it studies the use of language. As semantics, discourse analysis is interested in the side of language that represents meaning, but unlike semantics, it does not refer to the language as a closed system. The language is set in context and the analyst of the discourse is looking for the meaning of words in relation to that context. The context can be defined narrowly or broadly and, thus, it can refer to (1) the immediate situation of communication *hic et nunc*; (2) a certain social environment - family, school, company or political party; or (3) a whole political system or historical period. The meaning that the researcher finds inevitably expresses the choice of context in which the language used and discourse are studied. Linguists often study language on sentence level or even at the level of individual words. As we have seen, for discourse analysis these units are too small. To get to the sociological or interpersonal importance of language, it is necessary to focus on larger portions of text. The texts can be seen as separate discourses, but they also can come into interaction and thus create greater discourse.

---

[283]Harris, Z., Discourse analysis, Language (1952)
[284]Ibid
[285]Michell, T.F., The language of buying and selling in Cyrenaica, Hesperis (1957)

Foucalt's analysis showed that the discourse has a direct impact on social relations and power structures in society Which discourse with its concepts and classifications is prevalent in a certain period influences how it will be able to impose its will over others, including even compulsiveness over their bodies. An important part of the legacy of Foucault's subsequent discourse analysis is the strong emphasis on the importance of power.

Discourse analysis as a research methodology

The analysis of the discourse is characteristic of research in various academic disciplines, most of which are not related to linguistics. It is used as a research methodology in anthropology, rhetoric, cultural studies, media studies, sociology, psychology, pedagogy and related sciences. The common element of all these different approaches can be defined as the study of language and its impact on the world that surrounds us because the basic meaning of the language – the one that people first associate with the term - is *communication*. It should be noted that the discourse analysis is not only interested in the spoken discourse, but in principle examines social conditionality on the use of language in any medium (written, spoken language, sign language, etc.). However, discourse analysis is only one of the possible approaches to the study of language, and in order to be different from other related disciplines the meaning of the term discourse should first be kept in mind, which in different disciplines has a different meaning.

Here it is important to emphasize the difference between qualitative and quantitative research. Namely, discourse analysis is a very popular qualitative research method in the social sciences. While quantitative research methods use standardized instruments, such as (in social sciences) questionnaires, graphs and other instruments from which you can get statistical data, qualitative methods do not rely on statistics, but, above all, on the observations of the researchers. Qualitative research is always of an interpretative type, i.e., means that the description of a given phenomenon, its analysis and interpretation directly depend on the epistemological orientation, cultural patterns, attitudes and strategic goals of the researchers

(...).[286] The choice of topics depends on the personal interests of the researcher, his political beliefs, etc., which the discourse analysts do not consider bias, but a position that should be accepted. Furthermore, the identity of the researcher affects the process of data collection through the process of interaction with the participants in the interviews when the importance of awakening in terms of power is particularly emphasized. The worldview and general knowledge of researchers, of course, affect the interpretation and discourse analysts explicate their own positions of in the final report (via explanations regarding the topic, participants, and data).[287]

This qualitative component of discourse analysis is most apparent in the so-called critical discourse analysis. Critical discourse analysis is a modern analytical discipline that uses conceptual and analytical apparatus of traditional linguistics and so-called critical theories (which will be discussed at length in the next chapter). An example of this might be the case with the word "drug". Here not only the neutral word is challenged, but its definition is largely socially determined. Thus, the word "drug" does not mean only "a substance that affects the body and mind of the one who takes it", but our perception of the word drug is influenced by a whole range of social experiences: legislation, police, judiciary, medicine, charities and similar.

For Pål Kolstø discourse is, above all, an analytical tool that was invented by researchers to bring meaning of the text in its relationship with other texts in the social and political environment. Some discourse analysts tend to see language as a neutral aid, as a socio-political designation manifested only at the level of discourse. As Svenka Savic concludes, it is clear that there is a polarization between linguists and other researchers from other disciplines. The target of research for linguists has always been the language - its structure, functions and relationships between them. It indicates that linguists consider the discourse analysis a part that describes the language system, and all other disciplines are used as a favorable way to detect other features of human behavior. For other disciplines, the language is only a means to discover some other laws of human interaction

---

[286] Филиповић, Јелена, Моћ речи, Београд: Задужбина Андрејевић, 2009
[287] Павловић, Јелена. „Дискурс као нова тема у психологији" у ЗБОРНИК БЕОГРАДСКЕ ОТВОРЕНЕ ШКОЛЕ, 2005

and understanding. In other disciplines, with the assistance of discourse analysis, it is tended to learn about the natural, nonlinguistic aspects of human communication and language is just a tool in that.[288]

2. CRITICAL DISCOURSE ANALYSIS

Introduction

After we inspected the semantic discipline discourse analysis in the past chapter, in this section we continue to elaborate one of the main areas of discourse analysis, which is of great interest to be able to properly perform the analysis of political discourse and identify the presence of hate speech. It is critical discourse analysis or, as as we will further briefly use it - CDA.

In this chapter we are going to cover some of the principles, objectives and criteria of critical discourse analysis, but we will first look at its definition. In general, all that theoretically study CDA have jointly concluded that CDA presents an analysis of the relationship between discourse, power, domination, social inequality and the position of the discourse analyst in such social relations. Since this is a complex, multidisciplinary and still undeveloped domain of study, which can be called a "socio-political discourse analysis," we would process only the most relevant dimensions of this domain.

Although there are many directions in the study and critique of social inequality, the way in which CDA researchers approach these questions is by focusing on the role of discourse in the (re)production of power and challenge the dominance resulting from the application of such power. This reproduction process may involve different "modalities" of the relationship between discourse and power, such as direct or open support, implementation, advocacy, legitimiziing, concealment of domination, mitigation or denial. More specifically, critical discourse analysts want to know which structures, strategies or other characteristics of the text, speech, verbal interaction or communication events play a role in these modes of reproduction of power. But be reminded that the processing of

---

[288] Savic, Svenka, Diskurs analiza (1993)

CDA in this study, in some way, we will be half-way because we will devote more attention to the relations of domination that go "above down" rather than the relationships of resistance, compliance and acceptance that go" from down to above". This does not mean that we believe that power and domination are only unilaterally "imposed" on others. On the contrary, in many situations, sometimes paradoxical, power, and even abuse of power can make us seem "jointly produced", i.e. when the dominated groups are convinced that domination is "natural" or otherwise justified. Thus, although the analysis of the strategies of resistance and challenge is crucial for understanding the relationships of real power and domination in society, our critical approach prefers to focus on the social elites and their discursive strategies in maintaining inequality.

Theoretical approach to CDA

How to theoretically explain CDA? According to Kolstø CDA is another area of discourse analysis that developed near Foucalt's tradition. To him, CDA perhaps should not be described as a theory but as a set of theories and methods applied by several groups of researchers who think alike.[289] According to Woodak, CDA is fundamentally interested in the analysis of the opaque as well as the transparent structural relationships of dominance, discrimination, power and control that occur in language.[290] Kolstø notes that CDA analysts do not see language as an independent power, but believe that language acquires this power through its use by powerful people. At the same time, the language can be used to counter and undermine the power. Power can not be reduced to language nor can be derived from language, but the language can in time change the distribution of power.[291] According to Woodak language gives carefully articulated

---
[289] Kolstø, P. „Diskurs i nasilni sukob: predstave o „sebi" i „drugom" u državama nastalim posle raspada Jugoslavije", „Intima javnosti", Fabrika knjiga, Beograd, 2008
[290] Woodak, R (2005), "What CDA is about – a summary of its history, important concepts and Its Development", u: Wodak, R i Meyer, M., Methods of Critical Discourse Analysis, London: Sage
[291] Kolstø, P. „Diskurs i nasilni sukob: predstave o „sebi" i „drugom" u državama nastalim posle raspada Jugoslavije", „Intima javnosti", Fabrika knjiga, Beograd, 2008

means of differentiating power in hierarchical social systems.[292] Van Dijk assesses that CDA is a kind analytical research of discourse that, before all, studies the way in which society implements and reproduces abuse of social power, dominance and inequality, and resistance that is allowed by text and speech of those dominated. CDA for him has grown into one particular approach to the study of text and speech. This approach arises from critical linguistics, critical semiotics and in general from a socio-political conscious and opposite way to explore the language, discourse and communication.[293] Hence, we can draw several criteria that characterize the works associated with CDA:

- to study relevant social problems, such as those of gender discrimination, racism, colonialism and other forms of social inequality;
- to fully and adequately study the social problems or questions, CDA studies are usually interdisciplinary or multidisciplinary and focus particularly on the relationship between discourse and society (including social cognition, politics and culture);
- CDA is part of a wide range of critical research in the humanities and social sciences, for example, sociology, psychology, mass communication research, legal literature and political science;
- in studying the role of discourse in society, CDA especially focuses on group relations of power, domination and inequality and the ways in which they are reproducted or in which they oppose social group members through text and speech;
- consequently many of the CDA research deal with established or legitimized discursive structures and strategies of domination and resistance in the social relations of class, gender, ethnicity, race, sexual orientation, language, religion, age, nationality or world regions;
- much of the CDA research refer to the basic ideologies that play a role in the reproduction of power or resistance to domination or inequality.

---

[292] Woodak, R (2005), "What CDA is about – a summary of its history, important concepts and Its Development", u: Wodak, R i Meyer, M., Methods of Critical Discourse Analysis, London: Sage

[293] Van Dijk, T. A., Aims of Critical Discourse Analysis, Japanese Discourse Vol. I (1995)

In other words, CDA is specifically focused on strategies of manipulation, legitimization, production of consent and other discursive ways to influence the minds and, indirectly, the actions of people for the interests of the powerful;
- the attempt to discover discursive instruments for mental control and social impact, involves critical and opposite stance against the powerful and the elite, especially those who abuse their power;
- On the other hand, CDA studies try to formulate and maintain solidarity with the dominated groups, for example, by formulating strategic proposals for the adoption and development of contrast and counter-ideologies.

From the stated criteria, it is evident that with such dissident research, critical discourse analysts take explicit position, in order to understand, expose and finally, to oppose the social inequality. Of course the overall scientific activity dedicated to CDA is not characterized by these criteria. That is what CDA research should ideally try to realize and these criteria capture the main features of an approach which relatively well defer them from the other research on discourse. According to Van Dijk, CDA, essentially deals with the opposition study of the structures and strategies of elite discourse (discourse of those who dominate) and its cognitive and social consequences as well as the discourse of resistance against such domination.[294] According to him, the explicit awareness of their role in society is crucial for critical discourse analysts. Among other things, this may mean that the discourse analysts conduct the research as sign of solidarity and cooperation with groups being dominated. Thus, the typical vocabulary of many CDA researchers contains terms like "power", "dominance", "hegemony", "ideology", "class", "sex", "race", "discrimination", "interest", "reproduction", "institutions", "social structure", "social order ", despite most other familiar notions of discursive analysis.

As the main purpose with which CDA should handle, Van Dijk, points primarily the discursive dimensions of abuse of power and injustice and

---

[294]Ibid

inequalities deriving from it.[295] He points out some implications of such a goal of CDA.

- First, the focus of domination and inequality means that CDA is primarily interested in highlighting the social issues that it hopes will be better understood through discourse analysis. Central to this theoretical activity is the analysis of the complex relationship between discourse and dominance;
- Unlike other discursive analysts, critical discurs analysts take explicit socio-political stance: they explain their views, perspectives, principles and objectives, both within their discipline and within society as a whole. Their work is obviously political, **and their hope is social change through critical understanding.** ☐ Their perspective are those who suffer most from domination and inequality, and their critical goals are powerful elites who adopt, maintain, legitimize, approve or ignore the social inequality and injustice. In this sense, scientists of critical discourse, also need to be social and political scientists and social critics and activists;
- Critical discourse analysis is far from easy. It is the hardest challenge in the discipline and requires a multidisciplinary overview of the complex relationships between text, speech, social cognition, power, society and culture;
- This became particularly clear from the great processes of change such as class struggles, decolonization, the civil rights movement and the women's movement. Critical discourse analysts continue this tradition: even after the nineties of the last century, there are crowded regions of the world with constant problems of oppression, injustice and inequality that require attention;
- CDA researchers govern the choice of topics and their relevance. So if immigrants, refugees and other minorities suffer from prejudice, discrimination and racism, or if women continue to be subject to male domination, violence or sexual abuse, it will bw essential to examine and assess such events and their consequences from the perspective of the subordinates. Such events will be called

---

[295] Van Dijk, T. A., Principles of critical discourse analysis, Discourse & Society, 1993 SAGE (London. Newbury Park and New Delhi), vol. 4(2)

"racist" or "sexist" so if they call blacks or women despite denials by whites or members of the male sex;
- Critical scientists cannot have an unclear, let alone a neutral position. They should not care about the interests and perspectives of those in power who already are in the best position to take care of their own interests. Most male or white scientists showed that they despise or discredit such bias toward the dominated by which they showed how biased they are from the beginning, ignoring, mitigating, excluding or denying inequality. Some even cynically and directly cooperate with dominance, for example, with "expert" advice giving support and legitimizing powerful elites (the interests of Western civilization, the middle-class, white population, male members, heterosexual etc.). It is this plot which is one of the main research topics of critical discourse analysis.

Creation and application of CDA

Theoretical and descriptive, CDA should investigate which structures and strategies of text and speech should be processed in order to detect patterns of elite domination or manipulation in texts. Or, conversely, focusing on the major social and political problems and issues such as sexism and racism, CDA should thoroughly explain how such forms of inequality in text and speech are expressed, implemented, legitimized and reproduced. Consequently, Van Dijk makes the following differentiation: power, dominance and inequality between social groups are terms belonging to the macro-level analysis, while the use of language, discourse, verbal interaction and communication belong to the micro- level of social order.[296] This means that CDA should theoretically bridge the famous "gap" between micro and macro approaches, which is certainly the difference which is a sociological construction in itself.[297] In everyday

---

[296]Van Dijk, T. A., Aims of Critical Discourse Analysis, Japanese Discourse Vol. I (1995)
[297]Alexander, J. C., Giesen, B., Munch, R., and Smelser, N. J. (eds). (1987). The Micro—Macro Link. Berkeley, CA: University of California Press. Knorr–Cetina, K. and Cicourel, A. V. (eds). (1981). Advances in Social Theory and Universidad de Buenos Aires.

interaction and experience, the macro- and micro-level form a single unit. For example, racist speech in the Parliament is a discourse at a micro level of social interaction in the specific situation of a debate, but at the same time, you can bring or be part of the legislation or reproduction of racism at the macro level.

One key assumptions for an appropriate critical discourse analysis is understanding the nature of social power and domination. To shorten a lengthy analysis, we will assume that we're dealing here with relations between the social groups, i.e. while focusing on social power, we ignore personal power unless it is presented as a single realization of group power by individuals as group members. With the simplification of these complex relationships, we can divide the issue of discursive power in two basic issues important to CDA research: 1. How dominant groups control public discourse and 2. How such discourse controls the mind and actions of the dominanated groups and which are the social consequences of that control, such as social inequality?

Each issue will be considered separately.

Access and control of the discourse

The first major problem that needs to be processed is to examine the nature of social power and the abuse of power, especially the ways in which domination is expressed or enforced in text and speech. If social power is defined as a form of control of one group over another and if such domination or abuse of power implies that the control is in the interests of the dominant group, it means that the dominant social group members can also exercise control over the discourse.

If it is defined that the central idea in most critical discourse research is the notion of power, and, more specifically, the social power of groups or institutions, social power can be understood as control. That way, groups have the power if they are able to control the actions and minds of other groups. This capacity presupposes power base of privileged access to scarce social resources such as power, money, status, fame, education, knowledge, information, "culture" or different forms of public discourse and communication.[298] Different types of power may vary according to the different resources used to display such power: the coercive power of the military and violent men will be based on force, the rich have power because of their money, while the convincing power of parents, teachers or journalists can be based on knowledge, information or authority. Also, the power of dominant groups can also be integrated into laws, rules, norms, habits, and even the general consensus, and thus take the form of what Gramsci called "hegemony".[299] Or, under the hegemony we can understand if you think that the subordinate can be influenced in such a way that they accept domination and act in the interest of the powerful with their own free will.[300] One of the main functions of the dominant discourse is precisely to produce such a consensus that will lead to acceptance and legitimization of the dominance.[301] Typical examples of such hegemony are class domination, gender discrimination and racism. If you look at the historical evidence, the slaves accepted their duties and relationship to the rulers without resistance to, women suffered discrimination from men, blacks from whites. Until the moment when that general consensus was disrupted and a counterforce was created on the side of the dominant which contested their legitimacy.

The concept of hegemony and its related concepts of consensus, acceptance and mind control, also suggest that the relationship between critical discourse analysis and domination is far from simple, and does not always imply clear identification of villains and victims. In fact, we already pointed out that many of the forms of domination are "jointly produced" through complex forms of social interaction, communication and discourse. Therefore, power is not always manifested as a visible act of abuse by members of the dominant group and can be implemented in

---

[298]Lukes, S. (ed.) (1986). Power. Oxford: Blackwell и Wrong, D. H. (1979). Power: Its Forms, Bases and Uses. Oxford: Blackwell.
[299]Gramsci, A. (1971). Prison Notebooks. New York: International Publishers.
[300]Hall, S., Lumley, B. and McLennan, G. (1977) Gramsci on Ideology, in Centre for Contemporary Cultural Studies (ed. Politics and Ideology: Gramsci, pp. 45-76. London: Hutchinson.
[301]Herman, E.S. and Chomsky, N. (1958) Manufacturing Consent.- The Political Economy
of the Mass Media. New York: Pantheon Books.

everyday life through various forms of everyday gender discrimination and racism.[302]

Despite such complexities and subtleties in the relationship of power, CDA remains committed to its primary interest of abuse of power, i.e. of violation of laws, rules and principles of democracy, equality and justice by. those who hold power. Therefore we need to distinguish between abuse of power or domination by the legitimate and acceptable forms of power that allow the ensurance of smooth functioning of a social system. The social consensus which accepts to be dominated in democracy is achieved by voting on elections in which citizens give consent to be commanded. Such power and dominance is usually organized and institutionalized and is a major focus of CDA. CDA is interested in the social domination of the groups and not only for the one that is individually applied by members of the group (as is the case in many forms of everyday racism or sexual harassment), but it can be supported by other members the group, courts, be legitimized by laws, conducted by the police and ideologically maintained and reproduced by the media and textbooks.[303] This social, political and cultural organization of domination also implies a hierarchy of power: some members of dominant groups and organizations have a special role in planning and decision-making and control of the relations and the processes of implementation of power.[304] These small groups are called elites.[305] It is particularly interesting to note that such elites have special access to discourse because they are the ones who literally have the most to say. Accordingly, in a discursive analytical framework elites are defined precisely in terms of their "symbolic power", which is measured by the degree of their discursive and communicative capacity and resources.[306]

In the same way as the power and the dominance can be institutionalized to enhance their effectiveness, the access to discourse can be organized to enhance its impact. Given the important role of the media,

---

[302] Essed, P. J. M. (1991). Understanding
[303] Van Dijk, T. A., Aims of Critical Discourse Analysis, Japanese Discourse Vol. I (1995).
[304] Domhoff, G. W. (1978) The Powers That Be: Processes of Ruling Class Domination in America. New York: Random House (Vintage Books);
[305] Mills, C.W. (1956) The Power Elite. London: Oxford University Press.
[306] Bourdieu, P. (1983) Ce que parler veut dire (What speaking means). Paris: Fayard.

powerful social actors and institutions have organized their access to the media with their engagement with the press officers, press releases, press conferences, PR departments.[307] This is important in order to have control of public opinion and, therefore, to produce legitimacy, consent and consensus needed to reproduce hegemony.[308] It is clear that the power and dominance of the groups are measured by their control over the access to discourse. The key implication of this correlation is not just that discursive control is a form of social control of action, but also asumes the terms of control over the minds of other people. More control over text and context, including more control of over people is generally associated with greater impact, and therefore hegemony.

If the patterns of control of and access discourse are closely related to social power, analogously, a lack of power is also measured by the lack of active or controlled access to discourse. Ordinary people have active access and control only on the discursive genres such as everyday conversations with family members, friends or colleagues and the more pasive access to institutional discourse and media discourse. In other situations, they may be more or less controlled participants, bystanders, consumers, users, media audiences, suspects in court or a topic in the media (usually only when they are victims in disaster situations or perpetrators of crime). Modest forms of counter-power exist in some discursive and communication forms, such as letters to the editor, shouting slogans on protests, holding public speeches (the most famous example is *Speakers' Corner in Hyde Park* in London), or placing critical questions in the classroom. The elites, on the other hand, have access and control over a wide range of informal, public and institutional forms of text and speech. Politicians have control over the governmental and parliamentary discourse and preferential access to the means of public informing. In many situations, ordinary people are just passive targets of text or speech, from, for example, their bosses or teachers, or bodies such as the police, judges, welfare bureaucrats or tax inspectors who simply can tell them what to (not) believe or what to (not)

---

[307] See more: Gans, H. (1979). Deciding What's News. New York: Pantheon Books; Tuchman, G. (1978) Making News: A Study in the Construction of Reality. New York: Free Press.
[308] Margolis, M. and Mauser, G.A., eds (1989) Manipulating Public Opinion: Essays on Public Opinion as a Dependent Variable. Brooks/Cole.

do. On the other hand, scientists have active control over academic discourse, such as lectures, textbooks, courses and scientific publications. Corporate managers control the discourse on decision-making (fro example on Board Meetings), corporate reports and many other forms of text and speech in business context. Journalists have control over discourse in the media and preferential access to many other forms of official text and speech, such as press conferences, press releases, reports and so on. Judges not only have control over who can speak in the courtroom, but also have special access to discursive genres such as judgments. By definition, those who have control over more and more influential discourses are more powerful.

Control of subject, text and context

Besides control of the content, crucial in the implementation of the group power is also the control of structures of text and speech and the context in which it is realized. In this relation between text and context, members of powerful groups can decide on possible discursive genres or speech acts of an event. Thus, the teacher or the judge may require a direct response from the students or the suspect, and not a personal story or an argument.[309] Critically, we can even examine how powerful speakers can abuse their power in situations when, for example, police officers use force to extract a confession from the suspect[310], or when male editors exclude women from writing economic news.[311] Or to examine how power can be misused for censorship, intimidation or other means to restrict freedom of the less powerful participants. In fact, with some "voices" being censored, some opinions are not heard, some perspectives are ignored, the discourse becomes "segregated" structure. Blacks or women can, thus, not only not exercise their rights as speakers and holders of opinion, but they can also

---

[309] Wodak, R. (1984). Determination of guilt: discourses in the courtroom. In C. Kramarae, M. Schulz, and W. M. O'Barr (eds), Language and Power (pp. 89-100). Beverly Hills, CA: Sage.

[310] Linen, P. and Jonsson, L. (1991). Suspect stories: perspective-setting in an asymmetrical situation. In I. Markova and K. Foppa (eds), Asymmetries in Dialogue. The Dynamics of Dialogue (pp. 75-100). n.d. Barnes and Noble Books/Bowman and Littlefield Publishers: Harvester Wheatsheaf.

[311] Van Zoonen, L. (1994). Feminist Media Studies. London: Sage.

be expelled as listeners and triggers of power. Such exclusions may mean that the less powerful are less quoted less and less talked about, so that two other forms of (passive) access are blocked. Even when they are present as participants, members of less powerful groups may also otherwise be more or less dominated in discourse. At nearly every level of the structures of text and speech their freedom of choice may be limited by the dominant participants. This may be acceptable in the case of convention, rule or law, when the President organizes discussions, authorizes or prohibits specific speech acts, follows the agenda, sets or changes themes or regulates the order of speaking, which, more or less explicitly is the case with judges, doctors, teachers or police officers in discursive sessions they control (trials, consultations, classes, hearings etc.).[312] On the other hand, members of the less powerful groups may also be illegitimately or immorally limited in their communicative acts. Men can subtly or openly exclude women from taking a word or from the range of topics.[313] Judges or police officers can be banned from allowing entities explain or defend, immigration officers can prevent refugees tell their "story" and whites can criticize blacks for talking about racism (if they do even allow them to talk/write about it).[314]

Illegitimate control over the discourse, therefore, is a direct and immediate implementation of dominance, thus limiting the "discursive rights" of the other participants.[315] In fact, these more micro or "surface" structures can be less regulated by legal or moral rules, allowing more "unofficial" use of power, i.e. domination. For example, an impudent 'tone' 'of men, judges or police officers can only seem to break the rules of courtesy and not of law and, thus, can be one way to achieve dominance. Also precisely at this level of research was the emergence of a more or less

---

[312]Boden, Deirdre and Don H. Zimmerman. (eds.) 1991. Talk and Social Structure: Studies in Ethnomethodology and Conversation Analysis. Cambridge: Polity Press.; Fisher, Sue and Alexandra Dundas Todd. (eds.) 1986. Discourse and Institutional Authority: Medicine, Education, and Law. Norwood, NJ: Ablex.
[313]Kramarae, C. (1981) Women and Men Speaking: Frameworks for Analysis. Rowlev, MA:Newbury House.
[314]Van Dijk, T.A. (1993a) Elite Discourse and Racism. Newbury Park, CA: Sage.
[315]Kedar, L., ed. (1987) Power through Discourse. Norwood, NJ: Ablex.; Kramarae, C., Schulz, M. and O Barr, W.M. eds (1984) Language and Power. Beverley Hills, CA: Sage.

"powerful" style of conversation examined, whether in certain contexts (for example in court or classroom) or by members of specific groups (men against women) is presence or absence of fencing manifested, hesitations, pauses, laughter, interruptions, doubt, specific lexical elements, forms of address and use of pronouns etc.[316] Although such discourtesy can "signal" 'power, it does not necessarily have to mean social (group) power nor dominance.[317]. In other words, occasional incidents or personal violation of the discursive rules are not expressions of dominance. The same applies to the variation in intonation or "tone" 'lexical style or rhetorical figures. To determine that, we need a detailed textual and contextual analysis which can also determine the subtle forms of discursive domination.

Similarly, genres usually have conventional schemes that consist of various categories. The access to some of these may be prohibited or compulsory; for example, some greetings in a conversation may be used only by speakers from specific social rank, group, age or gender.[318] Also, what is vital for all discourses and communications is who will manage the topics and influence to change the topic, as when editors decide which topics will be covered in the news[319], teachers decide what lessons will be taught in class or men control subject or change the subject into conversations with women.[320]

---

[316] See more: Bradac, J.J. and Mulac, A. (1984) A Molecular View of Powerful and Powerless Speech Styles .Communication Monographs 51: 307-19.; Erickson, B., Lind, A.A., Johnson. B.C. and O Barr, W.M. (1978) Speech Style and Impression Formation in a Court Setting: The Effects of Powerful and Powerless Speech Journal of Experimental Social Psychology 14: 266-79.

[317] Brown, P. and Levinson, S.C. (1987) Politeness: Some Universals in Language Use. Cambridge: Cambridge University Press.

[318] Irvine, J. T. (1974). Strategies of status manipulation in the Wolof greeting. In R. Bauman and J. Sherzer (eds), Explorations in the Ethnography of Speaking (pp. 167-91). Cambridge: Cambridge University Press.

[319] Gans, H. (1979). Deciding What's News. New York: Pantheon Books; van Dijk, T. A. (1988a). News as Discourse. Hillsdale, NJ: Erlbaum. van Dijk, T. A. (1988b). News Analysis. Case Studies of International and National News in the Press. Hillsdale, NJ: Erlbaum.

[320] Palmer, M. T. (1989). Controlling conversations: turns, topics, and interpersonal control. Communication Monographs, 56(1); Fishman, P. (1983). Interaction: the work women do. In B. Thorne, C. Kramarae, and N. Henley (eds), Language, Gender, and Society. New York: Pergamon Press; Leet-Pellegrini, H. (1980). Conversational dominance as a function of gender and expertise. In H. Giles, W. P. Robinson, and P. Smith (eds), Language: Social Psychological Perspectives. Oxford: Pergamon Press;

Although most controls of the discourse are of contextual or global form, even local details of meaning, form or style can be controlled. For example, details of the response in class or the courtroom or the choice of lexical items or jargon in courtrooms, classrooms or editorial offices.[321] In many situations, the intensity of the sound can be controlled and the speakers can be ordered to "speak quieter" or to be "silent", women can be "silenced" in many ways[322], and in some cultures people should be "silenced" as a form of respect or fear of authority.[323] Public use of specific words can be assessed as subversive and banned during the dictatorship[324], and the dimensions of the action and interaction of discourse can be controlled by setting or banning specific speech acts and selectively giving a word or its interruption.[325] Thus, control of context can consist of control of the "call" to a communication event, schedule an appointment or setting the agenda. This may include making decisions about the time and location of the event and selective approach on who can participate in this event and with which role. Similarly, discursive control can be applied to all levels and dimensions of text and speech, such as linguistic variants, genres, themes, grammar, lexical style, rhetorical figures, speech acts, variability, politeness etc. In a word, practically all levels and structures of context, text and speech may be more or less controlled by powerful speakers and this power can be abused at the expense of other participants. However, it should be emphasized that the speech and text do not always implement or embody direct power relations between groups: the context is always the one which can stop, strengthen or otherwise transform these relations. It should be borne in mind that power is rarely absolute because some groups

---

Lindegren–Lerman, C. (1983). Dominant discourse: the institutional voice and the control of topic. In H. Davis and P. Walton (eds), Language, Image, Media. Oxford: Blackwell.
[321] Rojo, Martin, L. (1994). Jargon of delinquents and the study of conversational dynamics. Journal of Pragmatics, 21(3), 243-89.
[322] Houston, M. and Kramarae, C. (eds). (1991). Women speaking from silence. Discourse and Society, 2(4), special issue.
[323] Albert, E. M. (1972). Culture patterning of speech behavior in Burundi. In J. J. Gumperz and D. Hymes (eds), Directions in Sociolinguistics: The Ethnography of Communication (pp. 72-105). New York: Holt, Rhinehart, and Winston.
[324] Williams, J. (ed.) (1995). PC Wars. Politics and Theory in the Academy. New York: Routledge and Kegan Paul.
[325] Diamond, J. (1996). Status and Power in Verbal Interaction. A Study of Discourse in a Close-knit Social Network. Amsterdam: Benjamin.

could control others only in specific situations and social domains. Dominated groups can not only approve, accept or legitimize such power, or even think that it is "natural", they can also oppose, to reject or condemn it. Powerful group is not always and will not always be more powerful than the dominant group.

Mind control

However, discourse is not limited only to verbal action, but also includes meaning, interpretation and understanding. If discourse control is the first major form of power, control of peoples' minds is another fundamental way to reproduce the domination and hegemony. This means that the preferential access to public discourse or discourse control (for example: the right to representation of preferred themes) can also affect the mind of others, i.e. the powerful social actors not only control the the communicative action, but also indirectly control the minds of recipients. It is known that these processes of influence are too complex and mind control through text and speech is not a very clear and simple process.

Within CDA, "mind control" includes even more than just acquiring beliefs about the world through discourse and communication. To Van Dijk, such control can refer to the action and cognition, i.e. a powerful group may limit the freedom of movement of others, but also influence their minds. Besides the basic application of power to directly control the procedures (as in police violence against protesters or male violence against women), modern and often more efficient power is a strategic means to get to a change of opinion of others for own interest and it is mainly cognitive and conducted by methods of persuasion, desimilation or manipulation.[326] Exactly this is the key moment when discourse and CDA come into play: managing the minds of others is essentially a function of text and speech. However, such mind control is not always openly manipulative. Rather, domination can also be implemented and reproduced with subtle, routine, everyday forms of text and speech which seem "natural" and quite "acceptable". Therefore, CDA also needs to focus on

---

[326]Van Dijk, T. A., Principles of critical discourse analysis, Discourse & Society, 1993 SAGE (London. Newbury Park and New Delhi), vol. 4(2)

the discursive strategies that legitimize control or otherwise "naturalize" social order, especially the relations of inequality.[327]

Theoreticaly, several authors propose different ways in which power and domination are involved in mind control. First, the recipients tend to accept beliefs, knowledge and attitudes through the discourse of those considered authoritative or reliable source (unless they are contrary to their personal beliefs and experiences) as, for example, scientists, experts, professionals or credible media.[328] Second, in some situations, participants are obliged to be recipients of discourse as, for example, in education, the army and in different work situations when the discourse should be interpreted and learned as required by the institutional or organizational authorities (lectures, learning materials, work instructions, commands and other types discourse).[329] Third, in many situations there are no public or media discourses that can provide information on alternative beliefs.[330] Fourth, and closely related to the previous items, the recipients may not have the knowledge and belief needed to challenge the discourse or the information they are exposed to.[331]

Generally powerful speakers can control at least some parts of the minds of recipients. CDA studies the ways in which such influence and mind control is socially or morally illegitimate, that is when the powerful speakers control the minds and actions of other people for their own interests. For example, in the case of immigration, if European politicians and media accuse immigration and immigrants for the major social problems such as unemployment and lack of housing, thus, they can influence the beliefs of large segments of the majority, thereby also indirectly the patterns that underlie racism and discrimination, as well as other expressions of prejudice and intolerance which, on the other hand,

---

[327] Fairclough, N.L. (1985) Critical and Descriptive Goals in Discourse Analysis, Journalof Pragmatics 9
[328] Nesler, M. S., Aguinis, H., Quigley, B. M., and Tedeschi, J. T. (1993). The effect of credibility on perceived power. Journal of Applied Social Psychology, 23(17), 1407-25.
[329] Giroux, H. (1981). Ideology, Culture, and the Process of Schooling. London: Falmer Press.
[330] Downing, J. (1984). Radical Media: The Political Experience of Alternative Communication. Boston: South End Press.
[331] Wodak, R. (1987). "And where is the Lebanon?" A socio—psycholinguistic investigation of comprehension and intelligibility of news. Text, 7(4)

can be used by politicians to legitimize political decisions to limit immigration. Conversely, negative actions of the elites or "our group" can be less thematicly stylisticly or rhetorically highlighted, while "our" positive actions and properties can textually be highlighted for the positive self presentation. For example, strategic generalizations of discourse ("This always happens this way", "They are all the same ", etc.) may affect the generalization of *ad hoc* situational models for several abstract group attitudes and prejudices. In general, rhetorical figures, such as "hyperboles and metaphors" can similarly be used to highlight OUR good characteristics and THEIR poor characteristics, while forms of mitigation can reduce OUR negative characteristics and THEIR good characteristics. Narrative structures can be used to increase the credibility of the owner of the discourse, for example, through forms of "evidence from personal experience" in the arguments that emphasize THEIR negative characteristics.[332]

It is widely known that news reports, political propaganda, advertising, religious sermons, corporate directives or scientific articles have an impact on the minds of readers and listeners: they transmit knowledge, influence opinions or change attitudes. At the global level of discourse, topics can affect what people see as the most important information from text and speech, and thus meet the highest levels of their mental models. Thus, expressing a certain topic in a headline in the news can, to a large extent, affect how an event is defined in terms of "desired" mental model (cases when a criminal act committed by a representative of a minority is tendentious updated and put on the front page in the press).[333] Similarly, the argument can also be convincing because social attitudes that are hidden in the implicit premises and, thus, are taken for granted by the recipients. If in parliamentary debate it is implicitly predicted that all refugees are illegal, thus it can be influenced for the immigration to be

---

[332] Van Dijk, T. A., Aims of Critical Discourse Analysis, Japanese Discourse Vol. I (1995).
[333] Duin, A. H., Roen, D. H., and Graves, M. F. (1988). Excellence or malpractice: the effects of headlines on readers' recall and biases. National Reading Conference (1987, St Petersburg, Florida). National Reading Conference Yearbook, 37: Van Dijk, 1'. A. (1991). Racism and the Press. London: Routledge and Kegan Paul.

limited.[334] <u>A typical characteristic of manipulation is to communicate the views implicitly i.e. without being articulated, and thus also be less likely to run into resistance.</u>

These few examples show how different types of discourse structure can influence the formation and change of mental models and social representations. If dominant groups, especially their elites, largely control public discourse and its structures, they thus also have greater control over the minds of the public at large. All this is more or less known in cognitive and social psychology of language, discourse and communication. However, what is unknown is which properties of the speakers and the discourses are preferred and effective as means of implementing such forms of mind control (?). Certainly, political propagandists, the people who make the ads, journalists or professors have enough practical experience to have a guess about what kind of messages will cause which effects. They know how to effectively cause change of knowledge and attitudes of recipients and what kind of social activities will result from such mind control. However, such control has its limits because the complexity of understanding, formation and change of attitudes is such that it cannot always be predicted which characteristics of a text or speech will have effects on the minds of the recipients and what those effects will be. Also, recipients in a specific context and with regard to their existing knowledge and beliefs, can ignore, dismiss, not believe or otherwise mentally act contrary to the intentions of the powerful speakers or writers. Recipients have relative freedom to interpret and use discourses as they wish and as it is in their best interest, as is the case with media messages. The intention of the author of a news article or comment must not always be accepted by the reader, although this author's intention was recognized by him.

At the end of this section it is good to conclude two things from the above mentioned, which impose as a conclusion:
- First, access to specific forms of discourse, for example, those of politics, media or science is in itsellf a resource of power;

---

[334]Wodak, R. and van Dijk, T. A. (eds) (2000). Racism at the Top. Klagenfurt: Drava Verlag.

- and second, our action is controlled by our minds, that is, if we are able to influence the minds of people, for example, their knowledge or attitudes, we can indirectly control some of their activities. This means that those groups that control the most influential discourse also have more chances to control the minds and actions of others.

Social issues as a CDA subject for research

There are many social issues and phenomena which being discursive researched by CDA may reveal abuse of power, domination and social inequality. In the previous section, we often used as examples cases of pressure on immigration, the relationship between whites and blacks, discrimination against women bymen, the abuse of the media by the elite. All these cases represent topics of interest for CDA. Some of the topics will obly be superficially overviewed because they are out of our interests, and some will be covered in more details below.

Gender inequality

Gender belonging, although a wide area for critical research on language and discourse, however, is in the initial phase of research in terms of CDA. Feminist research became paradigmatic in many ways for many of the discourse analyses, especially since most of these studies explicitly deal with social inequality and domination of men.

Media discourse

The undeniable power of the media is a challenge for many critical studies in various disciplines to deal with media discourse. Traditional, often analytical approaches, focused on content in critical research on the media have found biased, stereotypical, sexist and racist images in the texts, illustrations and photographs or political use of the words US and THEM (and Our/Their actions and characteristics evaluated positively or negatively).

In one of his papers, Fowler also focused on the media.[335] The point of his research is to explain that certain events and activities can be described with syntax variations that serve to mitigate or hide the participation of the main actors. In later critical studies on the media Fowler pays tribute to British cultural studies, which "define the news not as a reflection of reality, but as a product shaped by political, economic and cultural forces".[336]

Van Dijk similarly applies the theory of discourse in critical studies on international news, racism in the press and coverage of *squatters* in the Dutch city of Amsterdam.[337]

Political discourse

Given the role of political discourse in passing, reproduction and legitimization of power and domination, there are numerous critical discursive studies on political text and speech. Here are the unavoidable research on political discourse by Paul Chilton, on the language that was used in the debate about nuclear weapons[338] and the later works of contemporary speech on nuclear power plants[339] (*nukespeak*) and metaphor.[340]

Although research on political discourse in English language is internationally famous (because of the hegemony of the English language), many papers have also been made on the German, French and Spanish language. Germany has a long tradition of political analysis of discourse

---

[335]Fowler, R., Hodge, B., Kress, G., and Trew, T. (1979). Language and Control. London: Routledge and Kegan Paul.
[336]Fowler, R. (1991). Language in the News. Discourse and Ideology in the Press., London: Routledge and Kegan Paul.
[337]van Dijk, T. A. (1988a). News as Discourse. Hillsdale, NJ: Erlbaum. van Dijk, T. A. (1988b). News Analysis. Case Studies of International and National News in the Press. Hillsdale, NJ: Erlbaum
[338]Chilton, P. (ed.) (1985). Language and Nuclear Arms Debate: Nukespeak Today. London and Dover, NH: Frances Printer.
[339]Chilton, P. (1988). Orwellian Language and the Media. London: Pluto Press.
[340] Chilton, P. (1996). Security Metaphors. Cold War Discourse from Containment toCommon House. Bern: Lang. и Chilton, P. and Lakoff, G. (1995). Foreign policy by metaphor. In C. Schaffner and A. L. Wenden (eds), Language andPeace, (pp. 37-59). Aldershot: Dartmouth.

focused primarily on the study of the language of war and peace[341] and acts of speech in political discourse.[342] Also, there is a strong tradition of studying the Nazi language, anti-Semitism and discourse (for example: lexicon, propaganda, media and language policies of Ehlich[343], as well as the use of language by immigrant workers and their language barriers in German society).

In France, the study of political language has a respectable tradition in linguistics and discourse analysis and a strong tendency towards quantitative analysis, often combined with critical ideological analysis (Pecheux[344]; Guespin[345]). Critical research on political discourse in Spain and especially in Latin America are very productive and, for the most part, oriented towards the regime of discourses "juntata" (Franco, Pinoche). These research have an influential sociolinguistic approach to political discourse, and are focused on authoritarian discourses.

We will return to the political discourse at length below.

Ethnocentrism, anti-Semitism, nationalism and racism

Studies of the role of discourse in the adoption and reproduction of ethnic and racial inequality have slowly appeared in CDA. Such an engagement was focused on ethnocentric and racist images in the media, literature and film. These representations are part of the centuries-old notions of dominance over others which were present in the discourse of European travelers, explorers, merchants, soldiers, philosophers and historians and are known as "elite discourse" (Barker[346]; Lauren[347]). Going

---

[341] Pasierbsky, F. (1983). Krieg und Frieden in der Sprache. (War and Peace in Language). Frankfurt: Fischer.

[342] Holly, W. (1990). Politikersprache. Inszenierungen and Rollenkonflikte im informellen Sprachhandeln eines Bundestagsabgeordneten. (Politician's Language. Dramatization and Role Conflicts in the Informal Speech Acts of a Bundestag Delegate). Berlin: Mouton de Gruyter.

[343] Ehlich, K. (ed.) (1989). Sprache im Faschismus. (Language under Fascism). Frankfurt: Suhrkamp.

[344] Pecheux, M. (1969). Analyse Automatique du Discours. Paris: Dunod.

[345] Guespin, L. (ed.) (1976). Typologie du discours politique (Typology of political discourse). Languages, 41.

[346] Barker, A. J. (1978). The African Link: British Attitudes to the Negro in the Era

from one extreme of the emphasis on exotic differences to another extreme for suprematic derogation, as well as emphasizing the intellectual, moral and biological inferiority of others, such discourses have also influenced public opinion and led to widely accepted social performances. Exactly the continuity of this socio-cultural tradition of negative images of the Others, it partly explains the existence of the dominant models in contemporary discourse, media and film.[348]

Later studies of discourse spread beyond traditional content analysis of images of the Others and entered in the linguistic, semiotic and other discursive properties of text and speech on rights of minorities, immigrants and other people. Besides the media, advertisements, film and books, which are genres that are commonly taught in CDA, newer research of CDA also focus on political discourse, scientific discourse, everyday conversations, talk shows and many other genres. Many studies of ethnic and racial inequality found great presence of stereotypes, prejudice and other forms of verbal harassment in various kinds of discourses and media.[349]

---

of the Atlantic Slave Trade, 1550-1807. London: Frank Cass.
[347]Lauren, P. G. (1988). Power and Prejudice. The Politics and Diplomacy of Racial Discrimination. Boulder, CO: Westview Press.
[348]Shohat, E. and Stam, R. (1994). Unthinking Eurocentrism. Multiculturalism and the Media. London: Routledge and Kegan Paul.
[349]Ter Wal applied this framework in a detailed study of the ways in which the Italian political and media discourse gradually changed from anti-racist commitment and benign representation of extracommunitari (non-European) to more stereotypical and negative view of the relationship between immigrants and crime, deviation and threat (Ter Wal, J. (1997). The reproduction of ethnic prejudice and racism through policy and news discourse. The Italian case (1988-92). Florence: PhD, European Institute). The main point is that racism (including anti-Semitism, xenophobia and other forms of resentment against racially or ethnically otherwise defined) is a complex system of social and political inequality that is reproduced by discourse, especially elite discourse. Another title is crucial for proper understanding of elite discourse, and it is „The End of Racism" by Souza (D'Souza, D. (1995). The End of Racism: Principles for Multiracial Society. New York: Free Press). This book embodies many of the dominant ideologies in the United States, especially on the right oriented and it is particularly aimed at a minority group in the United States - African-Americans (blacks). In it the author shows what kind of discursive structures, strategies and actions are used to manifest the power of the dominant group (white, Western world) and readers are manipulated to accept this picture, all in accordance with the existing conservative, supreme ideology. The overall strategy of the "The end of Racism" is a combination of a positive presentation of the group in itself and a negative presentation of the group

Discursive structures and strategies

Within the broader social and cognitive framework sketched above, the theory and practice of CDA are focus on the structures of text and speech. If powerful speakers or groups apply or otherwise "expose" their power in discourse, CDA researchers should determine how exactly is that done. Also, if in that way they are able to persuade or otherwise affect the audience, CDA researchers want to know which discursive structures and strategies are involved in the process. Therefore, the reproduction of domination through discourse, which is taken as a major subject of critical analysis, has two major dimensions: that of production and that of reception. In other words, on the one hand, we differentiate between application, expression or legitimizing dominance in producing different structures of text and speech, and, on the other hand, between the functions, consequences or results of such structures on the minds of the recipients. CDA has the duty to explain why, for example, a white speaker believes he can be impudent towarda a black person, but not towards a white speaker in the same situation, that is which models and social representations relate the social group domination to the choice of specific discursive forms? Van Dijk offers an explanation which might go as follows: (1) One white speaker understands, interprets and represents the current communication situation in a mental contextual model, including self-image (such as white) and the black man who he addresses. (2) To do so, the general attitudes about blacks are activated. If they are negative, it will also be shown in the representation of the black recipient in contextual model: the recipient may be given a lower status. (3) This "biased" contextual model follows the production and if all other parameters are equal (for example, If there is no fear of revenge, or there are no moral accusations), this can result in the

---

from the outside. In this book the main rhetorical means of the Others are hyperbole and metaphor (disease is called pathology and virus) and emphasizing the contrast between the civilized and barbarians. Semanticly and lexicalyl, the Others are related to deviation (illegitimacy) and threat (violence, attacks). The argued claims about the shortcomings of black culture are combined with denials of the shortcomings of whites (racism), then, with rhetorical mitigation and euphemisation of their crimes (colonialism, slavery) and semantic reshuffle of the blame (blaming the victim). Thus, social conflict is cognitively represented and reinforced by polarization and it is discursively maintained and reproduced by humiliation, demonizing and social exclusion of the Others by us, the civilized.

production of discursive structures that signal such fundamental bias and specific forms of impoliteness. However, it should be borne in mind that these socio-cognitive processes that underlie the production of racist discourse may be, largely automated.[350]

What you need to know is how discursive structures affect the structure and content of the models or the process of generalization that link models with views in a way that leads to the formation of social representations that maintain dominance. To Van Dijk there is no doubt that the reproduction of domination in modern societies often requires its justification or legitimization: it is simply "natural" that we have privileged access to valuable social resources. Another strategy for reproducing domination is denial: there is no domination, all the people in our society are equal and all have equal access to social resources. Such socio-cognitive strategies, will also appear in the discourse of justification and denial of inequality.

Modalities for US and against THEM

The justification of inequality involves two complementary strategies: 1). *positive presentation of the own group* and 2). *negative representation of the others*. This is also what we find in the discourses of whites on ethnic minorities. Arguments, stories, semantic moves and other structures of such discourse consistently and sometimes very subtly, have implications in everyday conversations, political discourse, textbooks or news reports.[351] Thus, models are expressed and transmitted convincingly which compare US with THEM, i.e. highlight our tolerance, support or sympathy, and focus on negative social or cultural differences, deviations or threats attributed to "them". If such polarized models are consistent with negative attitudes or ideologies, they can be used to maintain the existing views or create new negative attitudes. One of the strategic ways to ensure that such generalizations are made to stress that the current model is typical, not

---

[350] Essed, P.J. M. (1991) Understanding Everyday Racism. Newbury Park, CA: Sage.
[351] Van Dijk, T.A. (19187a) Communicating Racism. Newbury Park. CA: Sage.; Van Dijk, T. A. (1991) Racism and the Press. London: Routledge.; Van Dijk, T.A. (1993a) Elite Discourse and Racism. Newbury Park, CA: Sage.

exceptional or incidental and that the negative actions of the Others can not be explained or justified. Therefore, speakers or writers tend to be exceptional and to emphasize that "this is always so," that "we are not accustomed to it," and that the circumstances do not allow alternative interpretations of "deviant" acts of the Others.

Given these assumptions for the formation of models of events and schematic views that present US and THEM should examine in details which discursive structures are suitable for such processes. Clearly the simplest is by semantic content - statements which include negative opinions about THEM and positive about US. However, such statements should also be reliable because they are needed as well as other convincing moves, such as the following[352]:

- Argumentation: the negative assessment derives from "facts";
- Rhetorical figures: hyperbolic strengthening of their negative actions and our positive actions; euphemisms, denials, suppressing of our negative actions;
- Lexical style: choice of words that imply negative or positive assessments;
- Telling stories: retelling the above adverse events (for example, the idleness of blacks) as being personally experienced; provision of reliable details about the negative characteristics of events;
- Structured emphasis in the media of their negative actions in headlines, news summaries, news reports;
- Citing credible witnesses, sources experts, for example, in news reports.

These and many other subtle structures can be interpreted as the management of processes of understanding in such a way that the desired models are built by listeners/readers. Depending on the objectives of such discursive marginalization of dominated groups, generally, we can expect the structures and strategies of the dominant conversation to focus on different forms of positive self-representation and negative presentation of the others. For ethnic or racial issues, this may include, for example, denial of racism and discrimination by whites and systematic linking of ethnic

---

[352] Van Dijk, T. A., Principles of critical discourse analysis, Discourse & Society, 1993 SAGE (London. Newbury Park and New Delhi), vol. 4(2)

minorities with problematic cultural differences, illegal immigration and residence, illegal work and crime. Sometimes this happens in a direct and open way, and sometimes such attributions are much more subtle, which is a typical case in the liberal elite discourse.[353]

Another way to discredit the powerless groups is to devote too much attention to their alleged threat to the interests and privileges of the dominant group: we will have less or worse work, housing, education, or social assistance due to them and they are favored or positively discriminated. Such a strategy is suitable for the formation of models containing proposals known as "We are the real victims" or "We are discriminated, not them". In socio-economic situations of poverty among the white population, or uncertainty, of course it is easy to communicate convincingly on such proposals and they are accepted as general opinions which will be part of the general negative attitudes to ethnic minorities. In other words, there are few goals and values of the dominant ideologies of white groups that do not match these opinions.[354]

Liberal elites which declaratively always declare against discrimination and racism can also add humanitarian norms and values that would argue against "them". By highlighting their attitude of "equality for all" liberal elites, thus, can discredit the affirmative action programs or employment programs of a certain racial or ethnic minority. And by denial or mitigation of racism, they are able to marginalize those who claim otherwise. Let us remind you that in addition to the various semantic or other moves used in such discourse, the access to such discourse is a key requirement for power and counter-power: minorities or other groups dominated simply, are hardly allowed to present a different version of "facts," or the media of the whites or other elites will find a representative of the minority who will agree with their position.

Although every form of domination has its own historical, social, political and cultural characteristics, and thus different ways of discursive reproduction, we can assume that many of the observations above,

---

[353] Van Dijk, T.A. (1993a) Elite Discourse and Racism. Newbury Park, CA: Sage.
[354] Such discourse is easy to prove if you look at the election speeches of right-wing parties in Western countries, who always see one of the solutions to the economic crisis, the decline in the standard of the population and unemployment in taking restrictive measures on immigration.

universally apply in the areas of gender, class, religion, language ethnicity, political views or any other criteria, according to which groups may differ, be oppressed or marginalized. In creating discourse, especially when it is directed to the members of the dominant group, very often through direct abuse of power, we have violations of the rules of discourse that assume equality, free access to the communicative situation, to free choice of topics, alternate speaking, courtesy etc. In discursive understanding and reproduction, the dominant audience will generally expected the discourse to focus on the conviction of eligibility of marginalization of the "Other", by manipulation of models for the event and generalized negative attitudes arising from them.[355]

x x x

When it comes to critical analysis of discourse we should remember the following things: in every society elites are those who have control or preferential access to the most influential and important genres of discourse. Such an approach is defined as a consequence of their powerful social and institutional positions and functions; and conversely, their control or access to specific forms of institutional or public discourse maintains and reproduces their power in specific communicative situations. Because CDA focuses on abuse of power, critical studies specifically focus on ethically or lawfully illegitimate forms of control and access to the discourse - cases when politicians, journalists, teachers, managers or judges prevent others to use legitimate forms of text or speech, that is practice censorship. The exclusive right to access and control over the discourse, as one of the key forms of direct provision of social or institutional power, allows specific social actors (1) to engage in verbal action which is prohibited to others or (2) to be able to force or oblige others to engage in discourse or (3) to use the properties of the discourse in the manner the powerful person desires, and thus restrict the freedom and power of the less powerful. Among the many other resources that define the power of a particular group or institution access or control over public discourse and communication is important "symbolic" resource, as is the case with the possession of knowledge and information.

---

[355] Van Dijk, T. A., Principles of critical discourse analysis, Discourse & Society, 1993 SAGE (London. Newbury Park and New Delhi), vol. 4(2)

3. POLITICAL DISCOURSE

Introduction

There is no doubt that language is a powerful weapon and a means of gaining public support and social governance, especially at this time of information revolution. Or as Mills says, language is a powerful tool for the pressure of one group relative to another.[356] To Fairclough, however, discursive practices understood this way have enormous ideological effects on production and reproduction of unequal power relations between social classes, gender, ethnic, racial or cultural groups.[357] The tool of language - rhetorics can also be considered a cultural tradition and linguistic self-awareness and the skill and methods that form the beliefs of a particular audience are also a powerful weapon in the fight of a community against a community, worldview against worldview. Rhetorics is considered an instrument through which certain interests are represent and also a linguistic instrument for improving the lives of politicians.[358] The simplest example that politicians can gain their power or reproduce dominance exactly by using skillful language and rhetorical skill in political discourse, are the political campaigns during the elections, when politicians are deligitimized, that is the ruling party as well as the opposition are fighting for gaining legitimacy that would allow domination in society. It is often said that the winner in the election campaign won because he managed to convince voters in the correctness of his views and policies, he was more eloquent or acted more convincing in his speech in the TV duel. Means, he managed to win voters and earned power in society using language and different rhetorical skills. Analyzing interviews with former British Prime Minister Margaret ThatcherFairclough and Woodak[359] proved that the politician instead of establishing real interaction with journalists, managed

---

[356]Mills, S. (1995) Feminist Stylistics. london and New York: Routledge.
[357]Fairclough, N., Wodak R. (1997) Critical Discourse Analysis. In: Van Dijk, T.A. (ed.) Discourse as Social Interaction. Volume 2. London, Thousand Oaks, New Delhi: Sage.
[358]Zheng, Tongtao. Characteristics of Australian Political Language Rhetoric: Tactics of gaining public support and shirking responsibility, School of Asian Languages and Studies, University of Tasmania, Intercultural Communication, ISSN 1404-1634, 2000, November, issue 4.
[359]Fairclough, N. (1995) Critical Discourse Analysis: the Critical Study of Language. London, New York: Longman.

to hold political speeches and through various strategies managed to achieve rhetorics of political conviction (it is argued that Thatcherism has lingvisticly- discursive character); more recently, subject to such interpretations are the speeches of former US President Bush and so on.[360]

Studying the discourse Kolstø alsi comes to the conclusion that discourses can aim to preserve or to change the situation on the original condition. In terms of a given political or social situation, he distinguishes "conservative, revolutionary and reactionary discourses".

Political discourse and political cognition

In order to successfully perform an analysis of the political discourse it is first necessary to determine thee cognition, i.e. knowledge and understanding that the recipients have on the subject of political discourse. This is important because the efficiency and success of the political discourse is measured by how it was received and understood among those who have been targeted; because only successful end of that discursive process would mean acquisition or confirmation of power and domination. Cognitive linguistics is, in itself, a framework for analysis of a specific political language. The concepts in cognitive linguistics are equipped with one kind of equipment or a manual and it helps the critics - linguists to identify and analyze the linguistic and psychological strategies for manipulation of the political discourse. On the other hand, cognitive developmental (evolutionary) psychology sets the hypothesis as a kind of manipulative discourse - discourse which contains detailed information, it can activate and explore innate cognitive characteristics.[361] To Van Dijk, the study of political cognition widely deals with common ways of thinking of people as political actors.[362] Our knowledge and thoughts on politicians, parties or presidents is generally obtained, modified or confirmed by various forms of text and speech during our socialization, formal education,

---

[360]Ibid
[361]Hart, Christopher, (2005) Analysing Political Discourse: Toward a Cognitive Approach, Critical Discourse Studies 2 (2), University of Hertfordshire
[362]van Dijk, T. A., Political discourse and political cognition (paper) CHAPTER 7

monitoring the media and talks.[363] Political discourse is a mixture of personal development and relevant social environment in which the individual grows. Personal development is influenced by such factors as the impact that it has on the cultural environment in the process in which the individual develops its personality, their educational experiences, the influence of parents, social circles, political parties, economic status, etc. Thus, continues Dijk, political discourse is rarely just personal, though it should not be forgotten that the opposite is also true, i.e. it is not just social or political but also personal text and speech and itcontains personal characteristics. Only cognitive theory can explain the link between social and personal. Political groups or institutions are defined not only as socio-political, in the form of groups of related actors or groups and their interactions, but also socio-cognitive in the form of their collective knowledge, attitudes, ideologies, norms and values. Therefore, a biased text, for example, on immigrants can be drawn from personal beliefs about immigrants and these beliefs can be linked to the common racist views or ideologies of the larger group. A representative in Parliament speaks as an individual and, thus, expresses his personal political beliefs in a unique way and in a unique context. At the same time, this person speaks as a member of Parliament or Congress, as a member of a party and as a representative of an area, in which he reflects the views or ideologies of his group.[364]

As Dijk further explains, we assume that in the formation of discourse the speaker (or writer) generally starts from their mental model of an event or situation. This model organizes the subjective beliefs of the speaker on such a situation. Once such a personal model of an event or situation is established, the speakers can express fragments of that model in the discourse, using certain linguistic strategies and strategies in the formulation of the discourse that will be analyzed. It is important to realize that most speakers most frequently express only a fraction of their models, i.e. only the information relevant to the current context. In other words, the written text is just the tip of the information that speakers have about an event or condition about which they speak. On the other hand, the audience and the readers of the text, understand what is spoken primarily through a

---

[363] Merelman, R. M. 1986. Revitalizing Political Socialization. In M. G. Hermann (ed.), Political Psychology. San Francisco, Jossey-Bass:
[364] van Dijk, T. A., Political discourse and political cognition (paper) CHAPTER 7

complex process of decoding and understanding words and sentences and finally through the construction of own models of what was spoken. If they agree with him, they would also accept his models as true or accurate. If not, they can construct alternative models of the situation, depending on their personal knowledge of the current situation, as well as the social and shared knowledge of the group on the current situation. If recipients read or hear very similar discourses of politicians or the media and if there is no competitive, alternative information, such models can be generalized as generally accepted, abstract notions of a certain social phenomenon or problem (for example the Muslims, minorities, immigration, ethnic prejudice, nationalist or racist ideologies, etc.).

The study of political cognition is focused on different aspects of processing political information. It basically deals with the acquisition, use and structures of thinking about political situations, events, actors and groups. Typical research topics of political cognition are: "Organization of political beliefs", "Perception of political candidates", "political judgment and decision-making on practical cognition", "stereotypes, prejudices and other socio-political views", "political group identity", "public opinion", "formulation of impressions and many other various topics dealing with representation of memory and manner of thinking involved in political understanding and interaction".

After this brief discussion on the personal side of political cognition, below we will focus on the socio-political dimension of the common cognition. Social memory is composed of knowledge, attitudes, ideologies, values and norms.

Knowledge

Unlike the philosophical and psychological approaches to knowledge, in our case we should make a distinction between two types of knowledge: knowledge that is common to a specific group and general knowledge of the culture, spread among various groups in society. The second is the foundation for all interaction and communication in society and generally a prerequisite in discourse. This type of knowledge is generally undisputed, not controversal and as such it is learnt while socializing in schools in a certain society. We all know what "Parliament", "Muslim" and "immigration" means. Second, there are factual beliefs that are just accepted as "true" by certain social groups as scientists, experts, professionals, members of certain religions, members of parties or any other types of groups. This knowledge of the group is called "knowledge" (in quotation marks) within the group itself. Still, outside the group, such knowledge may not be appointed as knowledge, but as a "belief" or "opinion", i.e. beliefs that are not accepted as true according to the criteria of the general culture or those of other groups (which does not mean that that belief is wrong). Large part of political knowledge is knowledge of the group and is often seen as "pure political opinion" by the opposing groups. Typically, knowledge of feminists for male dominance in society can be rejected by many men; racist groups have their knowledge of the group, even when many people in society can argue such knowledge and treat it as a belief based on prejudices. As stated by Dijk, in political speeches, the speaker often knows to rhetorically claim that "we all know". For example, "We all know that the birth rate of Muslims is several times higher than the rate of the local population". We can assume that this is a "fact" for the speaker, while the members of other groups (for example: anti-racists) can also qualify it as an opinion based on prejudice or, at least, as an exaggeration or as a biased statement because it is incomplete. The fact that a speaker makes a statement about what "we all know" suggests that this is not common knowledge, because if so, he would have assumed that and not highlight it. He gives such a statement because he knows that others in the Parliament can perceive it as biased opinion or belief and its presentation of this knowledge as general and generic; basically, this is a well-known rhetorical move to convince the audience of the general validity of the "group" knowledge.

Common social knowledge of specific groups or entire cultures should be applicable in many situations and, thus, should be general. It may be about immigrants in general, but not for a specific immigrant. Therefore we have an unusual situation, known at the time of Nazi Germany, a Nazi has a negative or discriminatory attitudes towards the entire collectivity of Jews, based on his accumulated knowledge, but is a friend, even a protector to a specific person of Jewish ancestry. The same can also be found today when a white person has a racist attitude towards the black immigration, but quite correct, even friendly relationship with specific African-American settler. The reason for this is that he is guided towards the unwanted group by prejudices and stereotypes, while his personal relationship is based on the knowledge and experience from specific life situations. Therefore, it makes sense to distinguish not only between the knowledge of a group about culture, but also between social and personal knowledge.

Opinions and attitudes

The opinions and attitudes are still one of the elements necessary to allow the political discourse be successfully understood and if it does not interfere with the personal attitudes to be accepted. If personal views are not complimentary to the political discourse in one variant it would be rejected. However, in another, due to inconsistency of the positions and their variability, it is possible to come to evolutionary nature and acceptance of political discourse that was previously unacceptable. Empirical research suggests that such a consistency in attitude is more emphasized for those who have political experience in a particular area than for those new.[365] Attitudes most often change because of the desire to belong to a group (reference group) in which we want to become members or with which we identify (for example, if you are a member of the Social Democratic Party, and want to pass in the Conservative, it is clear that we will have to change our own political position and accept the views of other political community).[366] Reference group means a group to which we orient and which standards we use for self evaluation, and assessment of the world and events around us. A very important feature of the reference

---

[365] Judd, C. M. and Downing, J. W.. 1990. Political Expertise and the Development of Attitude Consistency. Social Cognition, 8(1):

[366] As early as in 1942 Newcomb made a study with which he confirmed that the change of attitudes is possible if there is a rupture of relations with the original reference group. He measured the change in the attitudes of conservative students of Bennington College and found that conservative students who disrupted the relations with the initial conservative group (family and friends), and enhanced relations with the new group (liberal) changed their attitudes and became liberal. That did not happen among conservative students who kept their contacts with family and friends (their original conservative reference group), and did not establish a quality relationship with the new (Liberal).(Franzoi, S. L. Social Psychology, drugo izdanje, McGrawHill, Boston, 2000).

group is that people have an emotional attachment towards it and turn on it/ turn on it for guidance/leadership even if they are not its members. The reference groups can be large (such as nations/peoples or religions), but can also be smaller (such as sections, parties, family and friends).

The beliefs that are described above as different kinds of knowledge can also be designated as "factual" because individuals, groups or entire cultures can consider them true based on their criteria for truth. However, there are group beliefs - opinions which are not reviewed in social memory in the light of the criteria of truth (good vs. bad, etc.). As we have seen, however, what may be actual belief of a group can be evoluationary belief or opinion of another. In terms of attitudes, they are basically social and related to groups. Individuals may have personal views, but the views can be shared only with a group or culture that they belong to. Knowing the position of a person, for example, on Muslims can tell us what that person thinks about the immigrant policy of the state. Or, for example, in the domain of politics in the United States, knowing the position of a person on abortion may help in assuming the position of the person on the death penalty.[367]

Ideologies

Ideology is another important factor that affects how will political discourse be accepted. Therefore, social representations (knowledge, attitudes) that are shared by a group can be organized by respective ideologies. Ideologies are by definition general and abstract because they need to be applicable to many different positions in different social domains. Thus, as assessed by Dijk, racist ideology may control attitudes about immigration, but at the same time also about residence, work, education or culture of immigrants or minorities. Or if we find the social democratic ideology acceptable , it is clear that it will be much easier to accept the political discourse that reflects tolerance of newcomers or the

---

[367] Taking sides: user classification for informal online political discourse. The Authors. Robert Malouf, Department of Linguistics and Asian/Middle Eastern Languages, San Diego State University, San Diego, California, USA, Tony Mullen, Department of Computer Science, Tsuda College, Tokyo, Japan

social policy to the poorer layers. This is only general characteristic of the acceptance of an ideology by the members of a group, which may not be affordable in the same detailed manner for all group members. Some experts of the group (ideologues) have broader ideologies than the "ordinary" members of the group. However, being a member of such an ideological group (and identifying with such a group), the individual has to accept some basic ideological beliefs. It is assumed that ideologies are initially organized by a group scheme, with categories as a criteria for membership, activities, goals, values/norms, social status and resources. These are the main categories under which information are presented and they define the group and its relations with other groups. who we are, what we do, which goals do we have and so on.? In the category - social status conflicting relationships with other groups can be presented. For example, knowledge of the group and the opinions stated with regard to Muslim immigrants can be organized in different ideologies as nationalism, ethnocentrism, racism or democracy. Therefore, the racist ideology emphasizes the knowledge of the group about the great number of immigrants, as well as the birth rate and the opposition of ordinary citizens to further increase of the number of immigrants. It also controls the attitude towards crime or aggression of minorities, especially Muslims. The nationalist ideology controls common social views on the positive social opinions on "us, the English or the French" (cultural, polite, tolerant, peaceful) and the (beloved) homeland. The democratic ideology organizes the major views about the needs of ordinary people to have a voice, to be able to vote, to be able to express their views on everyday life experiences, including immigration, concludes Dijk.

Structures of political discourse

After reviewing the various aspects of political cognition and the way they allow you to accept or reject political discourse we will now continue with the analysis of the structures of political discourse and their relations with political cognition and the functions they have in the political process. Taking into account the importance of contextualization of the definition of political discourse, at the beginning we will pay attention to (cognitive) analysis of context.

Context

Before referring to the the structures of political discourse, we must first briefly deal with their context. Contexts should be defined taking into account the mental models of the participants in the communication events. It should be noted that many genres of political discourse (parliamentary debates, laws, propaganda slogans, international treaties, peace agreements, etc.) are mainly defined more by contextual rather than a textual aspect. Political discourse is not primarily defined by theme or style, but by who speaks to whom, in which function, in what circumstances and with which objectives. In other words, the political discourse is especially "political" because of his functions in the political process.[368] Therefore, the speaker can only say what his speech will make "suitable" for a certain number of these contextual conditions that must be met. In the case of a parliamentary debate, the Chairman partially controls such criteria for the situation. For example, a speaker is only allowed to speak a certain time in the Parliament and for a specific debate or session of Parliament because he is a member of Parliament and as because he had received a word from the Chairman. His speech is also politically functional in the political process because his purpose is to defend the draft law of the government from the criticisms of the opposition. Moreover, the speaker usually knows more about the topic of speaking (for example: immigration) and has many more opinions about it, but because of the time constraints, the beliefs of the listeners, as well as the strategy for positive self-presentation determine some information on model which are selected for expression, while others remain implicit, assumed or just conceived. If it comes to a representative of the Conservative Party, the ideology of his party is included in the contextual model that favors emphasizing the belief in our good characteristics and their poor characteristics.

---

[368] van Dijk, T. A. 1997b. What is Political Discourse Analysis? In J. Blommaert and C. Bulcaen (eds.), Political Linguistics. Amsterdam, Benjamins

Referring to the "discursive polarization" of Us and Them, Dijk says that typical of political discourse is not only that it reflects the mental representations of the people being spoken of (for example: Englishmen against Muslims), but also categorizes the participants (presented in contextual models) being spoken of in the communication situation (we at power against those in opposition). So Woodak, was studying the Austrian nationalist and anti-Semitic discourse as two sides of the same pair. The practice of behavior included the disposition of solidarity with his own group and the exclusion of others from the constituted collective. Which individual features for distinguishing will be chosen by the racist discourse, depends largely on the context. Metaphors and metonymies are used to describe the own group - we, with terms and the other group with negative. Personal pronouns in the first person plural have a role to create a group identity. In another study, Bilig draws the attention on the essential status of other inconspicuous i words in the English language - the definite article the. In news reports, expressions such as people (the nation) or country (the country) usually do not have to be explained, they obviously refer to "our" people and "our" country. Even apparently such a harmless expression as "the weather forecast for today" can contribute to building an identity. We easily understand that the "weather" refers to the wether in "our" country. Such language thus sets the basics for what Bilig appointed as "banal nationalism 'as he considered "dangerous policy for us and them"[369]. It should be said that this way of structuring the language can be effective not only for building national identity in national states, of which Bilig speaks, but for the creation of ethnic identity within states.[370]

Furthermore, contextual models regulate the "pragmatic dimension of political discourse", for example the use of "voice forms as 'rhetorical' question", which will be discussed in more details below.

---

[369] Billig, M (2006), Banal Nationalism. London: Sage
[370] Kolstø, P. „Diskurs i nasilni sukob: predstave o „sebi" i „drugom" u državama nastalim posle raspada Jugoslavije", „Intima javnosti", Fabrika knjiga, Beograd, 2008

Themes

We will briefly discuss some structures of discourse, and show how are they relevant to the political process as well as the political cognition. Generally as we shall see, these structures follow the global ideological or political strategy for positive self-representation and negative representation of others. We will start with themes as a part of the structure of political discourse.

Which information is defined or emphasized as an important or thematic in (political and other type of) discourse is part of the function of the model for events or contextual models of listeners. Therefore, typically, negative information about Us, our own group (for example: the nationalism in our party) are not part of the theme of the speech of the speaker, while negative information about Them, the others (for example, their assumed aggressiveness) tend be part of the theme. Conversely, our positive characteristics (tolerance, hospitality) will be thematic, while their positive characteristics will be ignored, overlooked or mentioned only in passing. It is understandable that the participants in the discussion raise issues which they consider harmful to the opposite side, leading to the pattern in which the party people and issues are most likely mentioned by those who belong to the opposite political spectrum. Thus, for example, in a study of the on-line posts in the United States, publishers identified as liberal were very critical towards George Bush and the war in Iraq, while publishers identified as conservative preferred to concentrate on the shortcomings of Bill Clinton.[371] It is one of the constants when it comes to the thematic choice in political discourse on which Hana Arent generally concluded that no civilization, however perfect, was not able to see with the "same eyes" its friends and enemies, its success and defeat.[372]

---

[371] Taking sides: user classification for informal online political discourse, The Authors, Robert Malouf, Department of Linguistics and Asian/Middle Eastern Languages, San Diego State University, San Diego, California, USA, Tony Mullen, Department of Computer Science, Tsuda College, Tokyo, Japan

[372] Arent, Hana, "Istina i laž u politici", Filip Višnjić, Beograd, 1994

Schemes

The global schematic organization of discourse is also conventional because it is directly variable because of the contextual variable constraints. Thus, parliamentary speech has the same basic categories no matter whether it is made by a conservative or a social democrat. It's perfectly fine for the visibility, the type and volume of information included in these categories to vary and, thus, be emphasized or used in the function of positive self-representation and negative representation of others. Therefore, if such a speech would have a general structure of a problem - solution, the speaker could not keep longer to the side of the problem (the problem allegedly caused by immigrants) than the solution. Parliamentary debates are a typical kind of discourse that tries to convince, in which the members of Parliament who occupy political positions, express their opinions and attack those of others in the framework of "argument structure" - one of the most typical schematic structures of discourse. Therefore, the conservative speaker, who intends, for example, to support legislation that restricts immigration, argues that such a restriction is good for the country. The arguments are selected in his mental model as well as in his conservative views, so that they will optimally support the conclusion that: a) There are millions of immigrants; b) They have a higher birth rate; c) Our country is small and there are already a large number of immigrants; d) Our culture is under threat; e) Muslims are especially dangerous; f) Ordinary citizens will suffer etc. A liberal politician shall discuss according to the same Schematic presentation, in accordance with the attitudes and ideology which are immanent in his political party.

Techniques and tactics in the use of political discourse

After we examined the structure of the discourse aspects that need to be met for the political discourse be understood by those who have been targeted in this section we will continue to consider a more specific aspect, namely the techniques and tactics that are at the disposal of a speaker in the presentation of political discourse. We will focus on discovering how politicians use rhetorics as a powerful tool in the process of gaining political points and advantage. Several elements of the so called "public discourse" will be analyzed, but we will mainly concentrate on two areas of speech: how politicians use language skills to gain public support and how they avoid or reduce their liability. Starting from these two aspects in the speech of politicians, we can say that the behavior of political actors in political communication can reveal their characteristics. The way they address the citizens and the media reveals their internal democratic capacity but also their deficits. That relationship was emphasized long ago by now rarely quoted Karl Marx, who said: "Talking with blurred language, must hide some interest". Therefore political actors often mask their views and interests, trying to mask them with beautiful words or symbols acceptable for people. Publicly, they "show" false symbols, formulas and words to enter into negotiations and agreements intended not to say honestly what they want and what their interest is and in order to outwit or cheat other political entities. And, indeed, as Hana Arent syas truth and lies are relative in politics. The boundary line between them will always be pulled by the one who is in a position of greater power or historical winner. Therefore, as assessed by Dijk, the political discourse, especially in areas with low political culture is contaminated with heavy presence of euphemisms and lies, and suffers from chronic lack of dialogue. It can be noted with the rare willingness to truly hear the other, almost no desire to respect the better arguments or "the force of argument," but rather "the argument of force" is being applied. Therefore many agreements and negotiations of the political actors as well as their decisions are essentially rotten compromises, concludes Dijk.

In political discourse the following techniques can be applied to win the majority over the idea being represented:

Inclusive equipment: Typical for the technique technique is that through political discourses symbols of national identity are created. National identity is used as a means to gain as many supporters as possible. Most often, politicians speak to groups of people who share things in common and are connected on the basis of nationality, religion, race, sex, profession. Therefore, promotional campaigns for or against a proposal, look like Catholic, Orthodox, Muslim or Jewish campaigns depending on the dominant origin of the members of the group.[373] Politicians are trying to convince people that they and their ideas are the ideas "of the people". The main function of the inclusive also known as a plain-folks (ordinary people - technique of ordinary people) is to assimilate the speaker in the group or groups and then to gain the trust and support of this group/groups. This technique is especially used in the USA, where Presidents are mainly people of great wealth, but always trying to represent themselves as ordinary people to the voters. This phenomenon can continuously be observed on TV. Bill Clinton eats in "McDonalds" and reads cheap spy novels. George Bush hates broccoli and loves fishing. Ronald Reagan was often photographed chopping wood, while Jimmy Carter represented himself as a modest farmer and producer of peanuts from Georgia. There is a clear intention to present politicians as ordinary people and as part of the table. These tactics help politicians to "disarm" groups and to gain their affection for later support the policies of their parties.

Thus they awaken the sense of national identity, politicians, also develop the so called means of "transfer" in order to receive public support.[374] Since democracies are based on the decision of the majority, those who claim to represent the majority are more likely to be supported by the public. Therefore the transfer is a means by which the propagandists express their authority, implement penalties and put on a pedestal the thing which we will respect. For example, the majority of us respects the church and our nation. If propagandists win the affection and support of the church or nation regarding any proposal or program, they perform a transfer of their authority, permission and prestige of the proposal or the program. That way we can accept something that, otherwise, might be refused.[375]

Technique of witnessing: One of the most commonly used techniques by politicians is the so called technique of "witnessing" in which politicians list the achievements and accomplishments of their parties. This testifies that the technique can be used whenever a politician wants his audience to hear their accomplishments under discussion. The technique of witnessing

---

[373] Institute for Propaganda Analysis. The Fine Art of Propaganda. New York: Harcourt, Brace and Company, 1939. Pp 21
[374] Propaganda: http://carmen.artsci.washington.edu/propaganda/transfer.htm at March 12, 1995
[375] Ibid

is used to create a fair and proper balanced argument. But very often it is used arguments for unfair arguments and in the wrong ways, so the results are overstates and glorified, and the achievements of the opposing party are devalue, denied or, very often, the other party is blamed that they have no results. The populist method includes manipulating ordinary people or experts or people brought from abroad to testify to the achievements and successes of politicians by whom they were engaged.

Quoting historical speeches: In order to improve the illucitory[376] image of their speeches and to avoid the responsibility of bringing charges that may cause unexpected reactions in the public, politicians use historical speeches of previous politicians to support their arguments. Quoting historical speeches is used as a means of increasing the efficiency of the speech and to reduce the political risk for politician to be called an extremist. Therefore the politician who uses inaccurate information, you may notice an existing fear about the reliability of his statements. The best way to justify their views and demands to use a well-known historic speech. With this, his stale views become more acceptable to the public and, at the same time, release him from responsibility for everything he says.

Technique of inversion: The technique of inversion is a way by which the speaker uses certain expressions so that the meaning changes completely and it means the opposite of the original statement. It is very often used in political speeches when there is a conflict situation, whereby victims are converted into attackers, while attackers are presented as victims. Combined with historical speech, the politician can reinforce the illucitory force of his speech to avoid any responsibility for his statement, so that the victims of the conflict are seen through bad history, rather than irresponsible policy.

Technique of fear or intimidation: The technique of intimidation is another feature of the political discourse. This technique first causes a dose of fear and potential danger to the public, and then finds solutions from which the public can choose any. In reality, however, these solutions give choices offered by politicians, and not the public. In contemporary politics

---

[376]Illucitory: a linguistic act performed by the speaker in the production of a statement in terms of presenting a proposal, warning, promise or request.

this technique is widely used in political speeches. When a politician agitates the fear of the public about crime and proposes to vote for him in order to reduce that threat, then he/she will use this technique.[377] The intention of the speakers who use this technique to encourage the negative attitude of the audience towards certain issues such as reforms in the tax system, giving preference to minorities and racial tolerance by causing fear of higher taxes or immigration risk.

Logical delusions: In order to make the public accept their proposal, politicians also use the so called technique of "logical delusions". With this technique, the speaker has spectacular predictions about the future based on few facts. Simply, he promises what the voters want to hear while never explaining how he will achieve this.[378] Political experts named such predictions as logical delusions and warn that they should be carefully used. It is interesting to note that this technique is freely used in all political discourses, while such warnings are not taken into account.

Religious quotes: Politicians use proverbs in an attempt to win the public with vivid, suggestive and emotional words. In certain situations, the political discourse is trying to reassure to calm down the public by making the harsh reality more acceptable and sustainable. This is achieved by use of proverbs, idioms, and even biblical statements to attack the opponents. So often events in the Bible are inserted in political discourse or testimony of spiritual saints are cited and political leaders are attributed the role of Messiah or savior of the nation. However, this technique achieves an effect only when the audience accepts the incredibleness of what is said and has no doubt it will happen or is true.

---

[377] If we look at the speeches of Hitler, we will see that in his efforts he was trying to strengthen the illucitory force to gain public support: "The streets of our country are in chaos. Universities are full of students who strike and protest. Communists are trying to destroy our country. Russia threatens us with its power, and our country is in danger. Yes, in danger. Internal and external threats. We need law and order! Without that our nation will fail".

[378] In Macedonia, the most striking example of a logical fallacy was when one party in the electoral cycle in 1998 promised to the voters that if they win the election there will be one billion dollars foreign investment. The voters caught the cast hook, followed by recognition of Taiwan, for which several credit lines were obtained from Taiwan, but one billion dollars had never come to the country, and relations with China were completely disabled.

Technique of emotions: Politicians constantly use the so called "technique of emotions" in their attempts attract the public. Emotion can be considered as a kind of investment from which the speaker expects a lot in return. This technique is used in several ways. For example, when the speaker speaks whispering/suggestively or loud and uses exaggerated gestures and mimics, then he uses the technique of emotions. Hitler's speeches are full of such examples: he constantly raised his tone on important points in his speeches and fiercely gestured with his hands and shoulders. For a moment, it appeared as he was "fighting" with the audience. Emotional agitation is a favorite technique of propagandists because "every emotion can be 'turned' in any activity of skilled manipulation".[379]

Never talk about your disadvantages: One of the most common techniques for politicians is to ignore the strengths of their opponents and loudly emphasize their negative aspects and failures, and simultaneously reject the existence of any negative characteristics or beliefs of their own character. Politicians have always emphasized the wrong moves and poor management of their opponents, while at the same time, proudly giving themselves credit for their success (or seemingly successful) policies.

Special categories of words: Selecting the vocabulary can be used to refine the illucitory power. This is because some words can instantly activate certain assumptions, discover the views of the speaker and seek approval from the speaker for their interpretation. Certain "positive words"[380] as well as "insults"[381] are also used in political speeches. The language people use to describe their feelings about the art (for example) tends to be more specific than the language used to evaluate a product. It is reasonable to speculate that the language used in political discourse is sharper.[382]

---

[379] Wartime Propaganda: World War I Demons, Atrocities, and Lies, http://carmen.artsci.washington.edu/propaganda/war3.htm at March 12, 1995
[380] Propaganda Examples Gingrich's Glittering Generalities http://carmen.artsci.washington.edu/propaganda/newtname.htm at March 12, 1995
[381] Propaganda Examples, how Newt Gingrich Uses These Techniques. http://carmen.artsci.washington.edu/propaganda/newt.htm at March 12, 1995
[382] Taking sides: user classification for informal online political discourse.The Authors.Robert Malouf, Department of Linguistics and Asian/Middle Eastern

Contrasting statements: In many cases politicians use contrasting statements in political discourse to belittle their opponents and to elevate themselves. The use of contrasting statements is a technique used to extract the information that is already forgotten from the collective memory of the audience and be used for own purposes. This technique is often used when politicians want to influence voters by constantly reminding them of the mistakes the opposition party made when it was in power, by returning the past dissatisfaction of voters, and also to the defocusing them from critical observation of the current situation and the processes which the party that uses this strategy leads.

x x x

What is important in the analysis of political discourse is to know the profile of the audience to which it is intended. Since they are addressing various parts of the community, politicians use various strategies and techniques in their speeches to help themselves achieve their political goals. For example, a speech can be primarily oriented towards the upper middle and high class and the business community, and its style of expression may or may not have to be mostly "abstract", or simply put, vague and blurry (typical for the conservative politicians). On the other hand, another politician might predominantly addresses the middle and lower middle class. His way of expression will be very different from that of the first politician. On average, his statements will be shorter and his words will be easier to understand and grasp. This style of expression is more acceptable for theordinary voters (it usually refers to the Socialdemocrats and the Labourists). As regards the third possible style of political discourse, it competently uses many classical rhetorical techniques, including citing historical speeches, conversion technique, exaggeration, fear and logical delusions. The use of such extreme techniques is dedicated to satisfy a smaller percentage of voters who usually make up less than 10% of the voters in the country. These politicians are aware that their impact on the electorate is not very massive and therefore have the comfort of extreme political discourse because,

---

Languages, San Diego State University, San Diego, California, USA, Tony Mullen, Department of Computer Science, Tsuda College, Tokyo, Japan

although small, their voting potential is stable and non-fluctuating (Liberals, Greens and the extreme-left and extreme-right).

Political discourse and violent conflict

In this section we will look at several segments of the role political discourse on the conflict in society - from running political debate, through initiating conflict, its escalation, to the stage of reconciliation. Throughout this process, the political discourse is the tool that influences the management of the conflict in its various stages. At first glance, it might seem absurd as the one who is guilty of producing conflicting relationships can later appear as an actor to overcome the same, especially if you analyze the political discourse at the beginning and the end of a conflict process - striking will be the realization that two diametrically different discursive processes are spoken by a single politician. But it is the controversy of politics as the art of the possible (not to mention the metaphor of the oldest craft).

In the basics of a political discourse that is aimed to provoking conflict, always stands a discursive polarization or simplified story of good and bad guys, a story that always comes down to simplified display of "us" versus "them". It is clear that the conflict takes two sides, and in our own eyes we are always right and the other one is wrong and vice versa. In such discourse there is no room for nuance and a minimum of objectivity and empathy for the other side, as well as critical self-evaluation, disapproval or condemnation of your own policy. Therefore we have a paradoxical situation in which militant discourses of the two opposing sides mutually stimulate or any speech directed to the opposite side is followed by a response and so on indefinitely when insight is lost about who initiated the conflict discourse. In order to achieve such discursive polazrizacija of the population their emotions and the successful manipulating with them using political discourse by the ruling elite are important factors. However, in studying the role of discourse in conflicts, it would be wrong to assume that only those articles or speeches that advocate an escalation of violence or which result in this escalation are strategic. Both the texts with reconcilable with peaceful messages have to inevitably serve with a variety of (aggressive) rhetorical strategies to "win" the debate and have an impact on the wider discourse.[383] It is obvious that it is about a complex process of manipulation and creation of "own" truth based on lies and constructions. Therefore, in addition, we would enter in a theoretical debate that defines this situation.

Use of emotions in the political discourse for causing conflict

Known is the definition that if for an information you can easily see that it is a lie, it is told in a political language and if members of the electorate consider it completely accurate, then this language can be considered manipulative. Also, if individuals during such political discourse are convinced that they are endangered (for example: immigration), then such a feeling will influence the political process of decision-making that causes anti-immigration attitudes that can lead to conflict. Neurological studies present evidence that the language can activate the amygdala - the center responsible for emotions in the brain so that use of language can affect the awareness and thereby manipulate the individual and put it in a position to support the policy that is offered through discourse.[384] Roger Petersen dealt with the role of emotions in the conflicts, and he upgrades the "Posen's theory of 'endangered safety'". Petersen named the dominant emotion that manages the view of "endangered safety" as fear, but in his view, other emotions can also play a role in the deterioration of relations between two groups, such as resentment, hatred and anger.[385] Fear may occur when the other or the different is intentionally (based on personal experience or the experience of others, the media and/or promotional information) or seemingly random (prejudice) perceived as a potential threat to life, integrity, personal or social interest. In order to understand this specific manifestation of fear - fear of the other and the different (or xenophobia) the term reference group

---

[383]Kolstø, P. „Diskurs i nasilni sukob: predstave o „sebi" i „drugom" u državama nastalim posle raspada Jugoslavije", „Intima javnosti", Fabrika knjiga, Beograd, 2008
[384]Hart, Christopher, (2005) Analysing Political Discourse: Toward a Cognitive Approach, Critical Discourse Studies 2 (2), University of Hertfordshire
[385]Petersen R. D. (2002), Understanding Ethnic Violence:Fear, Hatred and Resentment in Twentieh-Century Eastern Europe. Cambidge: Cambridge University Press

is very important. In such a case, when considering the "usability" of individual reference groups for political manipulation by instrumentalization of fear, it seems that ethnic and religious differences are the most appropriate basis for such an activity - especially when there is a history of ethnic and religious conflicts, which is the case of the Balkans, Northern Ireland, the Caucasus, in Rwanda, in the horn of Africa and other areas. What is most characteristic for the said Roger's lists is that they relate primarily to situations when among people there is no fear and it should be created (this list is reduced when there is such a fear, or the memory of it is sufficiently fresh in the collective memory). If memories are a bit repressed, then fear should be re-called, while the reference is much easier in situations where fear is encoded earlier. This can be achieved when political discourse includes reminders of former frightening situations called – triggers (initiators) in psychological sciences.

Political manipulation or political marketing using established recipes for the other two conditions from the Roger's list, and those are: to offer a solution to their fear. The solution is a political option that is offered to solve their fears and minimal effort that should be taken is to go to the elections and vote for the political party that has offered a solution to their fear. The creative part of the work in the political manipulation with fear is the one that consists of recognizing the fear of the voting population, the use of triggers to provoke previous fears, or linking to frightening situations with a specific reason or reasons. Registration and recognition of the existing fear among citizens is achieved by qualitative or quantitative research, or a combination of them. The next step involves the use of the media - and they serve for the abovementioned linking of the existing fear with a specific reason or for the use of the trigger to provoke previously experienced fear. Thus the emergence of economic crisis will be an opportunity to explore the existing fear of worsening the crisis, increasing the unemployment rate and thus worsening the economic situation of individuals or voters. Then the reason for this fear is connected with the party or parties in power, then, according to the model, the solution that will be offered in the political discourse is giving confidence to opposition parties. Some other emergency situations (such as acts of violence or natural disasters) can bind to the current rulers, and some others may be suitable for association with other past traumatic events and be used as psychological triggers. Exactly the acts of violence are the ones that can best be used to generate fear through political discourse and, in such cases, political manipulation or politicization, is most apparent. The threat to human security can lead to war, but also poverty, unemployment and other factors, including natural disasters. The entire analysis of the conditions specified by the Roger's list, application of research for political purposes, the use of the media, the use of psychological initiators and other political methods is applicable both in countries with a long democratic tradition, and in countries where democracy has not taken root, or does not exist at all.

After fear, the use of political discourse for causing resentment among the population, is also suitable for causing conflict. Resentment arises when people are convinced of the discourse which they receive that they are dominated by another group which they consider inferior, and that affects the weakening of their self-esteem and leads to attempts to change this relation of power (this is especially susceptible in "Political speaks" by the Nazi propagandist Joseph Goebbels). Along with bitterness develops the feeling of hatred, which is the product of a long history of mutual hostility and violence. In the scenario driven by hatered, both sides feel they have a lot to sanctificate, and also expect the other group to commit new atrocities against them, as soon as there is a possibility for it. Finally, there is a fourth factor for creating preconditions for conflict, and it is anger, which is uncontrolled and, in essence, is a self-destructive emotion that leads to the fulfillment of any wish. The bitterness, hatred and anger are intermediary emotions so as to encourage individuals to achieve comprehensive objectives: improving the status of the group, historical revenge and security.

Gagnon developed analysis of "the cost and the benefits" to explain how the ruling elites, in order to maintain power could trigger violent conflict along the line of ethnic separation. According to him, when in an undemocratic society the ruling elites face the rival elites who dispute and threaten their power, they are often inclined to take such political steps the cost for which is later paid by the entire society. They present themselves in political discourse as the only true defenders of ethnic interests and create political context in which ethnicity is the only relevant political identity. Thus, what began as an internal struggle for power is transformed into conflict with other groups. The stronger the opposite political elites, the greater the fear the rulers feel and the more inclined are they to increase the price of their survival in power. At the same time they create a conflict and tend for it to have minimal consequences for that part of the population that gives them the crucial political support. Therefore, the conflict is provoked outside the area where their voting base lives.[386] In this regard Hana Arent assesses that if such experiments are made by people who have at their disposal the means of violence, then the results are terrible, but not because the lie replaces the truth. To her, it always comes to the point after which lying gives the contradictory results. That point comes when the audience, to which the lies are directed, in order to survive is forced to completely dismiss the difference between lies and truth. The difference between truth and untruth is no longer important if a man's life depends on the fact that he should act as he believes in the lie; then the factual truth of which he can rely completely disappears from public life, and therefore the most important stabilizing factor in the constant change of human behavior".[387] Hence, Ferdinand Tonnies assesses public opinion in a country that is in a state of war as the belief that "war is imposed as a defensive war, or necessary war".[388] According to Michael Kunczik the enemy must be represented as an aggressor, a monster. He cites as an example the war in the Persian Gulf (1991) when it was most easily attained through the method of propaganda of terror, through which extreme and multi-layer violence against the opponeny and the respective country and people wa propagated[389]. To him also there is no doubt that the media have a crucial role in the promotion of manipulation and lies that lead to readiness of the voting base to follow the leader in the conflict which is yet to come.

---

[386]Gagnon, V. P. (1997), "Ethnic Nationalism and International Conflict: The Case of Serbia", u: Brown, M. E. et al. (ur.), Nationalism and Ethnic Conflict. Cambridge MA: MIT Press.
[387]Arent, Hana, "Istina i laž u politici", Filip Višnjić, Beograd, 1994
[388]Tonnies, Ferdinand: Critics of public opinion, Berlin, 1922
[389]Kunczik, Michael: Introduction in publicity and communications, Friedrich Ebert Stiftung, Skopje, 1998

Recontextualization of own crimes

Politicization and care for security are discursive strategies and among the theories of ethnic violence, solely the Copenhagen school directly deals with the issue of discourse. The problem with this approach is that it neglects the role of language in the origin of the conflict, but that it fails to answer why nationalist propaganda can be as effective tool in some circles, and in others not. There are cynical politicians who are eager to manipulate its population even at the price of starting an ethnic war in all communities, but only in certain situations they are able to achieve their goals. The reason that such manipulators in some countries are marginalized, and are at the top of state power in others must generally be required beyond the discourse itself. It points to something important - the analysis of discourse cannot function independently and in itself it does not provide a complete theory of violence, but can function as a key element for analysis in other theories. In a similar direction is the thinking of Kolstø, who emphasizes that the discourse itself, does not determine the direction of the conflict and, therefore, the analysis of discourse is not an alternative to any of the current theories, but only their supplement because it can fit in various theories of conflict and be the "missing part". In theories in which the political leadership is in the spotlight, the analysis can explain how the leadership manipulates people, in some other theories that are more concerned with the reaction of the citizens as a whole, it can explain how the need to find security and support from the other members of their community is created among human.[390] Vetlesen approaches the problem of ethnic violence from a completely different angle. As a moral philosopher, he wants to understand why and how groups of people intentionally cause pain and suffering of other human beings, against their will, and thereby inflict very serious and predictable damage. In other words, why do they commit those crimes? Both paradigmatic cases of collective crimes in modern European history on which he focused were the Holocaust and ethnic cleansing in Bosnia in 1992-95. According to Vetlesen, one of the darkest driving forces behind ethnic cleansing is the one that he named the "logic of the original assignment". There are two

---

[390] Kolstø, P. „Diskurs i nasilni sukob: predstave o „sebi" i „drugom" u državama nastalim posle raspada Jugoslavije", „Intima javnosti", Fabrika knjiga, Beograd, 2008

sides of this logic: on the one hand, each individual is reduced to a "group member" and, on the other hand, each member of the group is responsible for all the acts committed by all other members of the group, not only in the present but also in the distant past. Hence, for example, the murder of five-year-Muslim child cannot just be justified by alleged Muslim crimes against Serbs hundred of years before.[391] However, when "enemies" are people who one knows and lives with them for years, such reductionism is not an easy task and presupposes the existence of significant preparatory ideological activities. To be convinced that their neighbors really belong to the enemy group that endangers, future criminals must be exposed to a political discourse with elements of systematic propaganda which, as we have seen, must include fear, resentment, anger and hatred. The history must be mythologized and individuals must be placed in a mold. To Vetlesen, verbal war precedes the physical war and it must produce an atmosphere filled with fear, hatred, distrust, contempt and so on against groups singled out for destruction and such verbal war must be created through a number of articles, books, speeches and talks. Such should be the dominance of the political discourse of the elite. Creating such an atmosphere is a necessary condition for the crimes that should follow[392]. In assessing the aforementioned theories, Kolstø first underscores the degree of focus on certain theorists on the structure of discourse, its significance for encouraging or preventing violence. So for example, Posen's "objective circumstances" leading to the acceptance of the sense of threat among individuals are not as "objective" if applied to individuals who have a positive experience of living near members of other nations and therefore need to be included in different discursive strategies (selection, interpretation, articulation) which will ensure acceptance of supposedly objective historical facts. Even in Gagnon's theory, there is no discussion on the "objective" situation of ethnic groups. Whether a group is really jeopardized or ,is in a way irrelevant to him, because the aspiration of conflict does not come from the broad masses, but from the leader, the elite. Same as Posen, Gagnon also deals with "perceptions of security," but

---

[391] Vetlesen, A. J. (2005), Evil and Human Agency: Understanding Collective Evildoing. Cambridge: Cambridge Uiversity Press.
[392] Ibid

from a completely different type: it is the perception of the elite that feels threatened by the other elite.[393]

Another aspect of the role of the political discourse in creating a conflict will be the possible relation between the context and text when the political situation changes from violent in nonviolent (or when mass violence becomes limited violence). Kolstø believes that violent conflicts can affect perception and discourse in such a way that following the cessation of hostilities, the situation cannot return to the situation before the outbreak of the war. On the one hand, institutional changes have happened: new frontiers, change of residence and citizenship, new media, new curricula in schools and so on. Whatt is least obvious, the experience of the war, the suffering inflicted on people with rough acts, but also with human deeds and heroism, are woven into the collective memory and can be read in the new ruling discourse.[394] The emergence of recontextualization in the representation of social events will become an active element of the new political discourse. The events of the past will be interpreted in a way that is acceptable to their own country, but provocative to the opposite. Members of society in their mental condition will regress again, the similar from before the conflict, except that there will be no violence and armed conflict - or it would be controlled incident and isolated. Although the conflict will be stopped, the new situation, very often, will not be accepted by the other side - those considered heroes by one party may be criminals to the other and vice versa. This unhealthy situation in the post-conflict society can lead to hidden tension that by simmering can easily trigger a new conflict initiated by a new militant discourse of political leaders, because in a post-conflict society, in parallel with the process of reconciliation and new realities among ethnic communities a collective bipartial consciousness of 'us and them' will be created . In his empirical research of the processes of recontextualization in post-conflict society and relativism of their crimes Wodak *analyzed the visitors - Germans* – at an exhibition of the German "Wehrmacht" on the strategies they have used to

---

[393] Gagnon, V. P. (1997), "Ethnic Nationalism and International Conflict: The Case of Serbia", u: Brown, M. E. et al. (ur.), Nationalism and Ethnic Conflict. Cambridge MA: MIT Press.
[394] Kolstø, P. „Diskurs i nasilni sukob: predstave o „sebi" i „drugom" u državama nastalim posle raspada Jugoslavije", „Intima javnosti", Fabrika knjiga, Beograd, 2008

justify the war crimes committed by German soldiers. She noted that they did it through: a) denial that there were war crimes, b) denial of the context itself (refusal to deal with the issue, claiming that they had no information or were themselves, in some way, victims), c) through the use of scientific rationalization, d) creation of "positive self-presentations" e) attempts to understand, f) justification or denial of war crimes: relativeness ("every war is terrible"), giving the (pseudo) rational informal explanation ("others forced us to it"), it is the military's fault ("I just served my duty"), recognition of the crimes, but transferring responsibility to other units.[395]

It is obvious from what has been stated that the application of political discourse is essential in the preparation of conflicts. It is made clear that it does not participate in decision-making but it is vital that such a decision should be effected among the population and start the preparing of the citizens for what is ahead. The same principle applies to the role of political discourse in the process of reconciliation and overcoming the conflict. The decision on truce/peace is brought out of the public political discourse, but only with its application can the process of post-conflict pacifization of society initiate.

4. LANGUAGE MANIPULATION IN POLITICAL DISCOURSE

It is commonly accepted that the strategy which a group of people uses (without the use of coercive and repressive means) to make another group of people act according to their interest known as linguistic strategy and it involves manipulation application of language. Theorists would define "linguistic manipulation" as conscious use of language on the sly way to control others.[396] It can be considered an influential political instrument of political rhetorics, because political discourse is primarily focused on provoking people take specific political activities or to make important policy decisions. Or, as Atkinson points out, linguistic manipulation is different feature of political rhetorics and it is based on the

---

[395] Wodak, R. (2006). History in the making/The making of history. Journal of Language and Politics, 5,
[396] Fairclough, Norman. Language and Power. London: Longman, 1989, p. 6

idea of persuading people, i.e. convinces people to take political activities or support a party or an individual.[397]

To convince a potential electorate, the policy must dominate the mass media, leading to the creation of new forms of linguistic manipulation, that creates such language that could easily be adopted by the mass media and without great effort be remembered the target audience (for example: modified forms of press conferences and press statements, modernized texts with slogans, input of striking phrases phrasal allusions, connotative meaning of words, the combination of language and visual metaphors). It is clear that language plays an important ideological role because it is an instrument with which assets manipulative intentions of politicians are becoming a reality. For that reason politicians are constantly interested in using the language and, therefore, they hold speeches, address the electorate in the newspapers or in other words, regimes, whether democratic or totalitarian, must communicate with the population in order to maintain their power. That relationship is one-way and in order for the person to whom it is addressed to understand the political discourse, he must have a political background knowledge which will allow him to understand the text and context of the situation, and be adept at decoding the foreign language: his style, the use of stylistic figures as metaphors metonymies, allegories, allusions and others. In a word, knowing all this presumes that the fact or contextual situation of the message sent by the politician to the audience will successfully be understood.

Accordingly, the purpose of political discourse varies and it can be:
- to persuade the followers to be loyal to the party and to appear on the ballot;
- to win the loyalty of the party undecided;
- to convince people to accept the general political and social attitudes in order to attract them to support the existing policy.

Given that the purpose of this research is the analysis of political discourse in the Macedonian media, with an emphasis on the eventual existence of hate speech towards Bulgaria, it is possible to meet the

---

[397] Atkinson, Max. Our Master's Voices. The Language and Body Language of Politics. London: Methuen,1984

selected media articles and manipulative language, which undoubtedly will have to be identified as an element of political discourse. The area of research will be very wide: from the description of the linguistic approaches used to influence the thoughts and emotions of the audience, to analyzing the rhetorical instruments used for creating persuasive and manipulative political discourse. The two main courses in the identification of such manipulative language will be determining (1) advertising and (2) misonformation elements in the text. Therefore, in the following we will focus on theoretical consideration of the principles, techniques and methods by which you can determine their presence in the selected media articles on research.

Propaganda techniques

The art of using language, symbols and other means of communication means are treated as a special power that, in history, has too often been abused by individuals or elite parts of society. Even just a superficial review of the historical process reveals to which extent the propaganda as a means to manage or to achieve certain goals, is gives meaning. From the Egyptian Pharaohs, through the Mayan culture, the medieval Catholic Church, until the Nazi Third Reich and contemporary Western democratic societies, propaganda appears as a powerful ally and a valuable asset in winning followers or sending messages about the power and size of the rulers, dictators or special interest groups. The so-called Four military ruses as a concept or principle were known as early as ancient Greece. In ancient Rome, Cicero mainly agreed with Aristotle's advocacy of conviction. Being famous for its attorney sermons used in defense of very notorious thugs and murderers, Cicero established his own ideas about the duty of the Orator named officia oratoris, in which he presented the main characteristics that an Orator must possess: charm (which establishes the credibility of the speaker), message (presenting the message together with sound arguments that lead the recipient to any cognition) and movement i.e. mobility (fill the audience with emotions)[398]. According to these basic settings, as explained by Darko Tadic a successful

---

[398] Tadic, Darko, Propaganda, , YU Spektrum, Beograd, 2005

propangandist can use many tactics to achieve the effects that are able to lead the target group to think positively about any issue. However, the maximum impact can be achieved in most cases even after you meet the four key conditions, namely: with good control of the situation and establishing the desired environment for presentation of the message through a process called "setting the propaganda scene". Second, the communicant must establish for themselves an image of credibility, which would be easily acceptable in the eyes of the public opinion. He should look likeable, authoritatively, as someone who can be trusted. Third, constituting and broadcasting a message that directs attention and consideration towards the target exactly on what the communicator wants. The ruse in the application of these procedures consists in the method of constructing the message, not only in its content. The message in these cases is "packed" together with elements of humor, pictorial metaphors, relevant comparison, adding some distinctive and desirable attributes to the theme of propaganda. Fourth, the effective impact of propaganda must control the emotions of the target group, using the simple rule - causing some emotion, then the target group is offered a response so that the emotion leads to the desired course of action. Whether it is a skilful use of words, visual symbols, music or their combination, once induced positive or negative emotions are always very efficient.

Besides these military ruses that are fundamental to creating an environment for propaganda, there is another important factor which is the basis for propaganda communication, and it is human trait that often colloquially call "lightmindedness" and, for the purpose of exploring propaganda communication, was first clearly defined the researchers Cacciopo and Petty in a research dedicated to building and changing human attitudes.[399] Namely, in propaganda practice it happens very often people to fall on amazing claims that are apparently false information, regardless that they can verify from other sources or with common sense. Also, it is confirmed in practice that people are absolutely able to with incredible ease and innocence firmly believe and accept completely inaccurate, illogical and contradictory claims which even go against their interests.

---

[399]Petty, R. E, and Cacciopo, J.T.: "Communication and persuasion: Central and peripheral routes to attitude change", Springer Verlag, New York, 1986

The other type of propaganda technique is probably the oldest and most applied technique in propaganda communication, known as word game - giving names. This technique consists of giving mainly "bad names", which connects people, things or ideas with the negative sense of the use of the appropriate symbols. This name giving can be realized in different forms and is usually carried out so that the subject of propaganda is attributed bad pejorative properties. Persons or ideas are usually exposed to insult or ridicule, in the context that does not necessarily have to do with the actual subject of the discussion. So people often are given negative names and even nicknames, such as "pig", "communists", "fascist", "deceiver", "fool", etc. Also frequent is the case when a person or object in propaganda are connected with appropriate stereotypes, myths and bad examples from history and the collective memory of certain nations. This group of word games also includes sophisticated words or phrases which carry negative emotional charge, referring to some kind of treatment or operation. These word games are very important in the propaganda campaigns because while creating the message great importance is attached to the selection of "key words" that will be contained in the propaganda message. The correct choice will provide that the recipient clearly and correctly understands the propaganda message.

Unlike the previous technique in which by giving names a person or object is brought in a negative context, the glaring generalizations are the opposite. The purpose of this technique is not to lead men to refuse or reject the objects of propaganda, but to indicate a positive attitude, approval and acceptance of the propaganda themes and messages. This technique uses different types of generalizations, stereotypes and generally accepted claims and moral premises in which, by definition, is not supposed to be suspect (Christianity, family morals, good, patriotism, homeland - classic examples of these dazzlingglaring generalizations that are usually not questioned). The essence of this technique is to make the public accept the propaganda claims disguised in brilliant generalizations, as a done deal without verification.

The technique of transfer, represents a transfer of meaning of one thing over another according to the desire of propangandists. This technique uses a kind of figurative meaning given to individuals or objects that do not have or do not naturally belong to such meanings. For example, when a politician has an appearance before the media or large political gatherings, mandatory decor in the background is the national flag. It has a clear objective for the significance of the nation, patriotism and the aura of the state authority to be transferred to a speaker who performs in front of it. Similarly, the cross symbols in religious ceremonies, then wearing appropriate uniforms, etc. This technique is quite effective because the expert use of symbols, mostly passes unnoticed, and the audience has a positive perception, given that usually it has generally accepted meanings which are not brought into doubt.

The testimony is one of the most popular advertising techniques. The essence of this technique is to ensure the source of information proper credibility, which can be a person or an institution of great trust. Testimony is usually implemented so that the communicant appears directly in communicating the message in a propaganda in the capacity of an expert or a favorite or popular person in the public (athlete, pop star, actor...) or is implemented in the form of listed or quoted statement and testimony of a credible source in a promotional context ("That institute said...", "The President of the Republic said...").

Application of the propaganda technique of mixing cards or exploitation of logical errors is based on the (ab)use of two basic things: ignorance of the basic facts about a propaganda theme that is general ignorance of the audience that does not posses adequate information about someone or something. This technique is also based on the propensity of thepublic opinion to quickly forget the presented facts and to make no effort to verify them from other sources. The essence of this technique is setting certain premises or claims during the propaganda communication, and then making intentional wrong logical conclusions. These premises may be deliberately inaccurately designed or partially correct, or simply torn out of their original context. The result is seemingly concluding properly based on the ratio of established claims, but, in fact, the final result is false logic as set allegations are designed to produce a result important for the propaganda purposes. In an experimental form, here is how it works:

a. All Christians believe in God;

b. All Muslims also believe in God;

c. Logical conclusion: all Christians are Muslims.

The first two premises are undeniably correct, but exactly because of that the (not) logical conclusion is also logically correct, but not true. Another, less radical example:

a. The politician X supports the legalization of weapons;

b. All fascist regimes in the 20th century supported the legalization of weapons;

c. Conclusion is that politician X is a fascist.

Manipulation of meanings that are torn out of their original context, quoting the generally known claims and their packing in brand new concepts, at first glance, always, seems perfectly logical and convincing.

Another possible use of the wrong logic is the technique of extrapolation, that is wrong prediction based on bad premises, that is inaccurate facts. This method of predicting incorrectly is a common process, especially when based on small or insufficient number of available elements based on which the propaganda wants to predict what events will follow in future. This propaganda technique is often used to address various utopian ideas or patterns of behavior, for which is enough to determine a few starting points that are connected in a logical order. An example is the behavior of a driver on a road while driving, at a short distance he passes several gas stations and concludes that the continuation of the journey there will be many new opportunities to refuel, although the next station may be only at the end of his trip or ever gone. This technique is especially used in political appearances, when based on general claims about the nature and quality of a nation grandiose ideas for a ideas for better future are presented.

The technique traveling orchestra or "join the majority" is a mechanism by which the individual is imposed a desired form of behavior that is characteristic of the group to which the individual aligns to avoid discomfort. Also, the incentive to accede to the majority may be the ability to gain some benefit from this form of behavior. Characteristic to this technique is the existence of a propaganda message or appeal which exploits already established group norms such as prejudices, values, attitudes, behavior patterns and emotions of the group being addressed. Basic psychological theme of this technique is "all others are doing this, so should you" and because of that it is based on mass. An example of application of this propaganda technique is massively visited grandiose party rallies during the Third Reich, most often organized in Nuremberg, where the pompous spectacle strengthened the unity of the present and performed the ideological indoctrination of the population by the fiery speeches of Hitler, Goebbels and other Nazi officials.

The special technique of appeal to fear is used by politicians in order to convince voters to vote for them as well as to avoid political and economic catastrophe of the country. Sometimes these appeals to fear can be based on legitimate grounds, but more frequently they are based on dark, irrational fears, whose roots are in different ideological prejudices or misconceptions. When using these illegitimate fears, the message promotes fraud, not to mention the brutality of the use of fear itself. For this propaganda technique to be used effectively it is not enough just to exist a topic that causes fear in people, but a very important factor is the way it shapes the message that contains an appeal to fear. To be effective this technique must meet four conditions: 1. Must have high intensity, 2. Must offer specific recommendation for overcoming the fear contained in a threat, 3. The recommended action must be understood as an effective method of overcoming fear, 4. The individual over which the propaganda is performed must be convinced that it is able to take the recommended action.

The use of emotions, is also characteristic of the propaganda technique attractive emotions - provocative baits, based on effectively attracting attention with unusual coloring of the real situation with attractive slogans, bouncing from the standard life situations, using provocative humor, fantasy or distorting the situation with unusual contrasts, which are not usually seen everyday. Such vivid propaganda appeals are usually personified in the message that is comprised of the following elements:

a. The message is always emotionally interesting and strongly attracts the attention and emotions of the audience,

b. It contains specific and imaginative provocations,

c. It is always immediate and personalized.

The essence of the technique of repeating are the large number of repetitions of the message over time to create a kind of knowledge in the audience, positive bias or preference to any idea. Although the knowledge of a political idea does not mean automatically more votes in the elections for the politician who promoted the idea, however, the notion of adequate knowledge and a positive reaction of the recipient have a pretty strong bond. The effects of this propaganda technique are not immediate and it is difficult to measure them precisely, but the power that derives from the repetition is not negligible.

Rumors, speculation and unverified speculations are examples of special type of communication, which is well known in the theory of propaganda and called "spreading false news" or psychology of factoids. In propaganda factoids are defined as claims or facts that are not supported by evidence, usually because the facts are false or simply cannot be checked. Also factoids are mainly displayed in such a light to become widely treated as truth, and the audience accepts them because it is prone to uncritically swallowing the factoids. In the media they are frequently met under the formulation "from well informed sources", "interlocutor, who wanted to remain anonymous" or "from the opposing camp leaked the information". One of the very dangerous forms of factoids may be false accusation, which is based on a tactics of designing constructed accusations that someone did something that actually we have done or we intend to do. History is full of such examples. Hitler regularly accused the leaders of foreign countries that they plan conspiracy and aggression against Germany, although, in fact, he was the one. who led the military campaign against other countries. Finally and most importantly, factoids are used to prepare the stage for propaganda activities, so that with its influence they create a certain social climate.

Methods of misinforming

The last section we will examine what are the tricks and what are the possible linguistic tricks with information. More simply, it can be said that one fact can be presented in "seven" different ways:[400]

- Denying the fact used when the public opinion has no way to check what really happened. However, when it is difficult to deny a fact because it is so obvious and the audience is familiar with it (for example, it is difficult to completely deny the atrocities of Pol Pot in Cambodia), the expert in misinforming instead of negation of the facts will resort to the following:
- Twisting the facts: This method is known as misinformation in which the victim is represented as a criminal and the criminal is presented as the victim. An example is the propaganda of Goebbels, in which the German people is presented as a victim of the Jews, and the Jews as a threat to the survival of the German people. Still, nowadays, manipulators seldom resort to so extreme methods such as twisting the facts. They are increasingly using the following methods:
- A mixture of truth and lies: whenever you assume that the public is, more or less, familiar with the event, it is familiar with the facts and that it would be inappropriate to imposes a 100 percent lie, truth and lies can skillfully be mixed. For example, in the civil war in Yugoslavia, all the warring parties did not deny that they made war crimes but also always relativized their blame with the fact that the opponent attacked them first while they were defending and in that defense it is possible to make crimes.[401]

---

[400] Волков, Владимир, „Од тројанског коња до интернета", Наш Дом, 2005, Београд, (Vladimir Volkoff, Petite historie de la désinformation, Editions du Rocher, Paris, 1998).

[401] As Vladimir Volkov writes, it should be noted that the term attack (aggression) can be extremely unclear. Germany in the Second World War looked as an aggressor to the allies. However, savage and humiliating provisions of the Treaty of Versailles created a sense among Germans that Germany was the first victim of aggression. It responded: the Treaty of Versailles was so strict only because Germany was the aggressor in the First World War. And Germany will answer that it is not it who killed the Austrian Archduke Ferdinand in Sarajevo. And the Serbs will answer that before that Austria wanted to colonize Serbia...

- Change of motives: This method means relativizing the motives for the crime, even their justification. Such examples are many in history: England as a colonizing power, has made several gruesome slaughter of Africans, but at the time, the colonizing policy was justified by being motivated to civilize people, teach them to enjoy the advantages of urban convenience and that it brings benefits and wellbeing. The similar happened in the USA when many Indian tribes were displaced and killed under the pretext that industrialization is implemented and a railway is being built from which they will benefit. It is clear that the aggressor wants to convince the victims are justified because of general and their own good with simplification.
- Change of circumstances refers to the strength of the opposing sides in which the aggressor falsely reduces his strength, and the victim increases his, so there would be an excuse for aggression. In its military interventions, USA rather use this method so that for the Iraqi army it was claimed that it was the fourth army in the world that possess nuclear weapons, for in the end, the army to be destroyed in just a few weeks, and nuclear weapons was not found. Similar overdimensioning of the real military is now created with regard to Iran, Syria and North Korea.
- The process of shading (mitigation) consists of diluting, dimmer and melting of the existing fact with other facts that have no connection with it and which, if possible, are more convenient to arouse interest among the audience. Thus, if a president produced some scandal or folly, this fact is suppressed in the second plan with a campaign that he is ready for honest, moral and democratic elections. An example is the scandal of Bill Clinton with Monica Lewinsky which was suppressed with the beginning of the military campaign against Yugoslavia, in which the media image of Clinton as a promiscuous husband and gullible man was changed in a protector of democracy and fighter against dictatorial regimes.
- Camouflage is a variant of darkening or shading, in which the atrocities of the opponent are highlighted, and the own are camouflaged. A similar technique was used by the USA during the invasion of Panama: cruel actions of President Noriega were

emphasized in order to suppress the fact that Americans, without any declaration of war, invaded an independent state and killed nearly 7,000 people. This was repeated with the bombing of Yugoslavia by NATO, with a campaign which had no legitimacy provided by the United Nations for intervention in a sovereign state - a fact that was suppressed by the news of the humanitarian refugee crisis in Kosovo.

- Interpretation: facts that are not subject to negation, change, darkening, concealing or camouflaging can be presented and commented on the favorable or unfavorable way. "Logomachia" (battle of words) specifically allows to ignite and cause positive or negative emotions depending on the preference. it can impose a whole range of accusation for a violator, in order to present him as cruel man, but he could also defend by presenting himself as an impulsive person or as mild and good person who had acted violently in self-defense, but after the violent act he reconcealed with the attacked person etc. The informant who occupied a position on a particular situation or event, will quite naturally try to prove that he is right, declaring only those events that confirm his view. This way, he bursts into auto-misinforming, even when it is no bad faith or intent for it.
- Generalization is one of the procedures which allows to reduce the responsibility of the abuser and it tends to show that he is not alone in this act, that there are many others who act the same way or that in certain situations it is considered necessary. For example, in a civil war one side is forgiven the atrocities ("It is sad, but it has always happened"), while simultaneously condemning those on the other side and presenting them as something that is gone out of it (the principle of bad guys and good guys).
- Illustration: with this method vandalism and looting are justified in the event of a political manifestation. In particular violence is relativized with the words "All these outbursts are just banal example of what could easily happen in such circumstances ... In fact, it could be worse ... It is ust shops being robbed and cars being burned ... No one is killed or ... just one man died".

- Unequal representation: allegations about the opponent will be announced very shortly after one minute in the TV news on a small area at the bottom of the paper, and praise for their preferred politician will take an hour on radio or television or will be published on a full page of magazine. Such inequality sometimes go up to 100 percent. For example, in general we have not seen that the press published anything on the position of President Noriega in the US-Panamanian conflict. Although the opposing side is given less space compared to the favored, it would still be present to create a fictitious impression that the argument is impartial. Let's uppose a newspaper publishes letters from readers: hundreds of letters can be received in favor of the opposing party, and only one will be published, and if ten are received for the favored party then all will be published.
- Equal representation: This procedure is used especially in the last phase of the operation misinformation when public opinion has already attracted and has a favorable reaction to the thesis of the misinformator and when it comes to achieving quasi equity because it plays with the card "herd instinct" (reaction of a member of the herd, most often the leader, usually causes an identical reaction to all other members of the herd). If in the previous procedure of unequal representation most important was quantity of published messages, here it is tight but more important is the quality of the content of the published text. Let's take a newspaper as an example: with the intention to be "objective", he will devote the same space for both sides, even the same number of rows. But for the opposing party it will publish worst written accusations, with worst arguments, to present it to the audience as completely antipathic person. On the other hand, as an alleged counterweight, it will publish letters with the most convincing defense for the favored politician.

5. NONVERBAL ASPECTS OF HATE SPEECH

If we agree with the subjective assessment of the American author Bruce Walker to whom man as homo politicus is a monstrous transformation of the homo sapiens in Frankenstein homo politikus[402] a consequential question would be whether the man as a political being, represents something positive. And the assessment of George Orwell, given 60 years ago that "today everything is politics" raises doubt. As he understood the times in which he lived, for him there was not a thing that was out of politics. "All issues are political issues, and politics itself is a set of lies, excuses, nonsense, hatred and schizophrenia" (Orwell). As correct as these obscure evaluations of the politics are, and as much as we agree that it is comprised of immoral things, from which most ordinary people are disguisted, however, unavoidable is the fact that the profession politician is one of the most attractive social professions. Therefore, in achieving this goal - to win power and to stay at the throne at any price - the contenders, often do not choose the means. Oratorical skills, good posture, style with which body language is practiced are just some of the legitimate means. We would not discuss the illegitimate (it is enough to recall that politics is compared with the oldest craft).

Gestures and nonverbal communication are an integral and important part of any political discourse and as such studied through the ages from different perspectives. The importance of the movements of the body for persuasive discourse is emphasized even in ancient rhetoric, and the examination of the gestures originates from ancient Rome. During the Roman Empire, Quantilian studied in his institution "Oratorio" how gestures can be used in rhetorical discourse. Cicero pointed out in "The Orator" (De Oratore) how gestures, face, eyes and posture are an important part of the activity (making a speech). Because of their ability of calling, promising, coercion, inducement, banning, approval and showing emotions, demonstrating fears, marking objects of the thought of the orator gestures were especially studied.

Another thorough study of nonverbal communication was published by John Bulwer in 1644 in which he analyzed a dozen gestures and provided a guide on how to use gestures to increase eloquency and clarity of public speaking. Andrea De Giorio published an extensive set of gesture expressions in 1832 and Charles Darwin, the author of "On the Origin of

---

[402] Walker, Bruce, Homo politicus, June 5, 2010, http://www.americanthinker.com/2010/06/homo_politicus.html

Species" published the first serious scientific study "The Expressions of the Emotions in Mans and Animals" in 1872. Common to all studies is the view that the gesture is a form of nonverbal communication in which visible bodily actions speak certain messages, in some cases replacing speech, in others, going along with the speech and parallel to the said word. Gestures include movement of the hands, face or other parts of the body, allowing the individual to communicate with many feelings and expresses thoughts from contempt and hostility to approval and affection, indicate aggression, attentiveness, boredom, relaxed state, pleasure and excitement.

Categorization of gestures

James Borg says that human communication consists of 93% body language and paralinguistic signals, while only 7% of communication consists of words. However, Albert Mehrabian whose work from the 1960s is the source of these statistics, said that it is a misinterpretation of the findings. Others argue that "studies suggest that between 60 and 70% of all meanings come from non-verbal behavior".

Although the study of gestures is still at the beginning, some broad categories of gestures have been identified by researchers. Several writers have tried to categorize gestures. Michael Argyle proposed five different functions that gestures can carry out, such as: − illustrations and other signals related to speech; - conventional signs and sign languages; - movements that can express emotions; - movements that express personality; - and movements used in various religious and other rituals. Paul Ekman and Wallace Freisen, also, consider that there are five groups, but categories are different: "emblems" (movements that replace words); "Illustrators" (movements that follow the speech); "regulators" (movements that maintain or signal a change in the role of the speaker or listener); "adapters" (movements such as scrubing head or rubbing hands or playing with an object that can indicate the emotional state of that person); and "indicators of affection" (movements that more directly express emotions like facial expressions). However categorized gestures can express a whole range of attitudes, emotions and other messages. Argyle gives many conventional gestures that have almost universal meaning (applause −

approval, yawns - boredom, patting on the back -encouragement). Gerald Nierenberg and Henry Callero suggest that gestures are used to express openness, defense reassurances, frustration, confidence, nervousness, acceptance, expectation, doubt. They suggest that gestures occur even when the other person is not present, or not seen, as when we use the phone or cassettes. In general, nouns and verbs can more easily be translated into gestures than adjectives, adverbs and other words. Gestures are probably most useful in the manifestation of attitudes and emotions, which is true for other aspects of body language.[403]

Hate speech through nonverbal communication

Although today there are many works on nonverbal communication, unfortunately, only a small number of them successfully merge the description of verbal and nonverbal behavior within the discourse analysis. We will not be interested in entering into detailed description and analysis of nonverbal communication in discourse analysis, but we will focus on one aspect - the possibility to express hate speech through nonverbal communication in public and political discourse. Most people agree that articulated body language in function of support to the political discourse began with "The Great Debate" - the first aired TV debate between the then presidential candidates Kennedy and Nixon in 1960.[404]

The interlocutors who do not know the language of the other, can through nonverbal communication exchange information and opinion, among other things, on their political views. It is important for both of them to have the knowledge to properly interpret and decode messages sent through such body language. This means that non-verbal communication must be universal, generally intelligible and transmit identical message in different cultures and social strata.[405] Translated in the area of our interest that would mean, in a situation where we have an international meeting or parade of neo-Nazis, for example, on the streets of Berlin, many of the

---

[403] Веинрајт, Гордон Р., Говорот на телото, практичен прирачник, (Body Language, Gordon R. Wainwright), Силсон 2002, Скопје
[404] Body Language in Politics By Pam Andes Campaign 2008 Professor Moran
[405] Savić, Svenka: Diskurs analiza, Filozofski fakultet, 1993, Novi Sad

foreign participants, although not speaking German with the typical sideways lifting of the the right arm in the air, will clearly will be able to express their political stance. And even if their procession passes beside a synagogue, Jewish, Roma or immigrant neighborhood, such Nazi gesture would represent a clearly articulated speech of hatred on ethnic or racial basis with nonverbal means. Or if a group of Christian worshipers are shown a clenched fist with straight index and little finger, which symbolizes the head of a devil with horns, it would represent a hate speech on religious grounds by nonverbal means. Another case could be the so called "Love parades" on which homosexuals publicly manifest their sexual choices. Such events, in more conservative Balkan areas, are always followed by counter-protests, in which Protestants who are "Strait" show a clenched fist with the middle finger straight, which symbolized the phallus, which in the given context is offensive connotation for homosexuals, that is represents hate speech on sexual base with nonverbal means. Also, hate speech can also be expressed by indirect support to groups that explicitly manifest hate speech with gestures. It is not necessary to always identically support neo-Nazis by greeting with the characteristic greeting, but with an extremely positive gesture - clenched fist, with thumb raise, which universally means acknowledgment, support, OK, in this context would have a negative meaning of gestural support of the nonverbal manifestation of hate speech on ethnic or other grounds.[406] A good example of gesture expression of hate speech was spotted at a football match in the United Kingdom in which a fan provoked a black player with movements of his hands that are characteristic of the monkey (Figure 1).[407]

---

[406] The Californian psychologist Paul Ekman (1987) was interested in studying these universal gestures, which are identically understood anywhere in the world.
[407] http://www.b92.net/sport/fudbal/vesti.php?yyyy=2012&mm=11&dd=01&nav_id=656766

Figure 1

Another good example is when the Croatian football hooligans group created Swastika with their bodies (Figure 2)[408]

Figure 2

---
[408] http://www.thesun.co.uk/sol/homepage/sport/football/66475/Nazty-Croats-form-swastika.html

Also interesting phenomenon is "gesture echo". In a group of people talking, when one person uses a gesture, others will do it a little later. The gesture echo can be a useful way of indicating the general sense of identity or sympathy with the group. Thus, in a religious rite, while the priest reads the prayer, at a certain part of the text he begins to make the sign ofcross, which as a gestural echo, reflects on the present believers who also begin to make the sign of cross. Or, a leader of the cheeing group of bullies, first begins with a gesture to insult the opponents (for example: an upright fist as a symbol of physical threat), which is then accepted by the other members of the group. In order to have a gestural echo, the group must have a clearly defined leader who will initiate the sign and will have sufficient authority for his sign to be accepted by the other members of the group as a gesture echo.

The gesture, or its echo, must be understood in the context in which they are manifested. Desmond Morris studied gestures with his research team from "Oxford" in 1979 and their findings indicated the importance of knowing the context in which a gesture is used before you try to interpret its meaning. Therefore, when using a gesture, we need to evaluate the context to ensure that the gesture suits. A single emblematic gesture can have different importance in different cultural contexts, from compliment to insult. For example, the gesture ring (joined thumb and index finger in the shape of circle – note – auth.) is interpreted differently in different cultures: in the USA is all correct, approval, which is accepted in most of Europe. In France it means "zero" or "nothing" in Japan it can mean "money" and in some Mediterranean countries it is an offensive gesture is used to denote "homosexuality".[409] In order to properly understand this gesture, one must know the culture of the environment in which it is used. As we have seen, the Nazi salute in a specific context can be a nonverbal expression of hate speech, but in another case, as was observed by the tabloids a few years ago, when Britain's Prince Harry was photographed in Nazi uniform, greeting with a Nazi salute it was interpreted as a comic, even cute photograph because the context in which the event occurred was a private party and carnival inherent in his growing years.

---

[409] Пис, Алан, „Говор на телото – Како да ги читате мислите на другите преку нивните гестови" (2009), Јазично студио Арт, Скопје (Body language-How to read others' thoughts by their gestures, Allan Pease, 1981)

Therefore, we should remember that all gestures should be taken and understood in the context in which they occur and which is determined either from discourse or social context that preceded such gestural activity. Otherwise, the gesture will stay misunderstood or misinterpreted.

6. SYMBOLISM IN POLITICAL DISCOURSE

Although the symbolism as movement is immanently associated with visual art, literature and music, it is also present in many other social areas. What we are interested in - political discourse and hate speech can also be in connotation with symbols. Ivan Cholovikj, begins the preface to his book "Politics of Symbols" (Politika simbola), with the statement that politics is mostly a matter of symbols, and the government is actually rule over symbols.[410] Symbolism is present everywhere and its general definition refers to the symbolism in art, literature, politics, certainly adjusted to their specifics. The general definition would be that symbolism is a representation of things through symbols or representation of things with symbolic meaning or character.[411] In Oxford Student's Dictionary of Current English symbolism is defined as the use of objects, activities, etc., to represent feelings, ideas and more.[412] In visual art, symbolism is defined as the systematic use of symbols or pictorial graphic elements to express an allegorical meaning. Hence, the symbol is subject, action or idea that represents something other than what it is itself, usually with abstract meaning.[413]

In everyday life we encounter many symbols – letters, numbers, mathematical signs, to more complex things like symbols for the management of technical devices, illustrations on walls, which for someone represent understandable information in the form of graffiti, and for another abstract drawings. Except illustrative and graphicly represented symbols that most often appear in written and illustrative form there are materialized symbols that are tangible, three-dimensional. Such are the cross as a

---

[410] Čolović, Ivan, „Politika simbola",„XX vek", Beograd 2000
[411] http://dictionary.reference.com/browse/symbolism
[412] Oxford Student's dictionarys of Current English, Second Edition by Christine Ruse, Oxford University Press, 1988
[413] Simbolizam - Umetnost XIX veka, http://www.krcky.com/simbolizam/index.html

symbol of religious beliefs, flags showing identification with the state, emblems as clothes accessories that represente certain meaning (belonging to a football club, horoscope sign, humanitarian organization - the Red Cross and Red Crescent).

Political symbolism is symbolism used to represent political views and attitudes and it can appear in many different forms such as flag, acronym, picture, title, slogan and many other forms. Thus, the red flag is traditionally flown by the Socialist, the left oriented parties and the Communist groups and symbolizes the "blood of the workers". The black flag has always been associated with the anarchists and left oriented radicals to present opposition to any repressive structure. The combination of black and red color has symbolic meaning of socialist anarchism, such as anarchocommunists or anarchosindicates. Different groups use political colors to associate their political philosophy such as, dark blue is usually associated with conservative parties. Different colors, arranged in horizontal lines are inherent to the LGBT community, and the rainbow flag hanging in front of an object, usually a café, restaurant or club, symbolizes that the local is "friendly for this population".

Symbolism may also be mystcial, invisible or unclear to the ordinary people. Many buildings built in Baroque and Neoclassical style in Europe, are in a discreet way marked with figures such as compass and protractor, which to most people are either insignificant or obscure, but they represent a symbol of Freemasonry and send a signal to those who know how to decode the message that the architect or the builder of the building belonged to the brotherhood of free masons (Figure 2).

Figure 2

The Fascist and Nazi movement paid much attention to symbolism and it had an inevitable role in the propaganda purposes, and its public presentation caused the reactions from both supporters and members, and those who were persecuted by it. Starting from the greeting - obliquely upright hand to the symbols worn on uniforms. Thus, special units for the elimination of the Jews, known as "SS forces", wore dead heads, which clearly symbolized their role in the regime. In fascist Italy "Blackshirts" have been specially trained for violence against political opponents and black symbolized death. The universal symbol of Nazism was the Swastika, which symbolized the racial superiority of the Aryan race, although initially the swastika was used in ancient India with a completely different symbolic meaning. Although, due to the discrediting of the swastika by the Nazis, today its public presentation is banned, it still continues to be a symbol of the American National Socialist Party of white people, and the skinheads everywhere. The communist movement symbolized its ideology with the hammer and sickle which meant that the government is fused into the hands of farmers and workers.

Symbolism is particularly present in the film industry (very often seen in genres as a political drama and political thriller) which aims to send (mostly) a hidden political message. This was particularly exercised by cinematographers in repressive regimes where political issues were banned in the public discourse. Many old movies were influenced by symbolism of which its creators took metaphors. German expressionist films were heavily influenced by symbolism. The Greek director, with dissident biography, Costa Gavras, became famous filming political thrillers in which he faught the dictatorial regime in Greece, the Junta of Pinochet in Chile, and racists in the USA. Best known for his movie "Z", with the title of the film representing a symbol taken from the protesters against the Greek military Junta in the sixties. Namely, the letter Z meant "he lives" for the protesters and symbolically associated to the left oriented politician Grigoris Lambrakis who was killed by supporters of the Junta. Z meant that the spirit of Lambrakis is still alive through the resistance represented by theopponents of the military regime. On the West American anthropologist James Birsk is widely known for his lectures on "King Kong and the Symbolism". His point is that the fate of the world's most famous gorilla, King Kong, IS today shared by all the other gorillas, and the development of modern civilization is threatening to jeopardize the many other animal species, and even man himself. According to him, the death of King Kong is an announcement of the extermination of his kind, and a dire consequence of accelerated technological development. His presentations represent the way this film hit of the 30s is connected with Darwin's theory of evolution and Freud's study of consciousness.[414] A strong symbolic message can be found in the movie "Planet of the Monkeys". George Orwell, in particular, was a master of symbolism, primarily filmed in his literary work "Animal Farm" and "1984".

Symbolism has great importance in military conflicts, which was noted at the recent military conflict in former Yugoslavia. As noted by Mitja Velikonja, all three sides in the conflict in Bosnia used equally universal religious symbols (cross, crescent, green color, quotations from the Bible and Qur'an), as well as symbols that were "nationalized" as symbol of Serbian Orthodoxy "four S's" arranged around a cross, with the meaning "only harmony saves the Serb", the Croats combined the national symbol red and white checkerboard with the cross and Muslims very often wore green ribbons around the head with quotations from the Qur'an. According to the eternal military logic, the victory on the battlefield is complete only if the opponent is also symbolically defeated. Thus, in the war in Bosnia not only civilian objects were destroyed, but also sacred objects as mosques, churches, chapels, cemeteries.[415] According to some estimates over 1,000 mosques, 340 Orthodox and 450 Catholic churches were demolished.[416] As usually happened in history, this time also, the winning symbols were laid out on the ruins of the defeated. In other words, the territory had to also symbolicly be conquered, and the emblem of victory "founded" concludes Velikonja. Strong military symbolism can befound in the destruction of the Old Bridge in Mostar (under UNESCO protection) by the Croatian military forces. The symbolism of the bridge is connecting two coasts and connecting people, and its destruction in Mostar

---

[414]Studio B, 24.08.2012, „King Kong i simbolizam", http://www.studiob.rs/info/vest.php?id=79879
[415]Velikonja, Mitja, "In Hoc Signo Vinces: Vjerski simbolizam u Ratovima u Hrvatskoj i Bosni i Hercegovini 1991 1995", Sarajevske Sveske br. 05
[416]Powers, Gerald (1998): Religion, Conflict, and Prospects for Peace in Bosnia, Croatia and Yugoslavia; u: Paul Mojzes (ur.): Religion and the War in Bosnia; Scholar Press; Atlanta; str. 218-245

has sent the message that both parts of the city, home to Muslims and Croats, and symbolically separated. The need for symbolic defeat of the opponent is found in other wars. The best known such cases during the Second World War are when Hitler in 1940 asked the French General Pétain to sign the capitulation of France in the same carriage in which Germany had conceded defeat in the First World War. One of the most famous photographies of World War II are the Red Army soldier as it sets the red flag of the USSR at the top of Riehstag in Berlin (Figure 3), and the rise of mast with the American flag on the island of Iwo Jima (Figure 4), as a symbolic designation the victories over the Germans and Japanese. The demolition of the Berlin wall, is undoubtly, a symbolic bursting of the "Iron Curtain" and end the Cold War.

Figure 3   Figure 4

Except as part of the political discourse, symbolism can be seen in hate speech that is the hate message can be sent by symbolic means, without the language used in voice function we covered that part with the nonverbal communication). Thus, the most common form of symbolic reference to hatred is when Nazis draw a swastika on a synagogue. During the war in Bosnia, a very common case was the Serbs and Croats to mark mosques with a cross and Muslims Orthodox and Roman Catholic churches with crescent and Arabic phrases. There was an identical case on Orthodox sites in Kosovo and Macedonia by the Albanians. During the war conflict in Kosovo, the media saw a case with bakery for in Pristina which was selling bread with a cross on it which, apparently, was a symbolic provocation for the Albanian Muslim population. Other case observed in Bosnia was leaving a pig's head at the door of Muslim families. O the sports fields, the most common form of manifestation of hate speech through symbolic means is observed through the audience throwing a banana on the ground, with a clear intention to harm the player with black skin (the allusion is banana - monkey). Illustrative is the case with the black hockey player from Canada, Wayne Simmonds, about whom the media broadcasted the news that he was pelted with bananas by the fans of the opponent club from Ontario.[417] Such provocations are identified by sports associations and strictly punished.

Clearly, however inventive abusers with the intention to offend an opponent on racial, ethnic, sexual or other grounds are, sports organizations and the state should also be prepared to detect such attempts in order to be able to sanction them. The tendency is that at the sports playgrounds explicit reference of hate speech through words leaves more space to more creative, covered, ways.

7. STYLISTIC FIGURES IN THE POLITICAL DISCOURSE AND PROMOTION OF HATE SPEECH

Introduction

Very often in political discourse - verbal or written – we can encounter ambiguous expressions, figurative descriptions, overcapacity of reality, hidden information which can just be sensed or implicity in the spoken which not only stylishly enriches the entire speech and makes it attractive for listening and reading, but also causes greater conviction or additional attention in the recipient. For example, the author mentions an example or description which differs from the previous (monotonous) content of the text and causes increased attention to the one who had reads/hears. He achieves such attraction in the text with the use of various stylistic figures which apart from their aesthetic role can be in operation for

---

[417] B92, 30.10.2012, Hokej: Česi kažnjeni zbog rasizma
http://www.b92.net/sport/zimski/hokej.php?yyyy=2012&mm=10&dd=30&nav_id=656
386

more efficient understanding of the message. However, precisely because the stylistic figures are often ambiguous, implicit, overstate or hide some data in the text, only if properly understood they will fulfill their purpose; otherwise they will affect the partial or complete uselessness of the text by the person to whom it was intended.

Hate speech, which is looked at as a segment that follows the political discourse, can also be realized through a stylistic figure or include a stylistic figure as an integral entity in its structure. That link between hate speech and stylistic figures has a specificity. Although hate speech is defined as a negative phenomenon in legal sciences, linguistically speaking, the use of stylistic figures can make it have a certain literary and aesthetic values. In terms of style it must always have a negative value because it does not deal with the effects it has in the disruption of the social order, but the content and the way the message was presented to the audience. Only with such an isolated use of the style it can be said that the literary work "Political speeches" by Paul Joseph Goebbels, has some publicist-linguistic values and is attractive in style for reading, although abounds with examples of hate speech.

In this part of the paper we will review the following stylistic figures that we believe are most suitable and commonly used in political discourse: "metaphor", "irony" "antithesis" "rhetorical question", "alusion", "litotes", "euphemia" and "onomatopoeia".

Methaphor

Metaphorical speech is especially present in political discourse. The impression is that of all stylistic figures it is most utilized by the actors in the political process. More often in situations where the intention is to offend and attack political opponents than to affirm personal success. It is understandable – one always seeks to clearly, explicitly and understandably promote his personal achievements, while the argument for denouncing the opponent may be hidden, ambiguous or just implied. The word metaphor originates from the 16th century from the old French word métaphore, and was built from the Latin metaphora, which means "transmission", "transmit", "to "transfer".[418] Historically, as an unusual appearance in language, metaphor is seen even in ancient times, the times of the beginnings of expression through language by people. The development of the notion of metaphor despite fluctuations, especially expressed in the Middle Ages, has moved forward from ancient times to modern trends.

The very idea of the existence of a metaphor can be found in Aristotle, who in his "Poetics" (Poetics) (about 335 BC) defined it as using a strange term transferred from the genus to the species, from the species transferred to the genus or from one species to another by analogy.[419] Hence, the main aspect of the metaphor is specific transferring of a word from one context to another. Aristotle pointed to the aesthetic function of metaphor and advocated for "true measure" in its use. Otherwise, the clarity of style is questioned.

For a long time in the history of speeches and the art of public speaking among the ancient Greeks and Romans and especially in the Middle Ages, the metaphor was treated as a linguistic tool that decorates and serves to influence the masses. The main division of the concepts of metaphor was hinted even at a time of blossoming of Roman oratory. It derived from the function of the metaphor: the first is one that aims to convince the interlocutor in something and to encourage any activity, means "instrumental - utilitarian" (Aristotle) and the second, which beautifies and decorates the word means "ornamental" (Cicero). Middle Ages are marked by the decline of democracy, and therefore the freedom of spoken expression. In the post-classical Roman era metaphor is reviewed only indirectly, in the works of philosophical and religious character. Rhetorical problems for St. Augustine and Thomas Aquinas are important only because speaking and "beautiful words" can be a powerful tool in the hands of the church to conquer the masses. These religious thinkers restored the thesis about the benefits from the symbolic language (metaphor) its the power of convincing the masses and generally the utilateral, pragmatic and instrumental function of the word, especially the "beautiful" one. According to Marco Fabio Quintilian, also, in "Education

---

[418] Phero, Henry George Liddell, Robert Scott, A Greek-English Lexicon, at Perseus
[419] Aristotle, Vol. 23, Harvard University Press; London, William Heinemann Ltd. 1932, 1457b.

of the speaker" (Institutio Oratoria), metaphor was used in order for "the meaning to be more clear and for artistic effects," and sometimes to replace another word. Although the metaphor "clarifies" the expression, it serves primarily for "things to be understood, and not said openly".[420]

- *The metaphor in political discourse and hate speech*

The metaphor is such a semantic figure which in various morphological syntactic forms (noun, adjective, verb, adverb), one or a group words is used in an unnatural assembly - context in which a relation of analogy or identifying is established between two otherwise distant/disparague terms.[421] The essence of metaphor consists in the duality of what it says, the ambiguity, i.e. polysemy on which it is based. (In the warning spoken in Macedonian political discourse, one political party addresses the other with the words: "We are here to tear your heads off". Clearly it is not thought that literally the head of the opponent will be torn off, but only figuratively that he will politically be eliminated. The metaphor is so structured to speak one thing, and think about another).

When it comes to political discourse, it is particularly difficult to identify hate speech which is pronounced with metaphorical language. Unlike the clear, explicit and direct speech, message of hatered, which is metaphorically addressed, is difficult to decode because it can be interpreted differently, and it is not excluded to be accepted as positive. As an example of the analysis we will take a statement from an Albanian politician in Macedonia, Menduh Thaci, given after a physical fight between fan groups of Macedonians and Albanians. For this incident politician said that it was the "Crystal Night for Albanians in Macedonia ...". With this metaphor he aluded on the historic event, in which thousands of Jews in Germany suffered, on the eve of World War II. In its comparison with the Crystal night, the politician has identified Albanians in Macedonia to be in an identical position with the Jews in Nazi Germany. He did not talk about specific local population from certain settlement or fan group, but generally about all Albanians in Macedonia. Logically the

---

[420]Kvintilijan, Marko Fabije, "Obrazovanje govornika", Veselin Masleša, Sarajevo 1967

[421]Кулакова, Катица, „Фигуративен говор и македонската поезија", Наша книга, Скопје 1984

question arises if they are the victims, then to whom he assigns the role of executioner since the Crystal night had an executioner? With this statement, the politician not only implicitly used hate speech to the Macedonian people, but if he was in Germany he would be charged with minimization and denial of the Holocaust victims (according to the legal provision "Lies about Auschwitz") by identifying the violent showdown with the sufferings of the Jews.

In order to create a metaphor at least two terms with the defined meaning (basic notions) are necessary between which a semantic act can be achieved, regardless whether "concrete" or "abstract", which will give birth to a new meaning that would give sense to the whole statement. However, in the statement in which "crystalline" and "night" are used in an unusual semantic connection, such as "crystal night", the statement is illogical if these terms are understood literally, only in their essential. For the unfamiliar observer crystal night does not have to mean anything or could mean something completely different (for example: "The night is crystal because the sky is crystal clear and the stars are seen"). To realize the effectiveness of the metaphor, the same words should be read differently, in a new way, their new meaning should be found in order to understand the meaning of the statement. That "designing" is not done by bringing to the basic meaning, but by moving away from it. Only by revealing the new, metaphorical meaning (sense) and finding their connotative value, the words and the statement become clear and logical again. So to be able to properly understand the statement "Crystal night for the Albanians in Macedonia ...", the listener needs to have some previous knowledge of the history first, and then project those facts on the specific political event in Macedonia. Otherwise, the Crystal night for the Albanians in Macedonia will mean nothing, or something wrong ("Night with crystal blue sky for the Albanians in Macedonia"). The new meaning - metaphorical concept – is realized on paradigmatic level in the associations of the recipient of the metaphorical message. Both ideas expressed in the words that make up the expression in which arise – the metaphor - intersect in a way that arouses a new idea. One idea – the Crystal night - as a synonym for suffering, and the other idea - the Albanians in Macedonia, create a new idea of the suffering of Albanians in Macedonia. Linking the two concepts which are alien to each other is done by abstraction of their established core meanings, thus expressing only one, just the one that may be common to both terms. This "common meaning" actually evokes and represents the metaphorical concept – the meaning of the expression.

Furthermore, metaphorical transfer and change of meaning have emotional and psychological nature. This extra linguistic aspect of the metaphor and its linguistic mechanism indicate the conditionality and subjective coloration of the metaphorical message from the person expressing it. Different people experience and express the same phenomena in different ways, and they will express their special individual attitude, emotional state, their intellect, affinity etc. So, a statement quoted by a member of the Albanian community, which successfully realized the metaphor will very likely cause attitude of approval, emotional excitement and identification with what was said, just as with a representative of the Macedonian people who also understood the metaphorical language, and it is likely to cause an attitude of condemnation and rejection of what was said as false. But for the representatives of both nations, who did not understand the metaphor, it will remain without effect and without any reaction from the audience. Therefore we have to remember that metaphors are different in different cultures, they are a reflection of our socio-cultural and cognitive schemes, so that every cognitive research should include the context, particularly the context of the Other and all consequences of that aspect.

Irony

One of the semantic figures that is often used in political discourse to express or substantiate certain political stance is irony. The irony is quite suitable because with its content is easy to understand and often because of the comic sense of its content and it is easily digestible for the audience. Ironic effects are commonly accompanied by laughter, which is related to dethrone of values - the difference between what you think and what you are told is identified. But precisely because of this characteristic of ambiguity that irony has, it can be very perfidious used as a means of promotion of hate speech, of which the audience may not always be aware, and its impact on building a position may be quite spectacular and effective. Experience tells us that most people will more easily accept easily understandable and entertaining, with a dose of irony, text, rather than their an information rendered with abstract philosophical and highly intelectual style.

Even Aristotle wrote about irony in his "Rhetoric" and he mentions it related to laughter, with which, under certain circumstances, you need to break the seriousness of the opponent in the dispute, just as to his laughter we should contrast with seriousness. Rhetoric even in the Roman Empire was intended to teach how to attract the listeners, and it was often used before the judges in front of whom you had to blame the opponent - and not just by the power of truth and arguments, but with your own speaking skills and persuasiveness. Then and even today it is believed that if irony is effectively used, it can serve to ridicule the opponent and as such it understands the rhetoric.

In order to successfully understood irony, several condition need to be fulfilled. It is necessary to follow the whole context – from the intonation of the said, to the gestures and articulation.[422] Another important aspect of irony is the specifics of historical consciousness in the time in which irony was important, which in modern times cannot be fully understood. The reflection on the meaning of the existence of ironic texts must include the context in which a text could be understood ironically. Something that is known and understood at a time, must not necessarily in be in another. Reflection of this kind can help to understand why a text was understood ironically in the past, but in the current moment it is difficult to ensure this effect, if appropriate context is no longer present and effective. The reason is that there is no ability to understand the text and context, which is necessary for real ironic effect. A good example is Shakespeare's work in which Hamlet's conversation with Rosenkanz and Guildestern for the contemporary theater surroundings was clear for the theater audience, but we today need an additional comment in order to be able to understand what was going on. To the audience then it was clear because it was familiar with the circumstances and that the author speaks through them about the current theater quarrels, competition and the emergence of children - actors that threaten the status and work of professional actors.

---

[422] Genette, Gerard, "Figures" II, èd, du Seuil, Paris, 1969

Shakespeare, through them, protested against and criticized the rash acting, immaturity, overstated theatricality, screaming on stage which at that time became general acting fashion. The irony theorist Muecke ascribes successful understanding of the context of irony, to the alerts with text, which touche in the cultural and socio-political reality of the particular society, directing viewers to a variety of actualities, which, in turn, over time, stop having meaning.[423]

Apart from the historical context that affects the successful understanding of irony, current social context in which irony is used is also important and it can be determined by current political, religious, cultural, social and other factors. For example, if we review the movie "Life of Brian", its basic text would be the crucifixion and death of Jesus Christ, but the context in which it is presented is ironic and comic, so that the viewer receives Christ's suffering with laughter and fun. On the other hand, although the intention of the context of the Muhammad cartoons published in a Danish newspaper, was also a dose of irony and humor, they were the cause of a severe reaction and violence and have been assessed as spreading hate speech on religious grounds. So, although the context in both examples of visual art is identical, their interpretation and performance are quite different.

As a powerful example of the use of irony in political discourse we would use the comments of Josef Goebbels in "Political speeches", in which he often used ironic metaphors that were later assessed as examples of hate speech. Wishing to describe the situation in English society during the Second World War, he borrowed someone else's speech as an ironic illustration of his political stance:

> *The average Englishman does not often have even the elementary knowledge of the map of Europe. However the problems of nationalities and races, which lately disturb the world, can not even become a topic. They are completely foreign and inexplicable for him. When recently so much fuss was raised about the events in Czechoslovakia, in one of the very popular English magazines "Punch" a caricature of a woman who reprimands her husband because he stayed for hours to listen to an orator*

---

[423] Muecke. D. C., Irony and Ironic, New York, 1982

> *in Hyde Park was moved, and her husband answers that he did not spent the time in vain because finally he learned that Czechoslovakia is not a flower, but – state.[424]*

In another political speech, Goebbels, through metaphor used irony:

> *We distinguish between good and bad people, as we distinguish between good and bad animals. The fact that Jews live among us is not evidence that they belong, such as flea can not be considered a farm animal just because they are found in the houses.[425]*

We would like to emphasize several points inherent to irony. Although irony is primarily encountered in the literary sphere, its wide application in rhetoric makes it applicative even in broader discourse. As already known, in its uncompromising and unscrupulous battle with opponents politicians do not choose the means they use in the public discourse. Whenever they assess that irony strengthens their political speech, affects its argumentation, persuasion, aesthetics and acceptance from the audience, no doubt that they will benefit from it. Therefore irony is very suitable because with its content (mostly) it is easy to understand, and, often, because of the comic sense of its content it is easily digestible for the audience.

For a (political) discourse to have irony in itself, it must always have an aura of ambiguity, according to the principle 'I think one thing and say something else". If it is effectively used, it can serve to ridicule the opponent. For this purpose politicians need oratorical skills as their main "weapon" in the promotion of irony. With different efficiencies irony is present in the daily political communication and often a politician or someone's political speech is bound by audience and remembered exactly through the irony expressed in the public appearance. Because of the attractiveness that it carries in itself through it a severe insult to the other side, or even perfidious promotion of hatred can easily be "swallowed". Although in different situations, semantically speaking, offense is different, however, its purpose in all cases identical - to discredit the other.

---

[424]Гебелс, Јозеф, „Политички говори", Скопје, 2003 (Josef Goebbels "Political speeches")
[425]Ibid

Therefore, from the person irony is intended to in the political discourse great skill and ability to reveal the core message of irony is required - whether behind the pleasant laughter, is subtly hiding something very dangerous and harmful. Indecent speech, offensive speech and defamation as well as hate speech is one of those traps that always follow us as active agents of political discourse.

Antithesis

The antithesis is a stylistic figure that is based on contrast. Two opposing terms placed side by side in order to emphasize their mutual contrast. The antithesis is a special kind of comparison/parallelism which rests on the relationship of contrast between the opposite manifestations/concepts. It is actually a negative parallelism. It is used to affirm the "aesthetics of diversity" and it is built in such a correlative pair in which "the opposite in the similar is emphasized".[426] Therefore Fonteiner sees it as a projection of one "subject through the prism of two opposing terms".[427] Cvetan Todorov defines it clearly as "convergence of two antonymous words (those that carry opposite seed)".[428] Morier emphasizes "the contrast between two ideas in order to shed light to the other".[429] two ideas, two words, two colors can be opposite. So for example, you put inhumanity, ferociousness, greed on the one side becomes , and honesty, common sense, fair play on the other. A very successful example to illustrate the use of antithesis in political discourse will be quoted from an excerpt from "Political **speeches**" by the Nazi propagandist Joseph Goebbels:

> *The Jews notice that now they are left to fend for themselves and try to use a new trick. They know the good heart of a German who is ready when he sees sentimental tears, to forget the injustice that has been done for years, so they are willing to cause pity ... We need to win the war. If we*

---

[426] Lotman, J. M., Predavanje iz strukturalne poetike, Sarajevo 1970
[427] Fontainer, Pierre, Les figures du discours, Flammarion, Paris, 1977
[428] Ducort, Oswald, Todorov, Tzvetan, Dictionnaire encyclopèdique des sciences du langage, èd, du Seuil, Paris 1972
[429] Morier, Henri, Dictionnaire de Poètique et de Rhètorique, deuxième ed., Presses Universitaires de France, Paris, 1975

> *lose all these Jews, who represent themselves as innocent and harmless, will suddenly turn into rabid wolves. They will come after our people, on our women and children, to avenge in an unprecedented way.*[430]

In the specified fragment of political speech by Goebbels it is clearly showen that the whole text promotes the thesis - antithesis and that it is actually the basis of the whole message: on the one hand, Germans are represented as good, humane, honest, and, on the other hand, the enemies – the Jews are greedy, ungrateful, vicious, rabid wolves who just wait for the opportunity to avenge to the Germans. There is a clear division of good and bad characteristics of the peoples, and the antithesis is only used to illustrate those characteristics with concrete examples. In political discourse, almost without hesitation, all politicians use antithesis and want to compare with their political opponents by emphasizing their good sides and the bad sides of the opponent in a so called discursive polarization of US and THEM ("we build, they destroy"). Even the discourse that emphasizes the ethnic division on US and THEM antithesis is the most important element that underlines our positive traits and their negative.

Rhetorical question

Rhetorical question is figurative speech that occurs in the form of a question to cause the effect of convincing those who listen, without expecting them to give any answer to the question.[431] Unlike the speaker, the listener of the rhetorical question prompts him to think which response can the question have (usually it is obvious, it is understood and without possible alternation). Very common form of rhetorical question is to be used as a metaphor for an question that has already been set. In dialectics, this form of rhetorical question, is commonly seen as "rhetorical affirmation" where the sute or obvious answer to the question is expressed by asking another question, often a humorous question, to which the

---

[430]Гебелс, Паул, Јозеф, „Политички говори", Скопје, 2007 (Josef Goebbels "Political speeches")
[431]Burton, Gideon O., Brigham Young University (http://rhetoric.byu.edu). "Rhetorical Questions" (http://rhetoric.byu.edu/figures/R/rhetorical%20questions.htm).

answer is more than obvious.[432] It is clear that the rhetorical question implicitly contains the answer in itself - it is the unity of question-answer, regardless of the formal "inquiring" illusion. With that, the rhetorical question emphatically approaches to semantic figures. Traditional rhetoric defined this figure as a figure of thought which does not expect an answer and therefore rhetorical question is highly functional in public speeches (it was a common speech action for ancient Roman speakers). In fact, his very name derives from the fact that it was a favorite in oratorical skills.

We are interested in it as an instrument very often used in political discourse. Practically for every politician who is talented with oratorical abilities and oratorical qualities, rhetorical question is an integral part of his discourse, eighter to verify the accuracy of their arguments through it or to challenge the arguments of the opposite side. Mass meetings, rallies, parliamentary tribunes are places where this stylistic figure is ultimately present. As an example for the analysis, we would use "Political speeches" by Goebbels who especially touching and emotionally uses rhetorical question on a rally, when the capitulation of Nazi Germany was becoming more certain. The despair of the defeat, which inevitably followed, was stated by a few rhetorical questions to boost the morale of the nation, but more as an encouragement that at critical moments it was not all lost.

> *Today I want to address the whole German nation with a series of questions and get answers from it ... I'll give you ten questions, which you will together answer before us and before the whole world, especially in front of our enemies, who are also listening to us ... The Brits claim that the German people had lost faith in victory. I ask you: do you believe, with the Fuhrer and with us all, in the final victory of the German people? Have you decided to follow the Fuhrer, whatever happens, despite major personal sacrifices? Are you ready to create, behind the army which is fighting an undaunted phalanx to achieve ultimate victory? The Brits claim that the German people did not want to take upon themselves the work that the government requires from it. I ask you: are you ready to work if Fuhrer*

---

[432] Powell, Chris; Paton, George E. C. (1988). Humour in society: resistance and control. Macmillan. p. 67. ; Moon, Rosamund (1998). Fixed expressions and idioms in English: a corpus-based approach (Oxford studies in lexicography and lexicology). Oxford University Press. p. 158. ; Fergusson, Rosalind; Partridge, Eric (1994). Shorter dictionary of catch phrases. Routledge. p. 25.

> *requires that, ten, twelve or even fourteen and sixteen hours a day, and to give your last strength to win?*[433]

Clearly the rhetorical questions Goebbels set only pro forma, and that the response to them is affirmative. First of all, it is a gathering of like-minded, in which the thinking and attitude of participants is provided in advance, determined and accepted. Second, it is a mass gathering, on which psychology of the masses is present, so that the created hysteria produces a reaction of the present which is driven by emotional, irrational and instinctive reasoning, not rational and sober thinking. Also, in such charged and militant atmosphere, it is obvious that there is no democratic atmosphere to pronounce an opinion different from the opinion of the masses, and thus not having repercussion on the lives of the possible "heretic". Then, and today, basically, rhetorical question uttered on mass gatherings excludes the democratic component and tolerance for an answer different from the one expected by the speaker from the egsalted masses. Therefore, such a rhetorical question functions only if set down in situation projected in advance where we know that the answer will be affirmative for the expectations of the one who asks. Otherwise, we do not have a rhetorical question, but an essential and speculative question that requires an answer, which is not pro forma and that is not provided in advance, but it is real because it searches for truth and offers one of the possible views.

Rhetorical questions are particularly present in the media discourse in which journalists in a skillful way manage to avoid the trap to directly enter in a debate with the other party, but by rhetorical questions successfully express their attitude and opinion. We distinguish several rhetorical questions:

- Erothema: question of which the answer is obvious or a claim that because of its stronger emphasis is put in the form of a question.
  Example: Why have thieves, meanwhile become politicians?
- Pusma: pusma question involves foreign dilemmas in the assumed rhetorical question to the recipients.
  Example: How many people should die for Assad to resign?

---

[433] Гебелс, Паул, Јозеф, „Политички говори", Скопје, 2007 (Josef Goebbels "Political speeches")

- Simbleusa: subsequent listing of several rhetorical questions that require some advice.
  Example: How should the domestic film look like to be found in the main program of the festival Manaki?
- Dialogic anacenose: Three forms of dialogue can be found in the media: 1. The journalist asks himself and gives the answer himself. 2. The journalist asks the interlocutor, but does not wait for the answer, instead he answers himself. 3. Ancenose in which by a question you forge the real conservation. Reporters often ask questions in advance to achieve condensed reporting and to avoid accidents and redundancy. In this way suggestive conversation is achieved, but lost in immediacy.
- Hypophor and antipophor: hypophor is a kind of dialogism when the speaker cites his question as one stated by another person. Antipophor goes even further: such question is annulled with an answer.
- Eperothesis: short, emphatic question for achieving special effects.
- Erothesis: is a rhetorical question that is fully realized even in the response.

Allusion

The allusion is figurative speech that refers to direct or implicit address in a specific place, event, literary work, myth or an artistic work. Abrams defines allusion as "explicit or indirect address to people, at places, on events, or to the whole literary work or its paragraph".[434] "The allusion (...) consists in feeling the ratio between one thing that is expressed and another that is not said whose idea arises in this ratio". [435] This stylistic figure is considered to be "a kind of enigmatic metaphor in which the one being compared must reveal the compared based on one or more common elements among them".[436] Allusion - unlike metaphor - implies certain

---

[434] Abrams, to Abe Linclon Gettsburg Adress A Glossary of Literary Terms 1971, s.v. "Allusion".
[435] Fontainer, Pierre, Les figures du discours, Flammarion, Paris, 1977
[436] Morier, Henri, Dictionnaire de Poètique et de Rhètorique, deuxième ed., Presses Universitaires de France, Paris, 1975

"foreknowledge" of the historical, political, current, mythical, private and other "extra-linguistic context". Otherwise, allusion will remain incomprehensible, uncommunicative.[437]

Although the allusion is a literary term, however, it is found in wider use. Depending on the subject matter that we "think of" the allusion is divided into political, verbal, mythical, literary, historical, social, religious and humorous. In "Political speeches" by Goebbels allusion can be found the following lines:

> *And the thought that between us is the man who, with the reform of German art, gave a new direction of German cultural history and who created values that will outlive centuries, fills our hearts with warm noble feeling.*
>
> *Because great men make history, a debt of the art is to recreate and exalt their works to remain a testament to future generations. So art will serve the eternal life of the people.438*

We note that in his speech Goebbels nowhere mentions the name, but it is clear that the allusion refers to Hitler. He can be located in the discourse in the epithet "great men". It is obvious to whom, in Nazi Germany, belonged to such an epithet. However, while on the one hand he refers to the Fuhrer, on the other hand, with the plural form of the noun man, he is placed in the wider context of the "great men of history". But all that has been said in an allusive way, without anywhere explicitly mentioning the name of the Fuhrer.

Even in the current political discourse frequent are the examples when the name is absent, and by allusion praise or criticism of political opponents is expressed. In the same way we can determine whether in a political discourse through allusion a message is sent which, basically, has offensive content or hate speech, which the general public could, but they does not have to understand as such. This stylistic figure shows that hate speech does not always have to be clear and explicit, but may also appear in subtly disguised and perfidious form. As such it is difficult to identify, and consequently will be sanctioned and publicly condemned.

---

[437] Кулакова, Катица, „Фигуративен говор и македонската поезија", Скопје, 1984
[438] Гебелс, Јозеф, „Политички говори" (Josef Goebbels "Political speeches")

Litote - Euphemia

Litotata (opposite of hyperbole) is based on the reduction, mitigation, modification of the meaning that consciously avoids work/performances to be shown in their real light and full intensity. It is a procedure by which "brutal and too bitter"[439] find an indirect, diluted and mitigated expression: instead of saying "he is old" it is said "he is not young". As "a quantitative reduction of one the properties of an object, condition and so on[440] litotate or euphemia is considered the type metalepsy or metonymy.[441] Litote is usually expressed in a negative construction. It is in that relationship that differences are made between litotate and euphemism: while the litote in a negative attitude expresses something positive, contrary to the negation[442], euphemy, with the same goal of mitigation, expresses uncomfortable truths in a "warm" - circumvent form, but without the use of negation. Euphemy, also appears as a sort of allusion: instead of saying that that a huge number of people died, it is said that a certain number survived.

Litote - euphemy contains metaphorical images. The tendency to avoid bare announcement of the facts, particularly the brutal and unwelcomed by metonymic-metaphorical and allusive excursions dominates in them. It is often present in political discourse, when we are aware that a deed that is done is contrary to the generally accepted norms of human behavior, so that, when it can no longer be hiden, we try to relativize it by presenting it as unimportant, minimized.

As an example for the analysis we will take two cases of political discourse from the French parliament.

We are neither racist nor xenophobic. Our goal is quite natural - just to have a hierarchy, because it is for France, and France is a country of the French. (M. Le Pen, July 7, 1986).

The French are not racists. But faced with the continuing increase in the foreign population in France, we have witnessed the emergence in

---

[439] Morier, Henri, Dictionnaire de Poètique et de Rhètorique, deuxième ed., Presses Universitaires de France, Paris, 1975
[440] Ducort, Oswald, Todorov, Tzvetan, Dictionnaire encyclopèdique des sciences du langage, èd, du Seuil, Paris 1972
[441] Fontainer, Pierre, Les figures du discours, Flammarion, Paris, 1977
[442] Kajzer, Volfgang, Jeziko umetnicko delo, Srpska knjizevna zadruga, Beograd 1973

certain cities and neighborhoods, of reactions which are on the border of xenophobia. M. Pascua, July 9, 1986).

From the statements it can be concluded that although racism, as such, is denied, however, it is recognized that there is a problem. This concession, however, largely mitigates and is incorporated in euphemism and indirectness. First, racism is redefined as "xenophobia" which sounds less worrisome. Second, even this concession is mitigated by the use of the phrase "reactions which are on the border of xenophobia". Third, xenophobia is limited by localization: "In certain cities and neighborhoods", which usually means poor urban neighborhoods inhabited by whites. So, as usual, the elites have transferred racism "down" to the lower class. Finally, xenophobia is described with the word semi-justified, with the initial clause "Faced with the continuous growth of foreign population in France".[443] This is a typical example of political discourse on interethnic relations: denial, derogation, mitigation and justification of racism.

Seeking to minimize any unacceptable phenomenon, with such discourse politicians do harm to the community because they relativize undesirable phenomena. Thus, if a party activist in his political discourse clearly and publicly promotes hate speech, and his party instead of condemning him and distancing from him, with selected words, litotes and euphemisms tries to relativize the case, thus it appears as an indirect accomplice and promoter of the language of violence, because if you do not emphasize something as unacceptable, then you send a message to your supporters that it is not such a bad occurance for them.

Onomatopoeia

Onomatopoeia derived from the corresponding Greek word and it is a word used to imitate or suggest the origin of the sound being described. It is characterized by the tendency to imitate the outer appearances and shapes, sounds, etc., but with "articulated voices to present natural sounds, to bring attributive values of the articulation – phonetic - layer first...".[444]

---

[443] Van Dijk, T.A. (1993a) Elite Discourse and Racism. Newbury Park, CA: Sage.
[444] Petkovic, Novica, Jezik u knjizevnom delu, Nolit, Beograd 1975

Most frequently onomatopoeia includes imitation of animal sounds as a dog barking, the cat endearingly, bleating of sheep, etc. Although animals have no nationality and the sound they make is identical anywhere in the world its onomatopoeia is not the same in all languages. For example, dog barking is expressed in the Central European Slavic languages as the "vau - vau" in Serbian, Bulgarian and Macedonian language it is "au - au" in English it is woof woof, in French is ouah ouah, in Italian bau bau in Japanese wan wan, in Turkish hauv hauv.

Types of onomatopoeia:

- Animal voices (meow-meow/cat au - au/dog, co-co-duck/hen, ku-ku-ri-ku/cock, meee/donkey, beee/sheep, kre-kre/frog).
- Sounds from the environment (boom/crash, bang/closing door, blah-blah/inarticulate speech, pljas/slap, fiu/wind, chuk - chuk/knock at the door, while in Serbian it is "kuc-kuc", and in English knock-knock).
- Onomatopoeia is particularly common in comics where the "clouds" display sounds of punches (boom, pljas, bang, pljus).

Although not often, its (mis)use can be found in political discourse, in the formal, institutional and official as well as in the informal, stret and spontaneous. There are cases on sports fields when the football ball is in possession of a black player, and the opposing fans in the stands chanti cries that imitate the sound made by monkeys (the most common onomatopoeia for cries of monkeys is "U-u-u-u-u u-u '). This way they direct insult the footballer on racial grounds, by relating him to an animal and considering hum a lower kind than whites. In his testimony, former football midfielder of Netherlands, Patrick Kluivert said that while he was playing in England fans insulted him on racial grounds. "When I had the ball, fans mimicked monkeys. It has not affected my play, but it was certainly not nice to hear something like that", explained Kluivert.[445] The English footballer Danny Rose had a similar unpleasant experience during a guest match in Serbia: "There was a monkey soundss every time I approached to t the out line".[446] On the territory former Yugoslavia, at a

---

[445] http://www.b92.net/sport/fudbal/vesti.php?yyyy=2012&mm=11&dd=05&nav_id=657870
[446] http://www.b92.net/sport/fudbal/vesti.php?yyyy=2012&mm=10&dd=17&nav_id=652513

time when nationalism was predominantly present, the sports competitions where athletes of Bosnia and Herzegovina played, because of their Muslim religion, opposing fans often insulted them by the use of onomatopoeia of pig snort, while in the opposite case, Muslim fans insulted Orthodox players with dog barking (identifying them as stated by themselves, with dogs). Such use of onomatopoeia and spread of hate speech, racism and religious intolerance is clearly detected by international sports associations and is strictly prohibited and sanctioned by instant discharge of the fan tribunes, to high penalties for the club whose fans used the onomatopoeia to spread hate speech. Therefore, we can conclude that onomatopoeia, although primarily a stylistic figure in literature, can be misused in political discourse in which it is usually regarded politically incorrect and banned language and is considered a promotion of racism, religious intolerance and hate speech.

* * *

There is no doubt that the inventiveness of man gives him unlimited achievements in literature, and the use of language is endlessly creative. In political discourse, of course, other stylistic figures can be used and through them contact can be made with hate speech. That does not mean that the mentioned figures are only through which it can be promoted, but are one of the most characteristic and according to frequency more used. Therefore, we decided they should be analyzed, without intention to claim that the other could not be put into operation in the processing of the problem that interests us.

8. CONCLUSION

In this chapter we reviewed some linguistic – sociocommunicational aspects of the relationship between political discourse and hate speech. We have seen how important and strong use of language by the political elite in its management with dominated groups in all phases of the exercise of power is: in the electoral process in the exercise of power and when power is won and the trust of voters gained. Throughout the process, language and linguistic methods of manipulation are inevitable to convince the dominated in the correctness of the political agenda offered. Critical discourse analysis is particularly important in order to successfully decompose the relation between those who dominate society and the dominated. It explains us how the dominating elite, through the use of various linguistic methods in political discourse retains its privileged position, as well as how the dominated are prevented from successfully changing their social position. Clearly theone that dominates the society and its resources will never accept to (easily) lose and leave the once acquired privileged position and comfort to others. Uncompromising are his manipulative language techniques through which elements of misinformation and propaganda are introduced in the political discourse, in order to extend the dominance. And this situation is immanent in all social systems - from totalitarian to democratic. We would say that for the democratic system it is most characteristic because in its essence of ruling and reproducing of power exclusively legitimate democratic means are used, which are, basically, based on public political debate and verbal confrontation of different arguments and pluralism of opinions. Hence, the public political discourse as a means of reproduction of domination is perhaps the least characteristic of totalitarian and undemocratic systems because there is a lack of open political debate and the unisonism and monolith of the dominirachkata elite is ensured through production of fear, repression and violent methods. Therefore the theorist Van Dijk based his views on CDA and political discourse on analysis of the political debate present in Western societies - in particular the British Parliament and the Western political discourse, and not on examples of undemocratic systems. However his focus is exclusively on the right-oriented political discourse, as holder of racial, nationalist and xenophobic discourse and with such an approach he gives the impression of being inconsistent because he creates the wrong impression that the political discourse of the left-oriented cannot be subject to CDA.

Except CDA and political discourse in this chapter we reviewed some other phenomena that characterize hate speech, and that is its public manifestation which must not exclusively be through verbal or written means. We have identified situations where hate speech can be expressedin non-spoken way with gestures, then using symbolic with the use of items that are replaced their essential meaning and are given a symbolic value, as well as with unarticulated application of the voice capabilities of man sending a clear message of offence. We reviewed a few more stylistic figures through which hate speech can be expressed, which must not be explicitly but in a sheltered, perfidious form, that is more difficult to identify, expose, condemn and finally sanction.

The overall theoretical consideration of the problem of this study in both chapters - hate speech and political discourse, in which it was multidisciplinary covered from several aspects (legal, politicological, linguistic and socio-communicational) allows if someone deals with empirical research on specific political discourse and possible presence of hate speech, to have a solid starting point, and the offered results and conclusions to be supported with strong scientific and theoretical base.

Bubliography

- A Communitarian Defense of Group Libel Laws, Harvard Law Review 101 (January 1988): 682-701
- Abraham, J. Henry, 'Freedom and the Court', 5th. Ed. (New York: Oxford University Press, 1988)
- ACLU, 'Shall We Defend?' (1934)
- Albert, E. M. (1972). 'Culture patterning of speech behavior in Burundi'. In J. J. Gumperz and D. Hymes (eds), 'Directions in Sociolinguistics: The Ethnography of Communication' (pp. 72-105). New York: Holt, Rhinehart, and Winston.
- Alexander, J. C., Giesen, B., Munch, R., and Smelser, N. J. (eds). (1987). 'The Micro—Macro Link'. Berkeley, CA: University of California Press. Knorr–Cetina, K. and Cicourel, A. V. (eds). (1981). Advances in Social Theory and Universidad de Buenos Aires.
- Alvin Day, Louis, „Ethics in Media Communications – Cases and Controversies".
- American Jewish Congress, resolution, January 8, 1978
- Anger over List of Names Divides Black from Their College Town, New York Times, September 27, 1992
- Arent, Hana. "Istina i laž u politici", Filip Višnjić, Beograd, 1994
- Arielli, Nir. (9 June 2010). 'Fascist Italy and the Middle East, 1933–40'. Palgrave Macmillan. pp. 92–99. ISBN 978-0-230-23160-3.
- Asbury, Mary Beth. and Haas, John, 2008: "An Exploratory Investigation of Whether Individuals Differentiate between Hate Speech and Offensive Language", Paper presented at the annual meeting of the NCA 94th Annual Convention, TBA, San Diego, CA, Nov 20, 2008: 4.
- Atkinson, Max. 'Our Master's Voices. The Language and Body Language of Politics'. London: Methuen,
- Atlagić, Siniša. 'Nacistička umetnost i propaganda', CM Časopis za upravljanje komuniciranjem, broj 11, godina IV, 2009, Beograd
- Babić, Dušan. "Jezik mržnje u javnoj sferi: fenomenološko-tipološke naznake karakteristične za ove prostore", Regionalni glasnik za promociju kulture manjinskih prava i međuetničke tolerancije, tema broja: Jezik mržnje, 15. august 2004.
- Barker, A. J. (1978). 'The African Link: British Attitudes to the Negro in the Era'
- Barović, Vladimir. "Mediji u Trećem rajhu", CM Časopis za upravljanje komuniciranjem, broj 5, godina II, Decembar 2007., Beograd

- Barron, S. (2001): „Modern Art and Politics in prewar Germany" in Barron (ed.), Degenerate Art: The Fate of the Avant-Garde in Nazi Germany. Los Angeles: County Museum, Pp 9 – 23.
- Beckford, James A. 'The Univeristy of Prophecy: A Sociological Study of Jehovah's Witnesses' (Oxford: Basil Blackwell, 1975)
- Berman, Paul. 'Debating PC' (New York: Dell, 1992)
- Billig, M. (1982) 'Ideology and Social Psychology'. Oxford: Blackwell.; Rosenberg, S.W.(1988) Reason, Ideology, and Politics. Princeton, NJ: Princeton University Press.; Windisch, U. (1985) Le raisonnement et le parler quotidiens. Lausanne: L Age d Homme.
- Billig, M. (2006), 'Banal Nationalism'. London: Sage
- Bloom, L. 'Language development: form and function in emerging grammars'. (1970),
- Boden, Deirdre and Don H. Zimmerman. (eds.) 1991. 'Talk and Social Structure: Studies in Ethnomethodology and Conversation Analysis'. Cambridge: Polity Press.; Fisher, Sue and Alexandra Dundas Todd. (eds.) 1986. Discourse and Institutional Authority: Medicine, Education, and Law. Norwood, NJ: Ablex.
- Boerefijn, Ineke and Oyediran, Joanna, "Article 20 of the International Covenant on Civil and Political Rights", in Coliver, Striking a balance
- Bollinger, Lee. 'The Tolerant Society' (New York: Oxford University Press, 1986)
- Borvik, Bjшrnar. 'The Norwegian Approach to Protection of Personality Rights: With a Special Emphasis on the Protection of Honour and Reputation' 133 (Bergen, Norway: Fagbokforlaget, 2004) (translating the Penal Code of May 22, 1909, No. 10, Art. 135a.).
- Bosworth, R. J. B. 'Mussolini's Italy', p134 ISBN 1-59420-078-5
- Bourdieu, P. (1983) 'Ce que parler veut dire' ('What speaking means'). Paris: Fayard.
- Boyle, Kevin, 2001, "Hate Speech-The United States Versus the Rest of the World?", Maine Law Review
- Bradac, J.J. and Mulac, A. (1984) 'A Molecular View of Powerful and Powerless Speech Styles'. Communication Monographs 51: 307-19.; Erickson, B., Lind, A.A., Johnson. B.C. and O Barr, W.M. (1978) Speech Style and Impression Formation in a Court Setting: The Effects of Powerful and Powerless Speech Journal of Experimental Social Psychology 14: 266-79.
- Brandenburg v. Ohio, 395 U.S. 444 (1969).
- Brendon, Piers. 'The Dark Valley: A Panorama of the 1930s', p322-3 ISBN 0-375-40881-9
- Brinkley. Voices of Protest
- Branković, Srbobran, „Uvod u metodologiju: Kvalitativni metodi istraživanja društvenih pojava", Beograd, mart 2007.

- Browing, Christopher R. 'The Origins of the Final Solution', University of Nebraska Press, 2004.
- Brown, P. and Levinson, S.C. (1987) 'Politeness: Some Universals in Language Use'. Cambridge: Cambridge University Press.
- Brownile, Ian. ed.., 'Basic Documents on Human Rights', 2d ed. (Oxford: Clarendon Press, 1980);
- Brownile, Ian. ed., 'Basic Documents on Human Rights' (Oxford: Clarendon Press, 1981)
- Brugger, Winfried, 'Verbot oder Schutz von Hassrede? Rechtsvergleichende Beobachtungen zum deutschen und amerikanischen Recht, u: Archiv des öffentlichen Rechts', vol. 128 (2003), s. 372-411.
- Brugger, Winfried. 'Ban On or Protection of Hate Speech'? Some Observations Based on German and American Law, 17 TUL. EUR. & CIV. L.F. 1 (2002)
- Cannistraro, P. V. (April 1972). "Mussolini's Cultural Revolution: Fascist or Nationalist?". Journal of Contemporary History (SAGE Journals Online) 7 (3)
- Carnegie Fund for the Advancement of Teaching , Campus Life (New York, 1990)
- Cecil, Robert. 'The Myth of the Master Race: Alfred Rosenberg and Nazi Ideology',
- Centril, Hadley. ed., 'Public Opinion', 1935-1946, (Westport, Conn.: Greenwood Press, 1978)
- Chaplinsky v. New Hampshire, 315 U.S. 568 (1942)
- Chilton, P. (1988). 'Orwellian Language and the Media'. London: Pluto Press.
- Chilton, P. (1996). 'Security Metaphors. Cold War Discourse from Containment to Common House'. Bern: Lang. и Chilton, P. and Lakoff, G. (1995). Foreign policy by metaphor. In C. Schaffner and A. L. Wenden (eds), Language and Peace, (pp. 37-59). Aldershot: Dartmouth.
- Chilton, P. (ed.) (1985). 'Language and Nuclear Arms Debate: Nukespeak Today'. London and Dover, NH: Frances Printer.
- Coates, Jennifer. 'Women, Men and Language'. London: Longman, 2004 (3rd edition)
- Coliver, 'Striking a balance', "Annexe B: Reservation and Declaration concerning Racist Speech and Advocacy of Racial and Religious Hatred"
- Coliver, Sandra. ed.., 'Striking a Balance: Hate Speech, Freedom of Expression and Non-discrimination' (London: Article 19, 1992)
- Čolović, Ivan, „Politika simbola", „XX vek", Beograd 2000
- Communist party (kpd) v. The federal republic of germany, decision of 20 july 1957, yearbook 1, p. 222
- Cortese, Anthony Joseph Paul, 'Opposing hate speech', Westport, Conn.: Praeger Publishers, 2006.
- Cox, Archibald, 'The Warren Court' (Cambridge: Harvard University Press, 1968)

- Cronicle of Higher Education, August 26, 1992
- Delgado, Richard, "Hate Cannot Be Tolerated", Usatoday.Com, March 3
- Delgado, Richard. "Campus Anti-racism Rules: Constructional Narratives in Collision", Northwestern University Law Review 85 (1991)
- Diamond, J. (1996). 'Status and Power in Verbal Interaction. A Study of Discourse in a Close-knit Social Network'. Amsterdam: Benjamin.
- Domhoff, G. W. (1978) 'The Powers That Be: Processes of Ruling Class Domination in America'. New York: Random House (Vintage Books);
- Downing, J. (1984). 'Radical Media: The Political Experience of Alternative Communication'. Boston: South End Press.
- Driscoll, J. Dennis, "The Development of Human Rights in International Law", in the Human Rights Readers, rev ed. Walter Laqueur and barry Rubin, eds., (New York: New American Library, 1989).
- Duin, A. H., Roen, D. H., and Graves, M. F. (1988). 'Excellence or malpractice: the effects of headlines on readers' recall and biases'. National Reading Conference (1987, St Petersburg, Florida). National Reading Conference Yearbook, 37: Van Dijk, 1'. A. (1991). 'Racism and the Press'. London: Routledge and Kegan Paul.
- Dworkin, Ronald (2005) 'Taking Rights Seriously'. Cambridge, Ma: Harvard University Press.
- Ehlich, K. (ed.) (1989). 'Sprache im Faschismus'. ('Language under Fascism'). Frankfurt: Suhrkamp.
- Encyclopedia of Associations, 26th ed. (Detroit: Gale Research, 1992)
- Essed, P. J. M. (1991). 'Understanding'
- Evans, R. J. (2003). 'The Coming of the Third Reich'. London: Penguin Books Ltd.
- Fairclough, N. (1995) 'Critical Discourse Analysis: the Critical Study of Language'. London, New York: Longman.
- Fairclough, N., Wodak R. (1997) 'Critical Discourse Analysis'. In: Van Dijk, T.A. (ed.) 'Discourse as Social Interaction'. Volume 2. London, Thousand Oaks, New Delhi: Sage.
- Fairclough, N.L. (1985) 'Critical and Descriptive Goals in Discourse Analysis', Journal of Pragmatics 9
- Fairclough, Norman. 'Language and Power'. London: Longman, 1989, p. 6
- Farr, R.M. and Moscovici, S., eds (1984) 'Social Representations'. Cambridge: Cambridge University Press.: Fiske, S.T. and Taylor, S.E. (1991) Social Cognition, 2nd edn. New York: McGraw-Hill.: Wyer, R.S. and Srull, T.K., eds (1984) Handbook of Social Cognition (3 vols). Hillsdale, NJ: Erlbaum.
- Forster, Arnold and Epstein, Benjamin, 'The Trouble Makers' (garden City, N.Y.: Doubleday, 1952, pp.225-26
- Fowler, R., Hodge, B., Kress, G., and Trew, T. (1979). 'Language and Control'. London: Routledge and Kegan Paul.

- Franzoi, S. L. 'Social Psychology', drugo izdanje, McGrawHill, Boston, 2000
- Gagnon, V. P. (1997), "Ethnic Nationalism and International Conflict: The Case of Serbia", u: Brown, M. E. et al. (ur.), 'Nationalism and Ethnic Conflict'. Cambridge MA: MIT Press.
- Gale, Mary Ellen. "On Curbing Racial Speech", Responsive Community 1 (Winter 1990-91)
- Gallo, Max. 'Mussolini's Italy', Macmillian Publishing Co. Inc., 1973 New York
- Gans, H. (1979). 'Deciding What's News'. New York: Pantheon Books; Van Dijk, T. A. (1988a). 'News as Discourse'. Hillsdale, NJ: Erlbaum. Van Dijk, T. A. (1988b). 'News Analysis'. Case Studies of International and National News in the Press. Hillsdale, NJ: Erlbaum.
- Gans, H. (1979). 'Deciding What's News'. New York: Pantheon Books; Tuchman, G. (1978) Making News: A Study in the Construction of Reality. New York: Free Press.
- Garfinkel, Herbert, 'When Negroes March' (Glencoe, Ill.: Free Press, 1959)
- Gillette, Aaron (2002). 'Racial Theories in Fascist Italy'. Routledge. p. 95. ISBN 0-415-25292-X.
- Giroux, H. (1981). 'Ideology, Culture, and the Process of Schooling'. London: Falmer Press.
- Glaser, "German American Bund"
- Glendon, Mary Ann. 'Rights Talk' (New York: Free Press, 1991)
- Glimmerveen and Hagenbeek v. the Netherlands, Nos. 8348/78 and 8406/78, decision of the Commission of 11 October 1979, D. R. 18, p. 187.
- Gould, Stephen Jay, 'The Mismeasure of Man' (New York: Norton, 1981)
- Graber, Mark A. 'Transforming Free Speech: The Ambiguous Legacy of Civil Libertarianism', 1991.
- Graham, Hugh Davis, 'The Civil Rights Era' (New York: Oxford University press, 1990)
- Gramsci, A. (1971). 'Prison Notebooks'. New York: International Publishers.
- Greenwalt, Kent , 'Speech, Crime, and the Uses of Language' (New York: Oxford University Press, 1989) p.298
- Gregor, A. James, 'The Search for Neofascism', New York, Cambridge University Press (2006). ISBN 978-0-521-85920-2
- Griffen, Roger (ed.). 'Fascism'. Oxford University Press, 1995. Pp. 59.
- Guespin, L. (ed.) (1976). 'Typologie du discours politique' ('Typology of political discourse'). Languages, 41.
- Hall, S., Lumley, B. and McLennan, G. (1977) 'Gramsci on Ideology', in Centre for Contemporary Cultural Studies (ed. Politics and Ideology: Gramsci, pp. 45-76. London: Hutchinson.
- Harris, Z., 'Discourse analysis', Language (1952)
- Hart, Christopher. (2005) 'Analysing Political Discourse: Toward a Cognitive Approach, Critical Discourse Studies 2 (2)', University of Hertfordshire

- Haupt, Claudia E. 'Regulating Hate Speech—Damned If You Do and Damned If You Don't: Lessons learned from comparing the German and U.S. approaches', Boston University International Law Journal [Vol. 23:299] 2005
- Helms-Liesenhoff, K.H.(1976). 'Gretchen u uniformi'. Zagreb: Globus
- Hentoff, 'Free Speech for Me but Not For Thee' (New York: Harper Collins, 1992)
- Hentoff, 'Free Speech for Me'
- Herman, E.S. and Chomsky, N. (1958) 'Manufacturing Consent.- The Political Economy of the Mass Media'. New York: Pantheon Books.
- Heuman, Milton & Thomas W. Church, 'Hate Speech On Campus' 6-7 (Northeastern University Press 1997).
- Higham, 'Strangers in the Land', chap. 6, "Toward Racism: The History of an Idea".
- Hollander, Ethan J (1997) (PDF). 'Italian Fascism and the Jews'. University of California. ISBN 0-8039-4648-1.
- Holly, W. (1990). 'Politikersprache. Inszenierungen and Rollenkonflikte im informellen Sprachhandeln eines Bundestagsabgeordneten'. ('Politician's Language. Dramatization and Role Conflicts in the Informal Speech Acts of a Bundestag Delegate'). Berlin: Mouton de Gruyter.
- Houston, M. and Kramarae, C. (eds). (1991). 'Women speaking from silence'. Discourse and Society, 2(4), special issue.
- Hunt, L. (2009). 'The Making of the West: Peoples and Cultures', Vol. C: Since 1740. Bedford/St. Martin's.
- Institute for Propaganda Analysis. 'The Fine Art of Propaganda'. New York: Harcourt, Brace and Company, 1939. Pp 21
- Irvine, J. T. (1974). 'Strategies of status manipulation in the Wolof greeting'. In R. Bauman and J. Sherzer (eds), 'Explorations in the Ethnography of Speaking' (pp. 167-91). Cambridge: Cambridge University Press.
- Jacobs, James B., and Kimberly A. Potter, "Hate Crimes: A Critical Perspective", In. M. Torny, ed. Crime and Justice: A Review of Research Chicago: University of Chicago Press, 1998
- Jaworski, A., Coupland, N. (1999) 'Introduction: Perspectives on Discourse Analysis'. In: Jaworski, Coupland. (Eds.) 'The Discourse Reader'. London, New York: Routledge.
- Johnson-Laird, P.N. (1983) 'Mental Models'. Cambridge: Cambridge University Press.; Van Dijk, T.A. (1987b) 'Episodic Models in Discourse Processing', in R. t Horowitz and S.J. Samuels (eds) Comprehending Oral and Written Language, pp. 161-96. New York: Academic Press.; Van Dijk, T.A. and Kintsch, W. (1983) 'Strategies of Discourse Comprehension'. New York: Academic Press.
- Judd, C. M. and J. W. Downing. 1990. 'Political Expertise and the Development of Attitude Consistency'. Social Cognition, 8(1):

- Kallis, Aristotle. 2000. 'Fascist Ideology'. London: Routledge
- Kalven, Harry, Jr., 'The Negro and the First Amendment', Phoenix ed. (Chicago: Univeristy of Chicago Press, 1966)
- Karst, Kenneth, "Equality as a Central Principle in the First Amendmant", University of Chicago Law Review 43 (1975)
- Kedar, L., ed. (1987) 'Power through Discourse'. Norwood, NJ: Ablex.; Kramarae, C., Schulz, M. and O Barr, W.M. eds (1984) Language and Power. Beverley Hills, CA: Sage.
- Klaric, Željko (ur.) 2009: "Govor mržnje u medijima", Cenzura, Novi Sad: 49.
- Kolstø, P. „Diskurs i nasilni sukob: predstave o „sebi" i „drugom" u državama nastalim posle raspada Jugoslavije", „Intima javnosti", Fabrika knjiga, Beograd, 2008
- Kramarae, C. (1981) 'Women and Men Speaking: Frameworks for Analysis'. Rowlev, MA: Newbury House.
- Кротошински, Ronald J. "A Comparative Perspective on the First Amendment: Free Speech, Militant Democracy, and the Primacy of Dignity as a Preferred Constitutional Value in Germany," 78 Tulane L. Rev. 1549 (2004).
- Kuk, A. Dejvid (2005). 'Istorija filma I-II.' Beograd: Clio.
- Kuljić, T. (2002). 'Prevladavanje prošlosti, Uzroci i pravci promene slike istorije krajem XX veka', Beograd: „Zagorac".
- Langshaw, Austin, J. 'How to do Things with Words: The William James Lectures delivered at Harvard University in 1955'. Oxford: Clarendon, 1962.
- Lasser, Williams. 'The Limits of Judicial Power: The Supreme Court in American Politics'. (Chapter Hill: University of North Carolina Press, 1988)
- Lauren, P. G. (1988). 'Power and Prejudice. The Politics and Diplomacy of Racial Discrimination'. Boulder, CO: Westview Press.
- Lee, Albert, 'Henry Ford and the Jews' (New York: Stein and Day, 1980)
- Leech, G. N., Short, M.H. (1981) 'Style in Fiction'. London and New York: Longman.
- Lehideux and Isorni v. France [GC], judgment of 23 September 1998, Reports of Judgments and Decisions 1998-VII, para. 53.
- Letter, Codman to Curley, October 11, 1923; Chafee Papers, box 30, HLS
- Levin, Abigail. 'The Cost of Free Speech Pornography, Hate Speech, and their Challenge to Liberalism', Niagara University, New York, 2010
- Linen, P. and Jonsson, L. (1991). 'Suspect stories: perspective-setting in an asymmetrical situation'. In I. Markova and K. Foppa (eds), Asymmetries in Dialogue. The Dynamics of Dialogue (pp. 75-100). n.d. Barnes and Noble Books/Bowman and Littlefield Publishers: Harvester Wheatsheaf.
- Lowenstein, Karlo. "Militant Democracy and Fundamental Rights, I", American Political Science Review 31 (June 1937).
- Lukes, S. (ed.) (1986). 'Power'. Oxford: Blackwell и Wrong, D. H. (1979). Power: Its Forms, Bases and Uses. Oxford: Blackwell.

- MacKinnon, Catherine. "Pornography, Civil Rights and Speech", Harvard Civil Rights-Civil Libertis Law Review 20 (1985)
- Malik, Kenan. 'From Fatwa to Jihad: The Rushdie Affair and Its Legacy', Atlantic Books, 2009.
- Malouf, Robert. 'Taking sides: user classification for informal online political'. Department of Linguistics and Asian/Middle Eastern Languages, San Diego State University, San Diego, California, USA, Tony Mullen, Department of Computer Science, Tsuda College, Tokyo, Japan
- Margolis, M. and Mauser, G.A., eds (1989) 'Manipulating Public Opinion: Essays on Public Opinion as a Dependent Variable'. Brooks/Cole.
- Matsuda, Mari J., Charles R. Lawrence III, Richard Delgado, and Kimberlè Williams Crenshaw (eds.) (1993) Words That Wound: Critical Race Theory, Assaultive Speech, and the First Amendment. Boulder, CO: Westview Press.
- Matsuda, Mary J. "Public Response to Racist Speech: Considering the Victim's Story", Michigan Law Review 87 (August 1989): 2320-81, esp. p. 2364
- Mc Houl, A. (1994) Discourse. In: Asher, R.E. (ed.) The Encyclopedia of language and linguistics. Vol. 2. Oxford, New York, Seoul, Tokio.
- McGonagle, Tarlach, "Wrestling (Racial) Equality from Tolerance of Hate Speech", Dublin University Law Journal (ns) 21, 2001.
- McLemore, S., and H. Romo. 2005. 'Racial and Ethnic Relations in America'. 7th ed. Boston: Allyn and Bacon
- Meiklejohn, Alexander, 'Free Speech and Its Relation to Self Government' (New York: Harper and Row, 1948)
- Merelman, R. M. 1986. 'Revitalizing Political Socialization'. In M. G. Hermann (ed.), Political Psychology. San Francisco, Jossey-Bass:
- Merton, Robert K., "Social Theory and Social Structure", Rev. ed. Glencoe, IL.: The Free Press, 1957
- Michell, T.F., The language of buying and selling in Cyrenaica, Hesperis (1957)
- Militants Back 'Queer', Shoving 'Gay' the Way of 'Negro'", New York Times, April 6, 1991
- Mills, C.W. (1956) The Power Elite. London: Oxford University Press.
- Mills, S. (1995) 'Feminist Stylistics'. London and New York: Routledge. of the Atlantic Slave Trade, 1550-1807. London: Frank Cass.
- Moran, Andes, Pam, "Body language in Politics Campaign" 2008
- National Socialist Party of America v. Village of Skokie, 432 U.S. 43 (1977)
- Nesler, M. S., Aguinis, H., Quigley, B. M., and Tedeschi, J. T. (1993). 'The effect of credibility on perceived power. Journal of Applied Social Psychology', 23(17), 1407-25.
- New York Times Co. v. Sullivan, 376 U.S. 254 (1964)
- Oxford Student's dictionary of Current English, Second Edition by Christine Ruse, Oxford University Press, 1988

- Palmer, M. T. (1989). 'Controlling conversations: turns, topics, and interpersonal control. Communication Monographs', 56(1); Fishman, P. (1983). Interaction: the work women do. In B. Thorne, C. Kramarae, and N. Henley (eds), Language, Gender, and Society. New York: Pergamon Press; Leet-Pellegrini, H. (1980). Conversational dominance as a function of gender and expertise. In H. Giles, W. P. Robinson, and P. Smith (eds), Language: Social Psychological Perspectives. Oxford: Pergamon Press; Lindegren–Lerman, C. (1983). Dominant discourse: the institutional voice and the control of topic. In H. Davis and P. Walton (eds), Language, Image, Media. Oxford: Blackwell.
- Palmer, T., Neubauer, H. (2000). 'The Weimar republic Through the Lens of the Press'. Könemann
- Pasierbsky, F. (1983). 'Krieg und Frieden in der Sprache'. ('War and Peace in Language'). Frankfurt: Fischer.
- Paull, Miller and Paull 2004, "Freedom of speech", Cambridge University Press: 24
- Pavel Ivanov v. Russia (dec.), No. 35222/04, decision of 20February 2007.
- Pecheux, M. (1969). 'Analyse Automatique du Discours'. Paris: Dunod.
- Penton, M. James, 'Apocalypse Delayed: The Story of the Jehovah's Witnesses' (Toronto: Univeristy of Toronto Press, 1985)
- Perrett, Geoffrey, 'America in the Twenties: A History' (New York: Simon and Schuster, 1982)
- Petersen R. D. (2002), 'Understanding Ethnic Violence: Fear, Hatred and Resentment in Twentieh-Century Eastern Europe'. Cambidge: Cambridge University Press
- Petkovic, Novica, 'Jezik u knjizevnom delu', Nolit, Beograd 1975
- Petty, R. E, and Cacciopo, J.T.: "Communication and persuasion: Central and peripheral routes to attitude change", Springer Verlag, New York, 1986
- Powers, Gerald (1998): 'Religion, Conflict, and Prospects for Peace in Bosnia, Croatia and Yugoslavia'; u: Paul Mojzes (ur.): Religion and the War in Bosnia; Scholar Press; Atlanta; str. 218-245
- R.A.V. v. City of St. Paul, 505 U.S. 377 (1992)
- Raz, Joseph (1992) 'Rights and Individual Well-Being'. Ratio Juris 5, 2 (July): 127–42.
- Riesman. David, "Democracy and Defamation", Columbia Law Review 42 (1942):
- Roberts, Jeremy (2006). 'Benito Mussolini. Minneapolis', MN: Twenty-First Century Books, p. 60.
- Rojo, L. Martin. (1994). 'Jargon of delinquents and the study of conversational dynamics'. Journal of Pragmatics, 21(3), 243-89.
- Rosenfeld, Michel, 'Hate Speech in Constitutional Jurisprudence: A Comparative Analysis', Cardozo Law Review (Vol. 24:4), 2003.

- Rutherford, Joseph F. 'Enemies' (Brooklyn, N.Y. : Watchtower Bible and Tract Society, 1937)
- Saunders, Kevin W. 'Degradation What the History of Obscenity Tells Us about Hate Speech', New York Universi t y Pre s s New York and London, 2011
- Savić, Svenka, "Diskurs analiza", Filozofski fakultet, 1993, Novi Sad
- Schmitt, Richard. 2000. "Radical Philosophy: 'Philosophers Combating Racism' Conference", American Philosophy Association Newsletter 99(20
- Sedler, R., "The Unconstitutionality of campus Bans on 'Racist Speech': The View from without and within", University of Pittsburg Law Review 53: 632-683, 1992
- Shohat, E. and Stam, R. (1994).' Unthinking Euro centrism. Multiculturalism and the Media'. London: Routledge and Kegan Paul.
- Smith, Denis Mack. 1982. 'Mussolini: A biography, Borzoi Book published by Alfred A. Knopf', Inc. ISBN 0-394-50694-4
- Smith, Mack, Denis, 'Mussolini's Roman Empire', p 28 ISBN 0-670-49652-9
- Snyder, L.Louis. (1998). 'Encyclopedia of the Third Reich'. Hertfordshire: Wordsworth Editions Limited
- Sumner, L.W. (2004) 'The Hateful and the Obscene'. Toronto: University of Toronto Press.
- Tadic, Darko, 'Propaganda', YU Spektrum, Beograd, 2005
- The Rights to Advocate Violence (New York: ACLU, 1931)
- Van Dijk, T. A. (1988a). 'News as Discourse'. Hillsdale, NJ: Erlbaum. Van Dijk, T. A. (1988b). News Analysis. Case Studies of International and National News in the Press. Hillsdale, NJ: Erlbaum
- Van Dijk, T. A. 1997b. 'What is Political Discourse Analysis'? In J. Blommaert and C. Bulcaen (eds.), Political Linguistics. Amsterdam, Benjamins
- Van Dijk, T. A., 'Aims of Critical Discourse Analysis, Japanese Discourse' Vol. I (1995)
- Van Dijk, T. A., 'Political discourse and political cognition (paper)' CHAPTER 7
- Van Dijk, T. A., 'Principles of critical discourse analysis', Discourse & Society, 1993 SAGE (London. Newbury Park and New Delhi), vol. 4(2)
- Van Dijk, T.A. (19187a) 'Communicating Racism'. Newbury Park. CA: Sage.; Van Dijk, T. A. (1991) 'Racism and the Press'. London: Routledge.; Van Dijk, T.A. (1993a) Elite Discourse and Racism. Newbury Park, CA: Sage.
- Van Dijk, T.A. (1989a) 'Social Cognition and Discourse', in H. Giles and R.P. Robinson (eds) Handbook of Social Psychology and Language, pp. 163-83. Chichester: Wiley.
- Van Dijk, T.A. (1993a) 'Elite Discourse and Racism'. Newbury Park, CA: Sage.
- Van Zoonen, L. (1994). 'Feminist Media Studies'. London: Sage.
- Vasović, Mirjana. „Govor mržnje", mesečne političke analize „Prizma", Izdavač „Centar za liberalno–demokratske studije", Beograd, oktobar, 2002

- Velikonja, Mitja. "In Hoc Signo Vinces: Vjerski simbolizam u ratovima u Hrvatskoj i Bosni i Hercegovini 1991 1995", Sarajevske Sveske br. 05
- Vetlesen, A. J. (2005), 'Evil and Human Agency: Understanding Collective Evildoing'. Cambridge: Cambridge Uiversity Press.
- Volkov, Vladimir, "Od trojanskog konja do internet", Nas Dom, 2005, Beograd (Vladimir Volkoff, Petite historie de la désinformation, Editions du Rocher, Paris, 1998).
- Walker, Bruce, "Homo politicus", June 5,2010,
- Walker, Samuel, 'In Defence of American Liberties: A History of the ACLU' (New York: Oxford University Press, 1990)
- Walker, Samuel. "Hate Speech: The History of an American Controversy" 8 (University of Nebraska Press 1994).
- Walter, G. Stephan, "Intergroup Relations", In Gardner Lindzey and Elliot Aronson, eds., Handbook of Social Psychology. 3rd ed. New York: Random House, 1985
- Weber, Anne, 'Manual on hate speech', Council of Europe Publishing, 2009
- Whitman, James Q. 'Enforcing Civility and Respect: Three Societies', 109 YALE L.J. 1279, 1281 (2000).
- Williams, J. (ed.) (1995). 'PC Wars'. Politics and Theory in the Academy. New York: Routledge and Kegan Paul.
- Wodak, R. (1984). 'Determination of guilt: discourses in the courtroom'. In C. Kramarae, M. Schulz, and W. M. O'Barr (eds), Language and Power (pp. 89-100). Beverly Hills, CA: Sage.
- Wodak, R. (1987). "And where is the Lebanon?" A socio—psycholinguistic investigation of comprehension and intelligibility of news. Text, 7(4)
- Wodak, R. (2006). 'History in the making/The making of history'. Journal of Language and Politics, 5,
- Wodak, R. and Van Dijk, T. A. (eds) (2000). 'Racism at the Top'. Klagenfurt: Drava Verlag.
- Woodak, R (2005), "What CDA is about – a summary of its history, important concepts and Its Development", u: Wodak, R i Meyer, M., Methods of Critical Discourse Analysis, London: Sage
- Woodak, R, (2002), 'Fragmented identities: redefining and recontextualizing national identity, Politics as Text and Talk: Analytic Approaches to Political Discourse'. Amsterdam/Philadelphia: John Benjamins 1984
- Working, Russell. "Illegal Abroad, Hate Web Sites Thrive Here: 1st Amendment Lets Fringe Groups Use U.S. Sites to Spread Their Message around the World," Chicago Tribune A1 (Nov. 13, 2007), available at 2007 WLNR 22413864.
- Wyman, S. David, Paper Walls: 'America and the Refugee Crisis, 1938-1941' (New York: Pantheon Books, 1985)

- Yahoo! Inc. v. La Ligue Contre le Racisme et L'antisemitisme, 433 F.3d 1199 (9th Cir.) (en banc), cert. denied, 547 U.S. 1163 (2006).
- Zheng, Tongtao. 'Characteristics of Australian Political Language Rhetoric: Tactics of gaining public support and shirking responsibility, School of Asian Languages and Studies', University of Tasmania, Intercultural Communication, ISSN 1404-1634, 2000, November, issue 4.
- Zimmer, Anja, 'Hate speech im Völkerrecht - Rassendiskriminierende Äußerungen im Spannungsfeld zwischen Rassendiskriminierungsverbot und Meinungsfreiheit', Heidelberg: Max-Planck-Institut für ausländisches öffentliches Recht und Völkerrecht, 2001.

INTERNET

- Beham, Mira. 2004: "Govor mržnje u politici i medijima". Objavljeno u Vacic, Z. (ur.) 2004 Etika javne rijeci u medijima i politici, Centar za liberalno demokratske studije, Beograd, 2004., http://www.clds.rs/pdf-s/s-ETIKA.pdf
- Budimir, V. 2009, 'Odgovornost medija za ratne zlocine',
- CoE hate speech Factsheet, достъпно на
- Fahrenheit 9/11, http://www.youtube.com/watch?v=chj5R0Izt9s
- Hate Speech in Political Discourse, 01.07.2004, http://karmalised.com/?p=549 http://carmen.artsci.washington.edu/propaganda/newtname.htm at March 12, 1995
- http://dictionary.reference.com/browse/symbolism
- http://dromvidin.org/images/webpics/ok_Vseobshta.pdf
- http://kzd-nondiscrimination.com/proektuchilista/religioznitesimvoli.pdf http://sacp.government.bg/normativna-uredba/mejdunarodni-konvencii/evropeiska-socialna-harta/
- http://www.americanthinker.com/2010/06/homo_politicus.html
- http://www.b92.net/sport/fudbal/vesti.php?yyyy=2012&mm=10&dd=17&nav_id=652513
- http://www.b92.net/sport/fudbal/vesti.php?yyyy=2012&mm=11&dd=01&nav_id=656766
- http://www.b92.net/sport/fudbal/vesti.php?yyyy=2012&mm=11&dd=05&nav_id=657870
- http://www.b92.net/sport/zimski/hokej.php?yyyy=2012&mm=10&dd=30&nav_id=656386
- http://www.bghelsinki.org/index.php?module=news&id=1312,
- http://www.coe.int/t/dghl/standardsetting/t-cy/ETS_185_Bulgarian%20.pdf
- http://www.dnevnik.com.mk/default.asp?ItemID=45876693D08A064FA7427B03864CF212
- http://www.echr.coe.int/NR/rdonlyres/F84D2B7F-0F2E-403B-892F-8CA51C30A8B3/0/Convention_BUL.pdf

- http://www.krcky.com/simbolizam/index.html
- http://www.media.ba/bs/etikaregulativa-novinarstvo-ratni-zlocini-etika/odgovornost-medija-za-ratne-zlocine-1
- http://www.mediatimesreview.com/september05/ataka.php,
- http://www.osce.org/documents/odihr/2005/11/16836_bg.pdf,
- http://www.osce.org/publications/rfm/2004/12/12239_94_en.pdf
  http://www.studiob.rs/info/vest.php?id=79879
- http://www.thesun.co.uk/sol/homepage/sport/football/66475/Nazty-Croats-form-swastika.html
- http://www.usconstitution.net/xconst_Am1.html
- http://www.usconstitution.net/xconst_Am14.html
- http://www.utrinski.com.mk/default.asp?ItemID=67A15FD461B23542AA2175032D63B79F
- http://www.vbox7.com/play:a258eb80
- Kaminskaya, Elvira, 2008: "Hate Speech: Theory and Issues", CASE-UC Berkeley Field Project - spring 2008 Work Products: 3-4; страница 2. http://iseees.berkeley.edu/sites/default/files/u4/iseees/caseproject_/KaminskayaFR.pdf
- O'Neill, Brendan. "After Hate Speech, the war against 'Mate Speech'", Spiked, 13. 03. 2007, http://www.spiked-online.com/site/article/2953/
- OSCE/ODIHR, Hate Crime Laws: A Practial Guide, OSCE / ODIHR, 2009 или на http://legal-dictionary.thefreedictionary.com/bias+crime
- Propaganda Examples Gingrich's Glittering Generalities,
- Radoja, Žarko. „Uloga medija u ratnim sukobima na prostoru bivše SFRJ, Kako kazniti ratno huškanje?", http://www.enovine.com/drustvo/36020-Kako-kazniti-ratno-huskanje.html
- Sandy Starr, „Understanding Hate Speech, Hate Speech on the Internet", December, 2004,
- Schenk v. US, 249 U.S. 47, 1919, http://caselaw.lp.fi ndlaw.com
- Wartime Propaganda: World War I Demons, Atrocities, and Lies, http://carmen.artsci.washington.edu/propaganda/war3.htm at March 12, 1995
- www.coe.int/t/DC/Files/Source/FS_hate_en.doc,December 2009
- Всеобща декларация за правата на човека, Издадена в сборник от международни документи, 1992 г.,
- Дневник, 12.03.2007, Скопје,
- Европейска социална харта (ревизирана), Държавна агенция за закрила на детето,
- Европейската конвенция за защита на човешките права и основните свободи на Съвета на Европа (ЕКПЧ),
- Конвенция за престъления в кибер-пространството,

- ❖ М е ж д у н а р о д е н   п а к т за граждански и политически права, http://www.minedu.government.bg/opencms/export/sites/mon/left_menu/strategies/documents/pakt-grazhdaski-prava.pdf
- ❖ Международна конвенция за ликвидиране на всички форми на расова дискриминация, http://www.minedu.government.bg/opencms/export/sites/mon/left_menu/strategies/documents/konvencia-rasova-discriminacia.pdf
- ❖ Реч на омразата в медиите на България и Македония: прояви, фактори, решения, http://osi.bg/downloads/File/HateSpeech_Report_BG.pdf
- ❖ Символизам - изкуство XIX – тог века,
- ❖ Студио Б, 24.08.2012, „Кинг Конг и символизам",

CYRILIC

- ❖ Веинрајт, Гордон Р. 'Говорот на телото, практичен прирачник', ('Body Language', Gordon R. Wainwright), Силсон 2002, Скопје
- ❖ Гебелс, Јозеф, „Политички говори", Скопје, 2003 (Josef Goebbels "Political speeches")
- ❖ Златева, Минка. Мостове към консенсуса. Пъблик рилейшънс: проблемни области и конфликтни зони. Унив. изд. „Св. Кл. Охридски", 2008
- ❖ Кършакова, Рада. Връзки с обществеността. Русе, 2002
- ❖ Кършакова, Рада. Основи на комуникацията. Русе, 2002
- ❖ Мавродиева, Иванка. Политическата реторика в България: от митингите до онлайн социалните мрежи /1989 – 2011/. Парадигма, 2012
- ❖ Мангейм, Дж., Р.Рич. Политология. Методы исследования. Пер. с англ., М., 1997
- ❖ Михаилова, Елена, „Јазикот на омраза и културната различност", Темплум, 2010
- ❖ Павловић, Јелена. „Дискурс као нова тема у психологији" у ЗБОРНИК БЕОГРАДСКЕ ОТВОРЕНЕ ШКОЛЕ, 2005
- ❖ Пис, Алан. 'Говор на телото – Како да ги читате мислите на другите преку нивните гестови' (2009), ('Body language-How to read others' thoughts by their gestures', Allan Pease, 1981), јазично студио Арт, Скопје
- ❖ Попова, Юлиана, Е.Коларов. Субективна култура. Субективни права. Русе, 2006
- ❖ Рот, Юлиана, Ю. Попова. Ръководство по интеркултурна комуникация. Русе, 2010
- ❖ Стаменов, Максим. Проблеми на значението в субективната семантика. С., 1993
- ❖ Стаменов, Максим. Съдбата на турцизмите в българския език и българската култура. С., 2011
- ❖ Филиповић, Јелена, 'Моћ речи', Београд: Задужбина Андрејевић, 2009

❖ Хинсик против Австрия ном. 25962/94, решение на Комисията от 18 октомври 1995 D.R. 83, pp. 77-85, също така и Мараис против Франция ном. 31159/96 решение на Комисията от 24 юни 1996 D.R. 86.

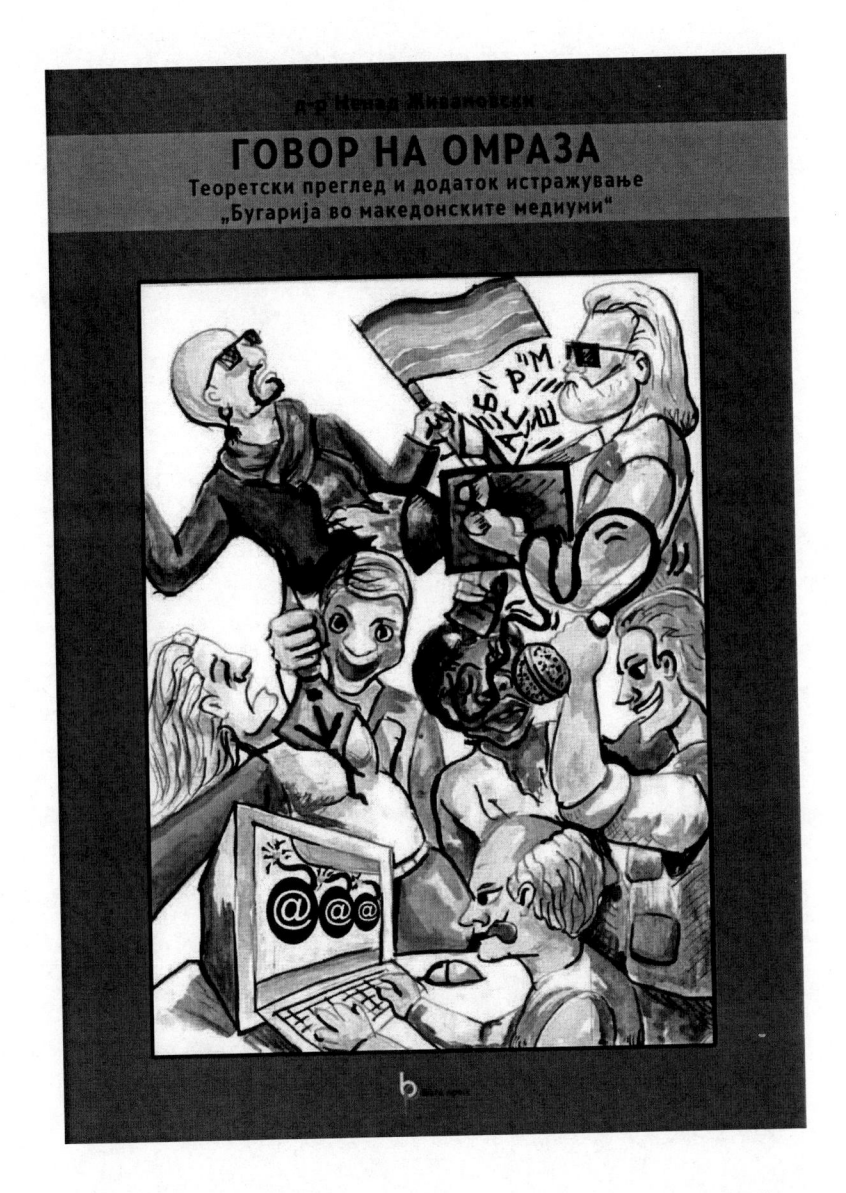

Cover page of Macedonian issue of the book published in 2014 in Skopje.

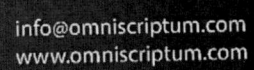